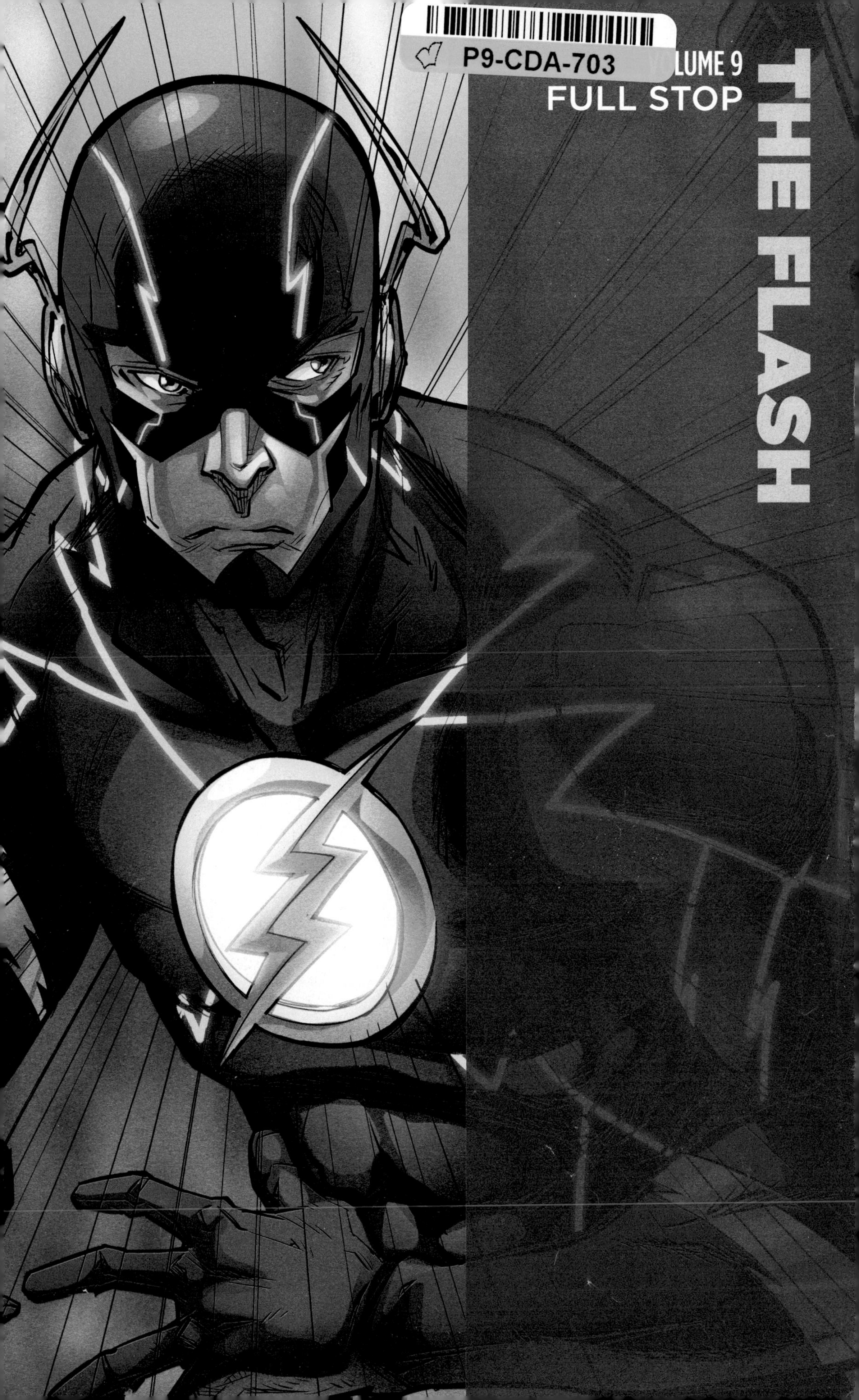
LUME 9
FULL STOP
THE FLASH

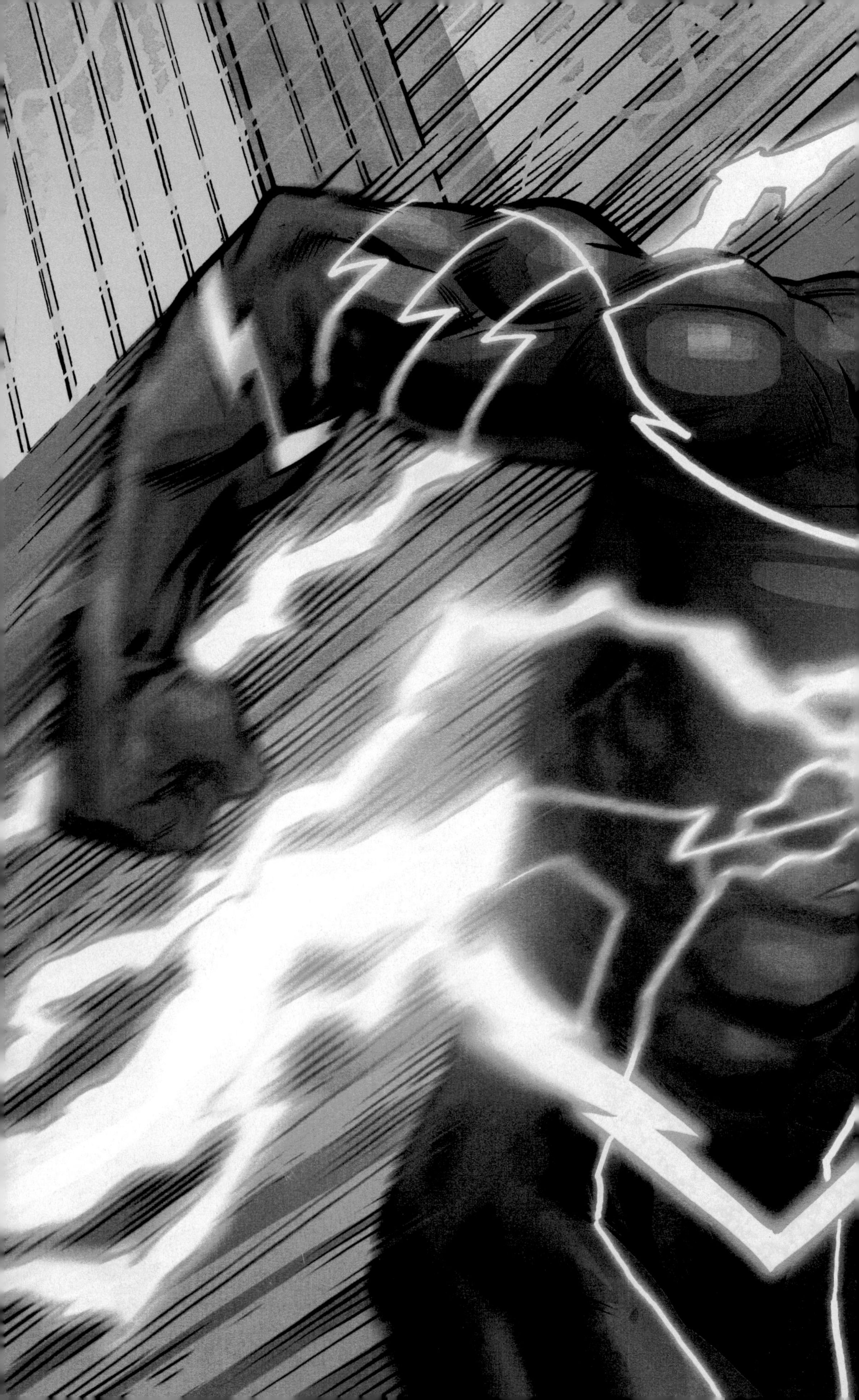

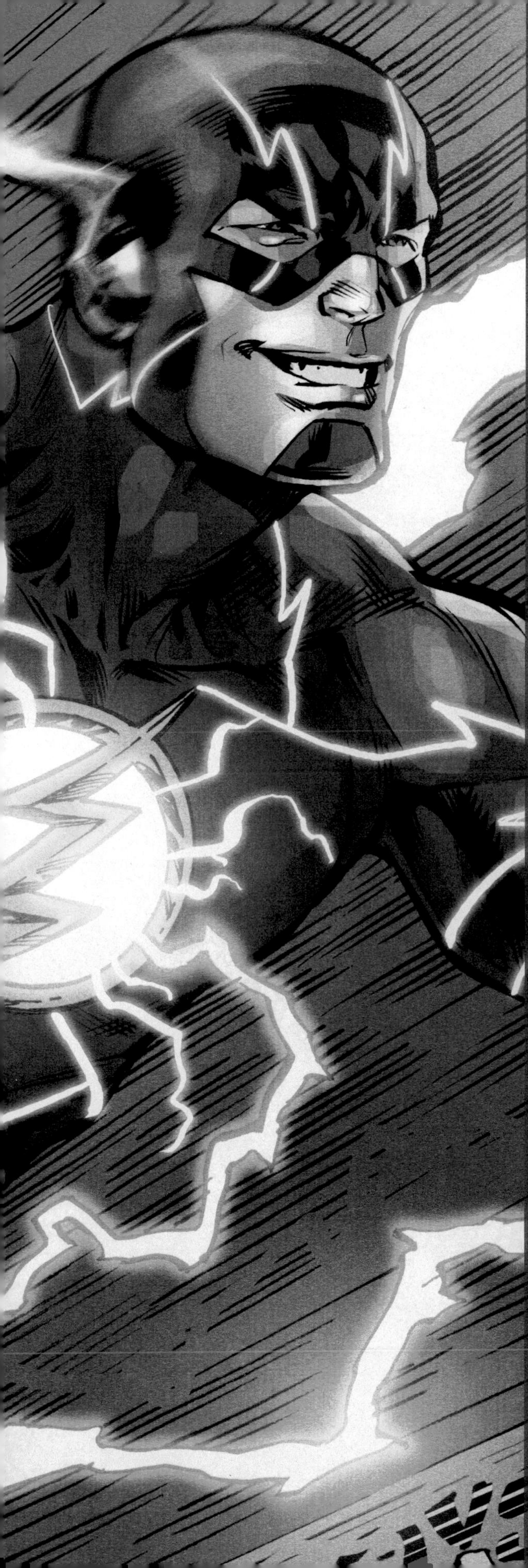

THE FLASH

VOLUME 9
FULL STOP

WRITTEN BY
VAN JENSEN
ROBERT VENDITTI

PENCILS BY
PHIL BRIONES
JOE EISMA
JESÚS MERINO
PAUL PELLETIER
GUS VAZQUEZ

INKS BY
PHIL BRIONES
JOE EISMA
WAYNE FAUCHER
SCOTT HANNA
TONY KORDOS
JESÚS MERINO
GUS VAZQUEZ

COLOR BY
GUY MAJOR
PETE PANTAZIS

LETTERS BY
PAT BROSSEAU

COLLECTION COVER ART BY
JOE PRADO
IVAN REIS

BRIAN CUNNINGHAM Editor – Original Series
AMEDEO TURTURRO Assistant Editor – Original Series
JEB WOODARD Group Editor – Collected Editions
SUZANNAH ROWNTREE Editor – Collected Edition
STEVE COOK Design Director – Books
DAMIAN RYLAND Publication Design

BOB HARRAS Senior VP – Editor-in-Chief, DC Comics

DIANE NELSON President
DAN DiDIO Publisher
JIM LEE Publisher
GEOFF JOHNS President & Chief Creative Officer
AMIT DESAI Executive VP – Business & Marketing Strategy, Direct to Consumer & Global Franchise Management
SAM ADES Senior VP – Direct to Consumer
BOBBIE CHASE VP – Talent Development
MARK CHIARELLO Senior VP – Art, Design & Collected Editions
JOHN CUNNINGHAM Senior VP – Sales & Trade Marketing
ANNE DePIES Senior VP – Business Strategy, Finance & Administration
DON FALLETTI VP – Manufacturing Operations
LAWRENCE GANEM VP – Editorial Administration & Talent Relations
ALISON GILL Senior VP – Manufacturing & Operations
HANK KANALZ Senior VP – Editorial Strategy & Administration
JAY KOGAN VP – Legal Affairs
THOMAS LOFTUS VP – Business Affairs
JACK MAHAN VP – Business Affairs
NICK J. NAPOLITANO VP – Manufacturing Administration
EDDIE SCANNELL VP – Consumer Marketing
COURTNEY SIMMONS Senior VP – Publicity & Communications
JIM (SKI) SOKOLOWSKI VP – Comic Book Specialty Sales & Trade Marketing
NANCY SPEARS VP – Mass, Book, Digital Sales & Trade Marketing

THE FLASH VOLUME 9: FULL STOP

DC Comics, 2900 West Alameda Ave., Burbank, CA 91505
Printed by LSC Communications, Salem, VA, USA. 5/26/17. First Printing.
ISBN: 978-1-4012-7412-2

Library of Congress Cataloging-in-Publication Data is available.

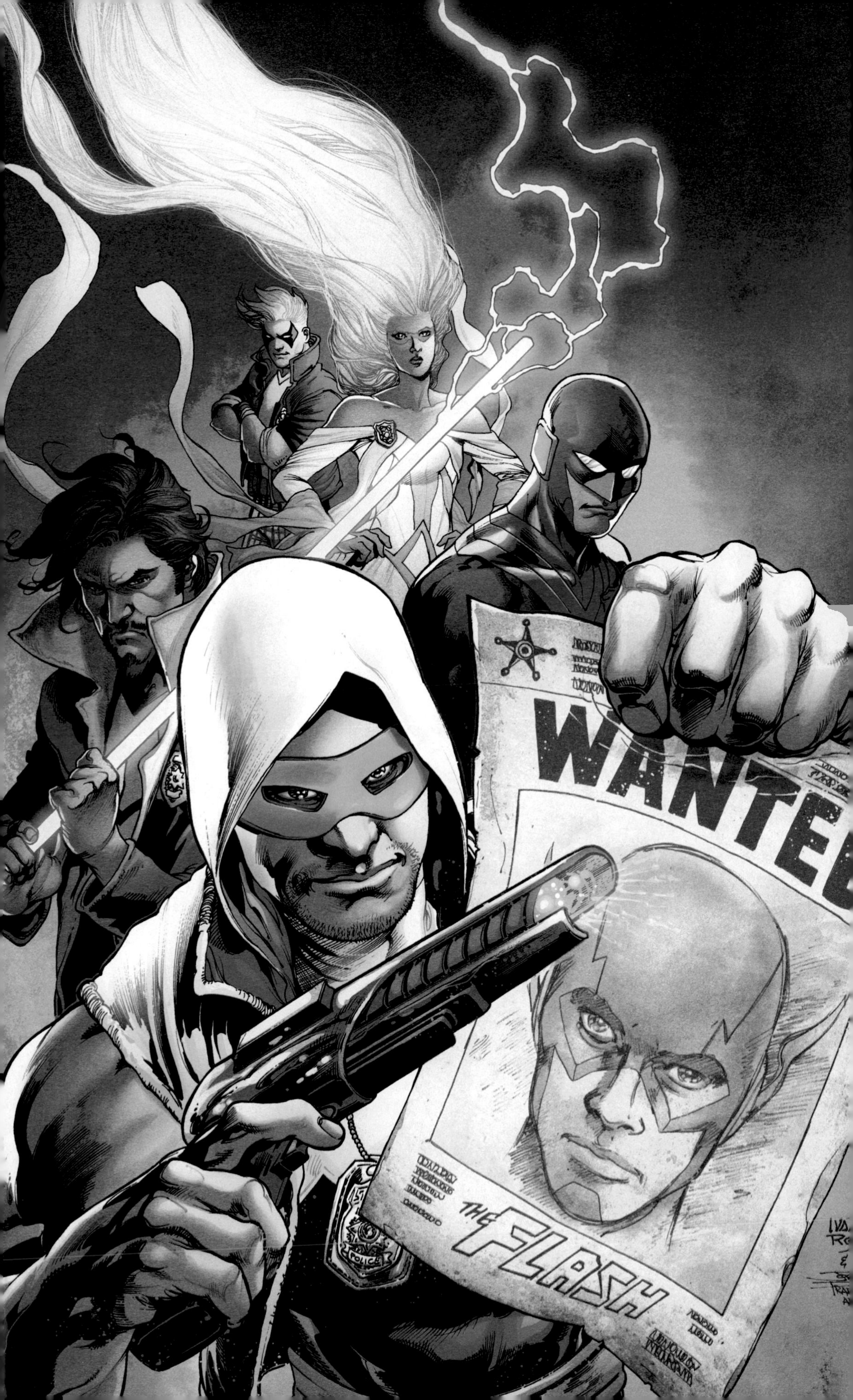
THE FLASH

PUBLIC ENEMY

ROBERT VENDITTI VAN JENSEN writers JESÚS MERINO artist GUY MAJOR colorist PAT BROSSEAU letterer IVAN REIS JOE PRADO cover

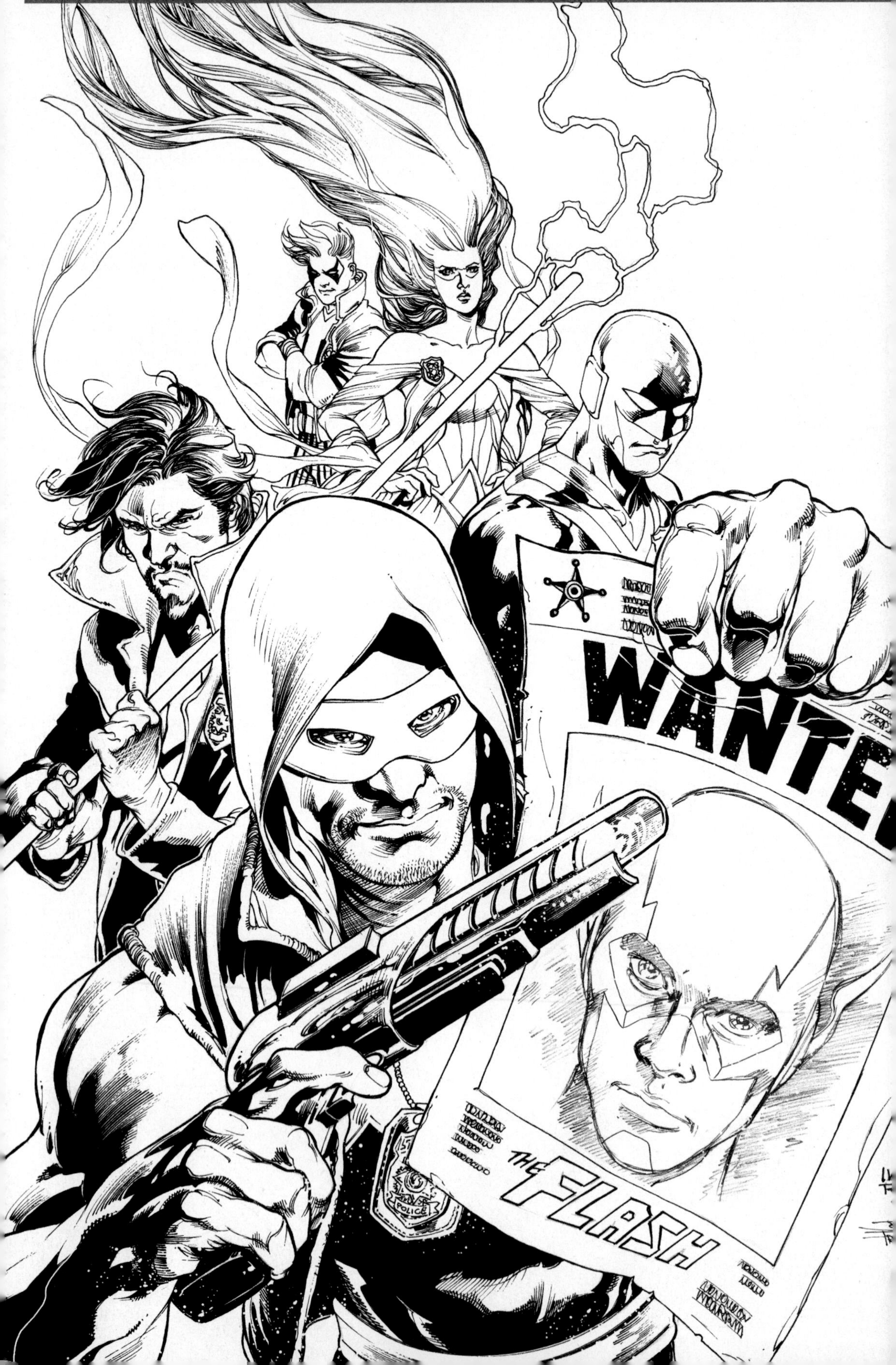
THE FLASH

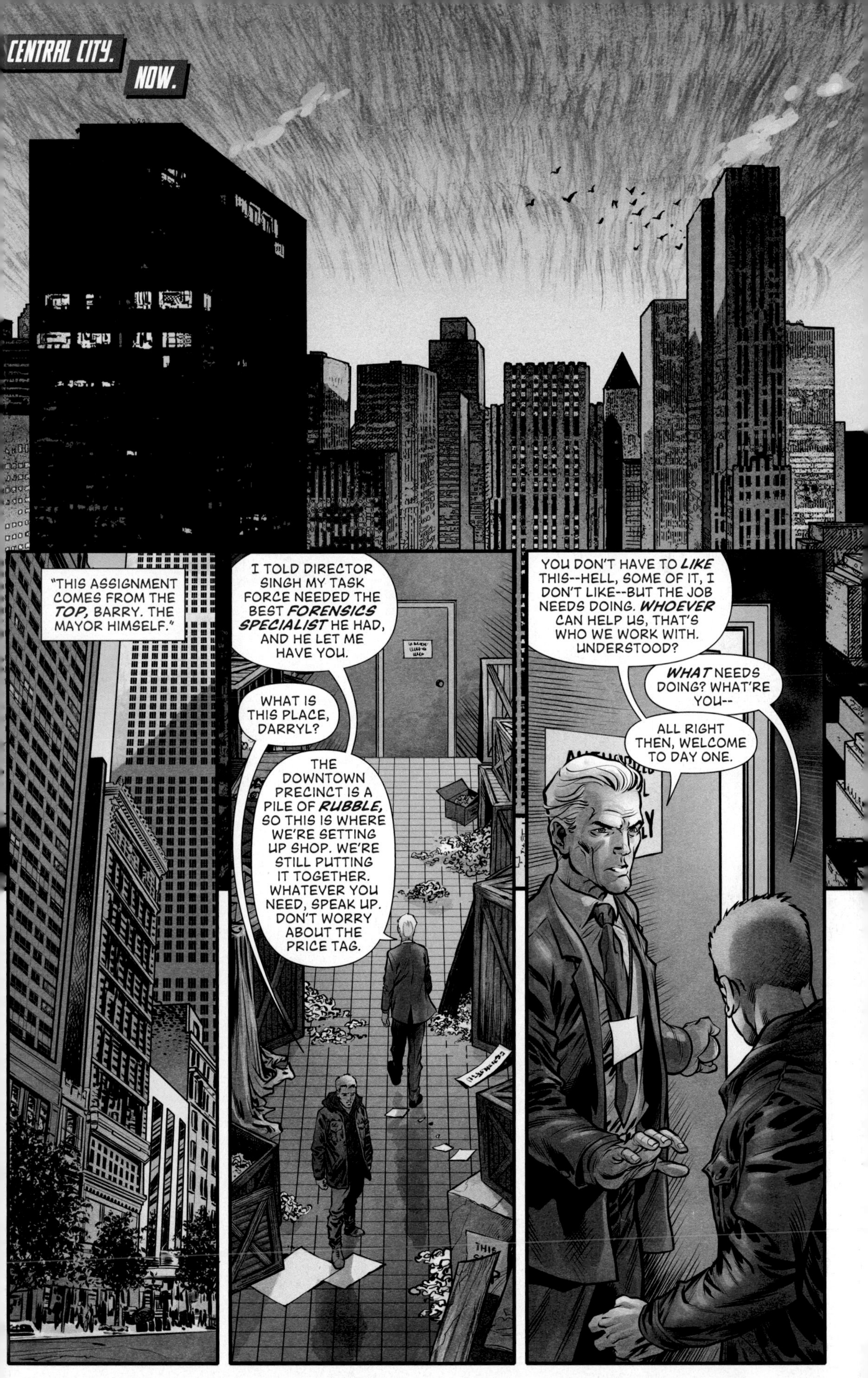
CENTRAL CITY.
NOW.
"THIS ASSIGNMENT COMES FROM THE TOP, BARRY. THE MAYOR HIMSELF."
I TOLD DIRECTOR SINGH MY TASK FORCE NEEDED THE BEST FORENSICS SPECIALIST HE HAD, AND HE LET ME HAVE YOU.
WHAT IS THIS PLACE, DARRYL?
THE DOWNTOWN PRECINCT IS A PILE OF RUBBLE, SO THIS IS WHERE WE'RE SETTING UP SHOP. WE'RE STILL PUTTING IT TOGETHER. WHATEVER YOU NEED, SPEAK UP. DON'T WORRY ABOUT THE PRICE TAG.
YOU DON'T HAVE TO LIKE THIS--HELL, SOME OF IT, I DON'T LIKE--BUT THE JOB NEEDS DOING. WHOEVER CAN HELP US, THAT'S WHO WE WORK WITH. UNDERSTOOD?
WHAT NEEDS DOING? WHAT'RE YOU--
ALL RIGHT THEN, WELCOME TO DAY ONE.

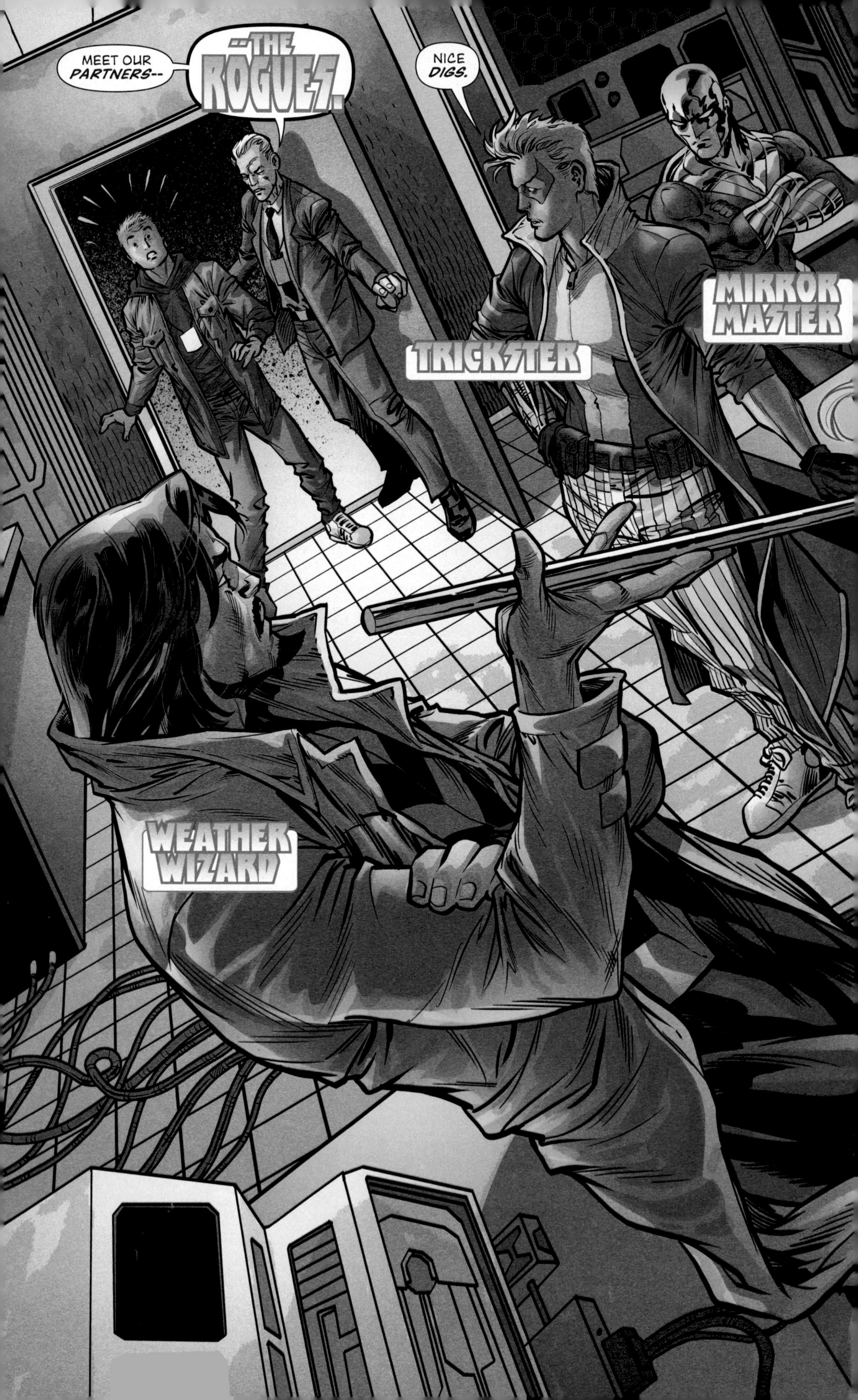
MEET OUR PARTNERS--
--THE ROGUES.
NICE DIGS.
MIRROR MASTER
TRICKSTER
WEATHER WIZARD

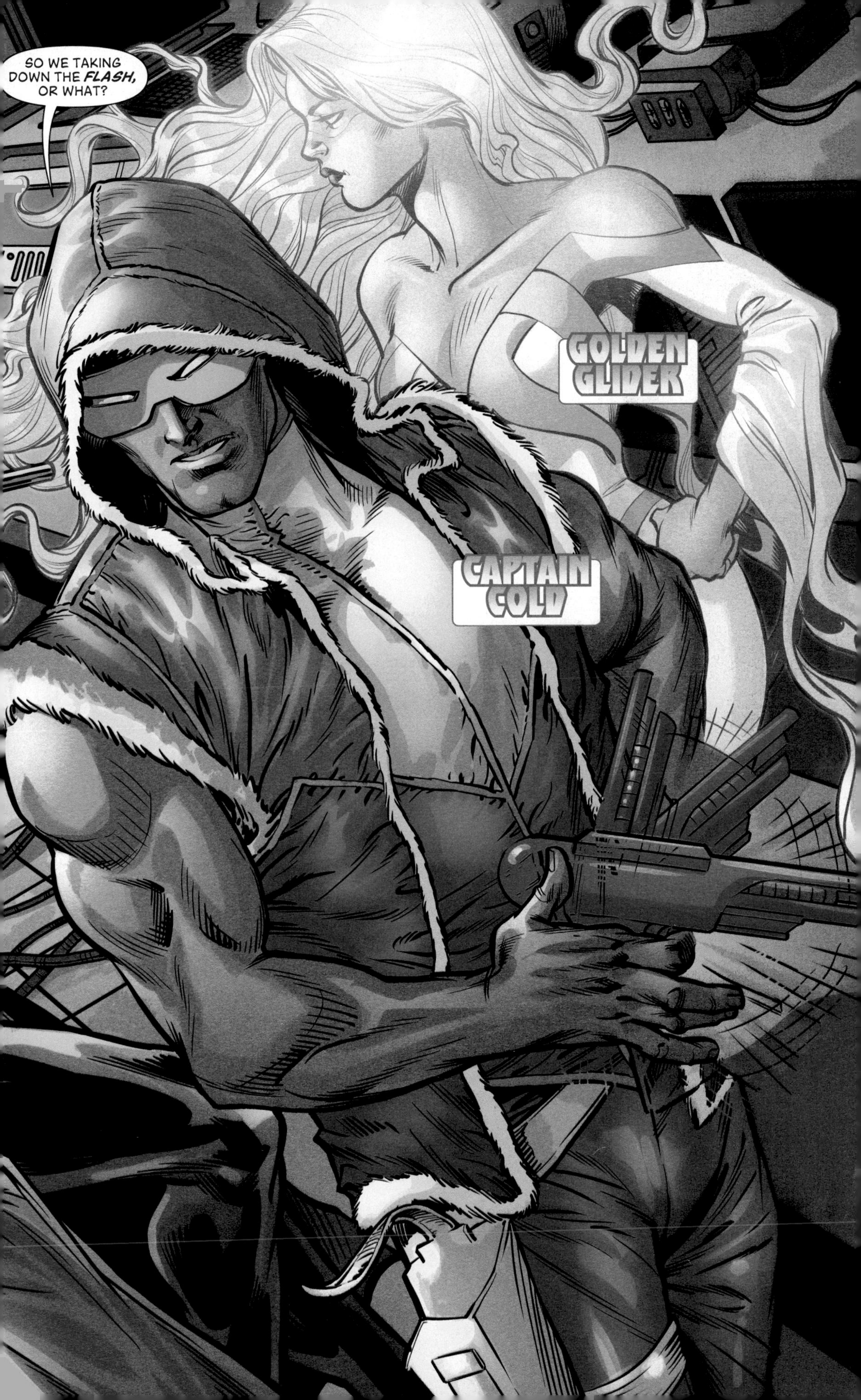
SO WE TAKING DOWN THE *FLASH,* OR WHAT?
GOLDEN GLIDER
CAPTAIN COLD

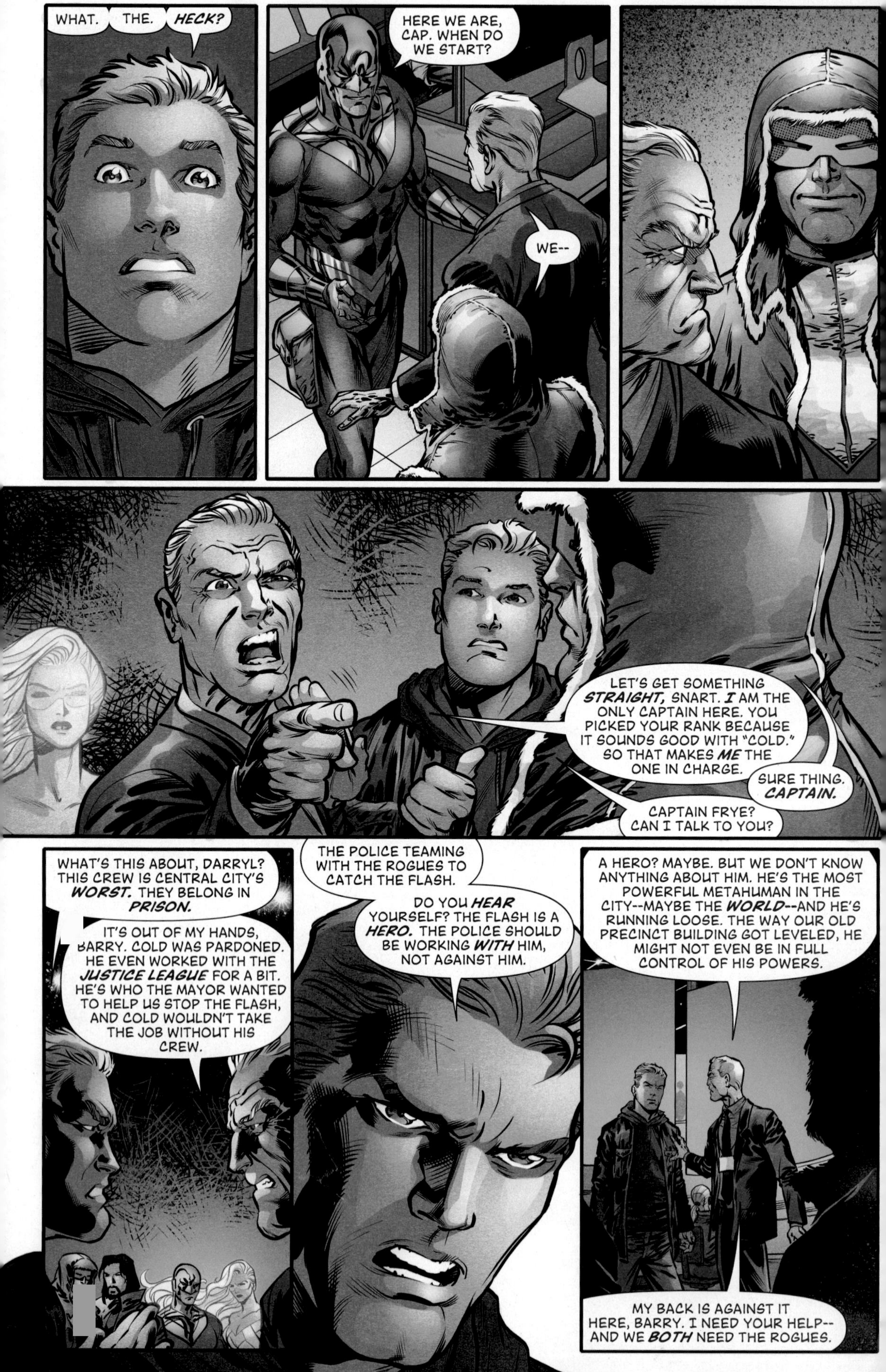
WHAT.
THE.
HECK?
HERE WE ARE, CAP. WHEN DO WE START?
WE--
LET'S GET SOMETHING STRAIGHT, SNART. I AM THE ONLY CAPTAIN HERE. YOU PICKED YOUR RANK BECAUSE IT SOUNDS GOOD WITH "COLD." SO THAT MAKES ME THE ONE IN CHARGE.
SURE THING. CAPTAIN.
CAPTAIN FRYE? CAN I TALK TO YOU?
WHAT'S THIS ABOUT, DARRYL? THIS CREW IS CENTRAL CITY'S WORST. THEY BELONG IN PRISON.
IT'S OUT OF MY HANDS, BARRY. COLD WAS PARDONED. HE EVEN WORKED WITH THE JUSTICE LEAGUE FOR A BIT. HE'S WHO THE MAYOR WANTED TO HELP US STOP THE FLASH, AND COLD WOULDN'T TAKE THE JOB WITHOUT HIS CREW.
THE POLICE TEAMING WITH THE ROGUES TO CATCH THE FLASH.
DO YOU HEAR YOURSELF? THE FLASH IS A HERO. THE POLICE SHOULD BE WORKING WITH HIM, NOT AGAINST HIM.
A HERO? MAYBE. BUT WE DON'T KNOW ANYTHING ABOUT HIM. HE'S THE MOST POWERFUL METAHUMAN IN THE CITY--MAYBE THE WORLD--AND HE'S RUNNING LOOSE. THE WAY OUR OLD PRECINCT BUILDING GOT LEVELED, HE MIGHT NOT EVEN BE IN FULL CONTROL OF HIS POWERS.
MY BACK IS AGAINST IT HERE, BARRY. I NEED YOUR HELP-- AND WE BOTH NEED THE ROGUES.

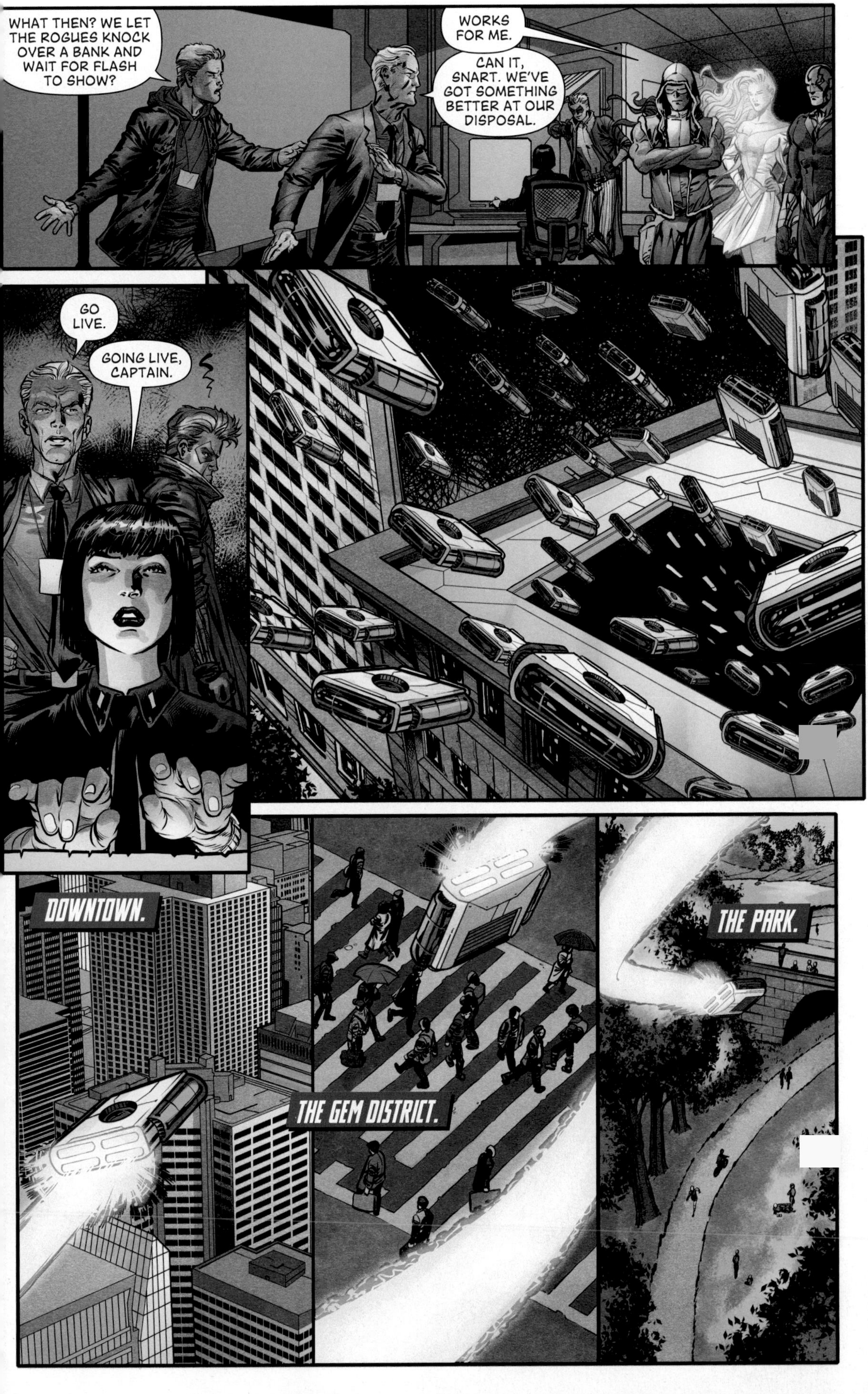
WHAT THEN? WE LET THE ROGUES KNOCK OVER A BANK AND WAIT FOR FLASH TO SHOW?
WORKS FOR ME.
CAN IT, SNART. WE'VE GOT SOMETHING BETTER AT OUR DISPOSAL.
GO LIVE.
GOING LIVE, CAPTAIN.
DOWNTOWN.
THE GEM DISTRICT.
THE PARK.

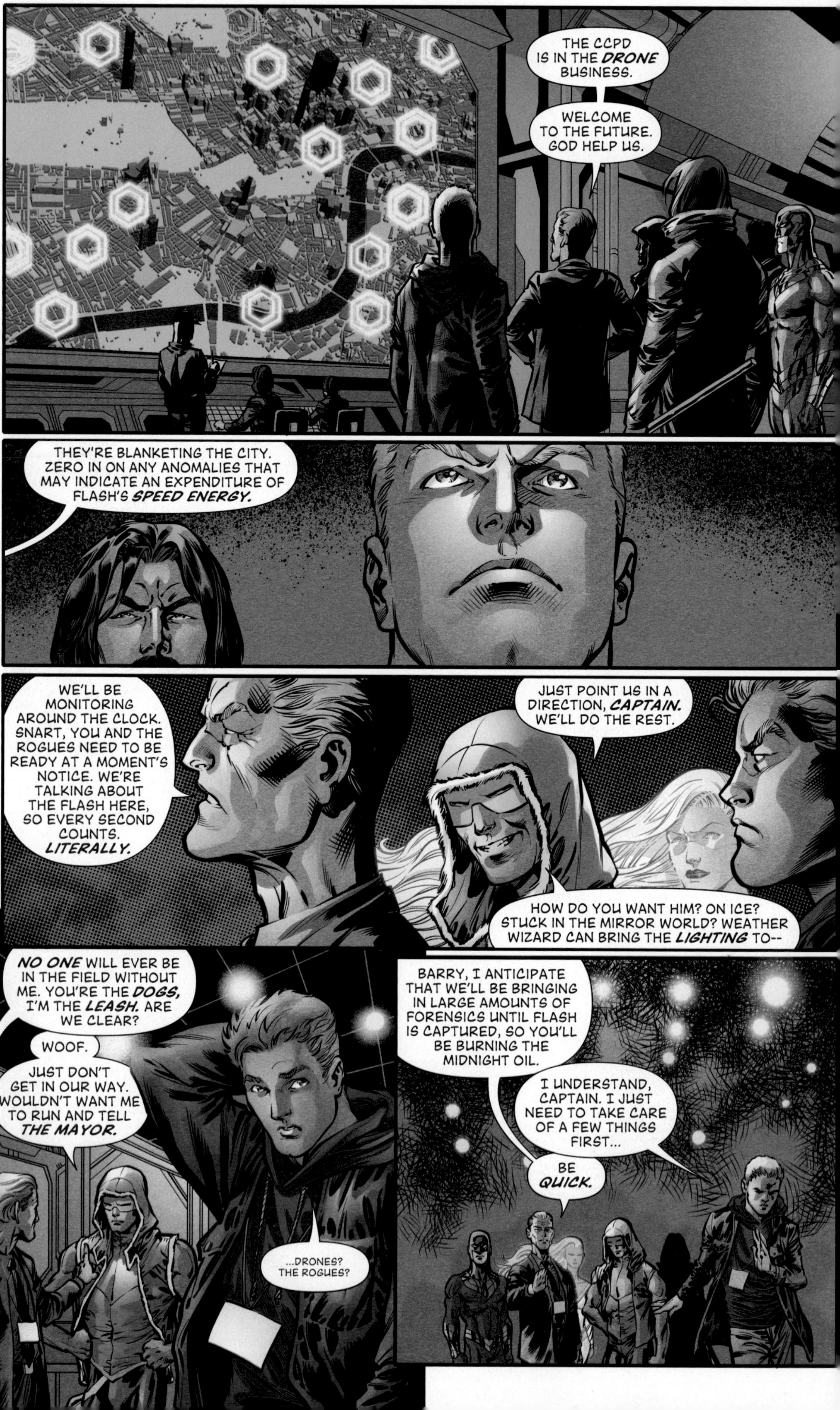
THE CCPD IS IN THE DRONE BUSINESS.
WELCOME TO THE FUTURE. GOD HELP US.
THEY'RE BLANKETING THE CITY. ZERO IN ON ANY ANOMALIES THAT MAY INDICATE AN EXPENDITURE OF FLASH'S SPEED ENERGY.
WE'LL BE MONITORING AROUND THE CLOCK. SNART, YOU AND THE ROGUES NEED TO BE READY AT A MOMENT'S NOTICE. WE'RE TALKING ABOUT THE FLASH HERE, SO EVERY SECOND COUNTS. LITERALLY.
JUST POINT US IN A DIRECTION, CAPTAIN. WE'LL DO THE REST.
HOW DO YOU WANT HIM? ON ICE? STUCK IN THE MIRROR WORLD? WEATHER WIZARD CAN BRING THE LIGHTING TO--
NO ONE WILL EVER BE IN THE FIELD WITHOUT ME. YOU'RE THE DOGS, I'M THE LEASH. ARE WE CLEAR?
WOOF.
JUST DON'T GET IN OUR WAY. WOULDN'T WANT ME TO RUN AND TELL THE MAYOR.
...DRONES? THE ROGUES?
BARRY, I ANTICIPATE THAT WE'LL BE BRINGING IN LARGE AMOUNTS OF FORENSICS UNTIL FLASH IS CAPTURED, SO YOU'LL BE BURNING THE MIDNIGHT OIL.
I UNDERSTAND, CAPTAIN. I JUST NEED TO TAKE CARE OF A FEW THINGS FIRST...
BE QUICK.

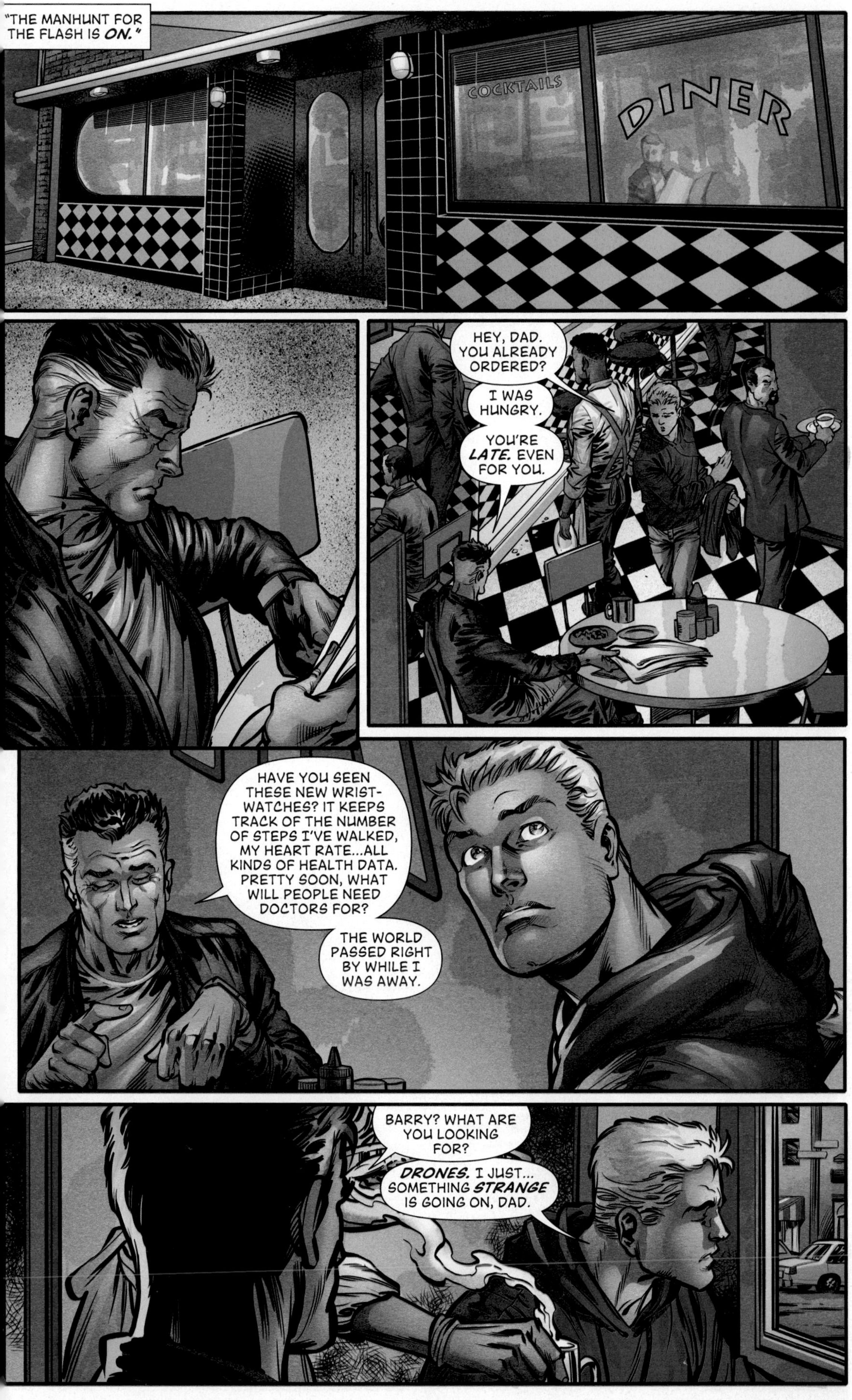
"THE MANHUNT FOR THE FLASH IS *ON.*"
COCKTAILS
DINER
HEY, DAD. YOU ALREADY ORDERED?
I WAS HUNGRY.
YOU'RE *LATE.* EVEN FOR YOU.
HAVE YOU SEEN THESE NEW WRIST-WATCHES? IT KEEPS TRACK OF THE NUMBER OF STEPS I'VE WALKED, MY HEART RATE...ALL KINDS OF HEALTH DATA. PRETTY SOON, WHAT WILL PEOPLE NEED DOCTORS FOR?
THE WORLD PASSED RIGHT BY WHILE I WAS AWAY.
BARRY? WHAT ARE YOU LOOKING FOR?
DRONES. I JUST... SOMETHING *STRANGE* IS GOING ON, DAD.

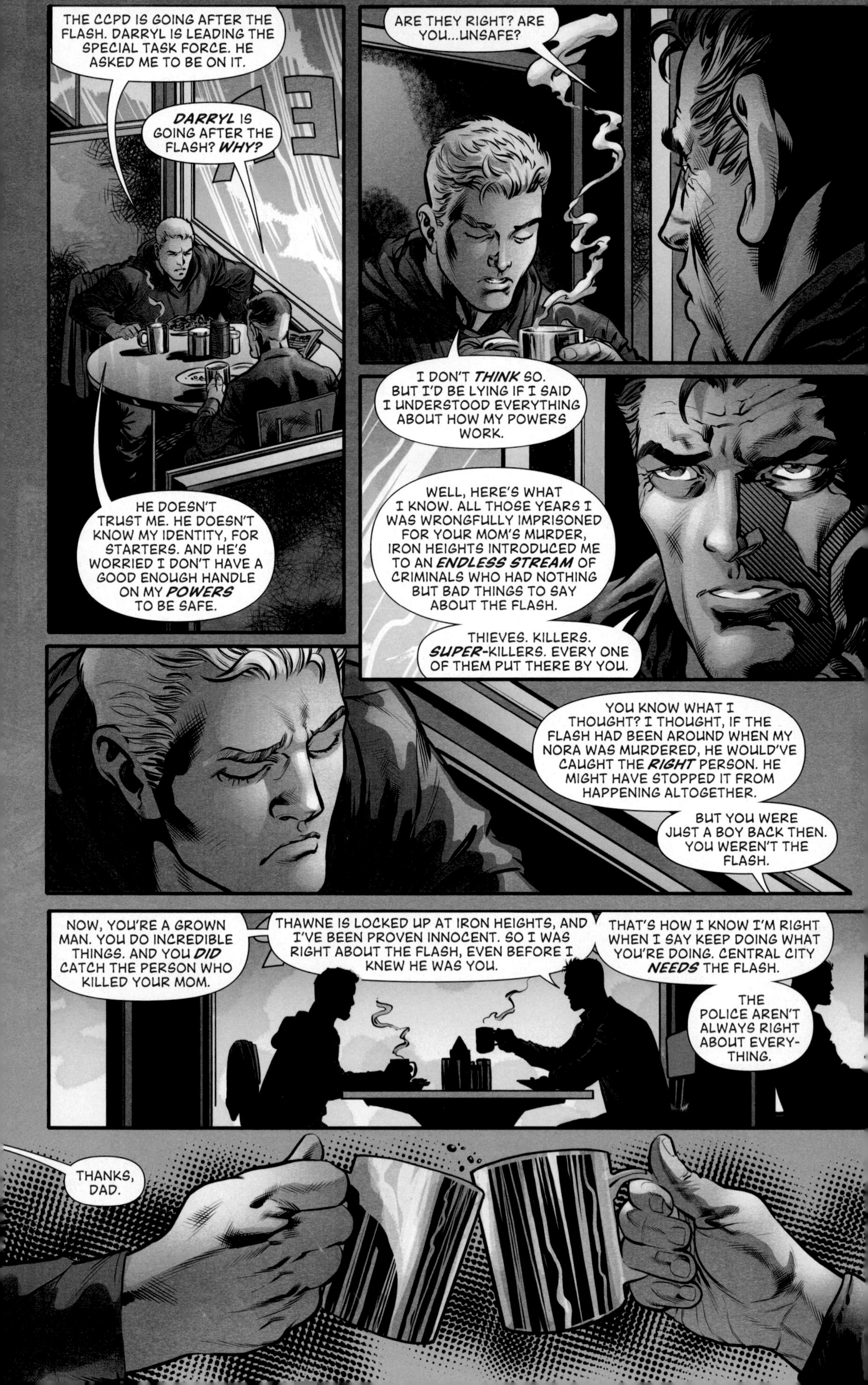
THE CCPD IS GOING AFTER THE FLASH. DARRYL IS LEADING THE SPECIAL TASK FORCE. HE ASKED ME TO BE ON IT.
DARRYL IS GOING AFTER THE FLASH? WHY?
HE DOESN'T TRUST ME. HE DOESN'T KNOW MY IDENTITY, FOR STARTERS. AND HE'S WORRIED I DON'T HAVE A GOOD ENOUGH HANDLE ON MY POWERS TO BE SAFE.
ARE THEY RIGHT? ARE YOU...UNSAFE?
I DON'T THINK SO. BUT I'D BE LYING IF I SAID I UNDERSTOOD EVERYTHING ABOUT HOW MY POWERS WORK.
WELL, HERE'S WHAT I KNOW. ALL THOSE YEARS I WAS WRONGFULLY IMPRISONED FOR YOUR MOM'S MURDER, IRON HEIGHTS INTRODUCED ME TO AN ENDLESS STREAM OF CRIMINALS WHO HAD NOTHING BUT BAD THINGS TO SAY ABOUT THE FLASH.
THIEVES. KILLERS. SUPER-KILLERS. EVERY ONE OF THEM PUT THERE BY YOU.
YOU KNOW WHAT I THOUGHT? I THOUGHT, IF THE FLASH HAD BEEN AROUND WHEN MY NORA WAS MURDERED, HE WOULD'VE CAUGHT THE RIGHT PERSON. HE MIGHT HAVE STOPPED IT FROM HAPPENING ALTOGETHER.
BUT YOU WERE JUST A BOY BACK THEN. YOU WEREN'T THE FLASH.
NOW, YOU'RE A GROWN MAN. YOU DO INCREDIBLE THINGS. AND YOU DID CATCH THE PERSON WHO KILLED YOUR MOM.
THAWNE IS LOCKED UP AT IRON HEIGHTS, AND I'VE BEEN PROVEN INNOCENT. SO I WAS RIGHT ABOUT THE FLASH, EVEN BEFORE I KNEW HE WAS YOU.
THAT'S HOW I KNOW I'M RIGHT WHEN I SAY KEEP DOING WHAT YOU'RE DOING. CENTRAL CITY NEEDS THE FLASH.
THE POLICE AREN'T ALWAYS RIGHT ABOUT EVERY-THING.
THANKS, DAD.

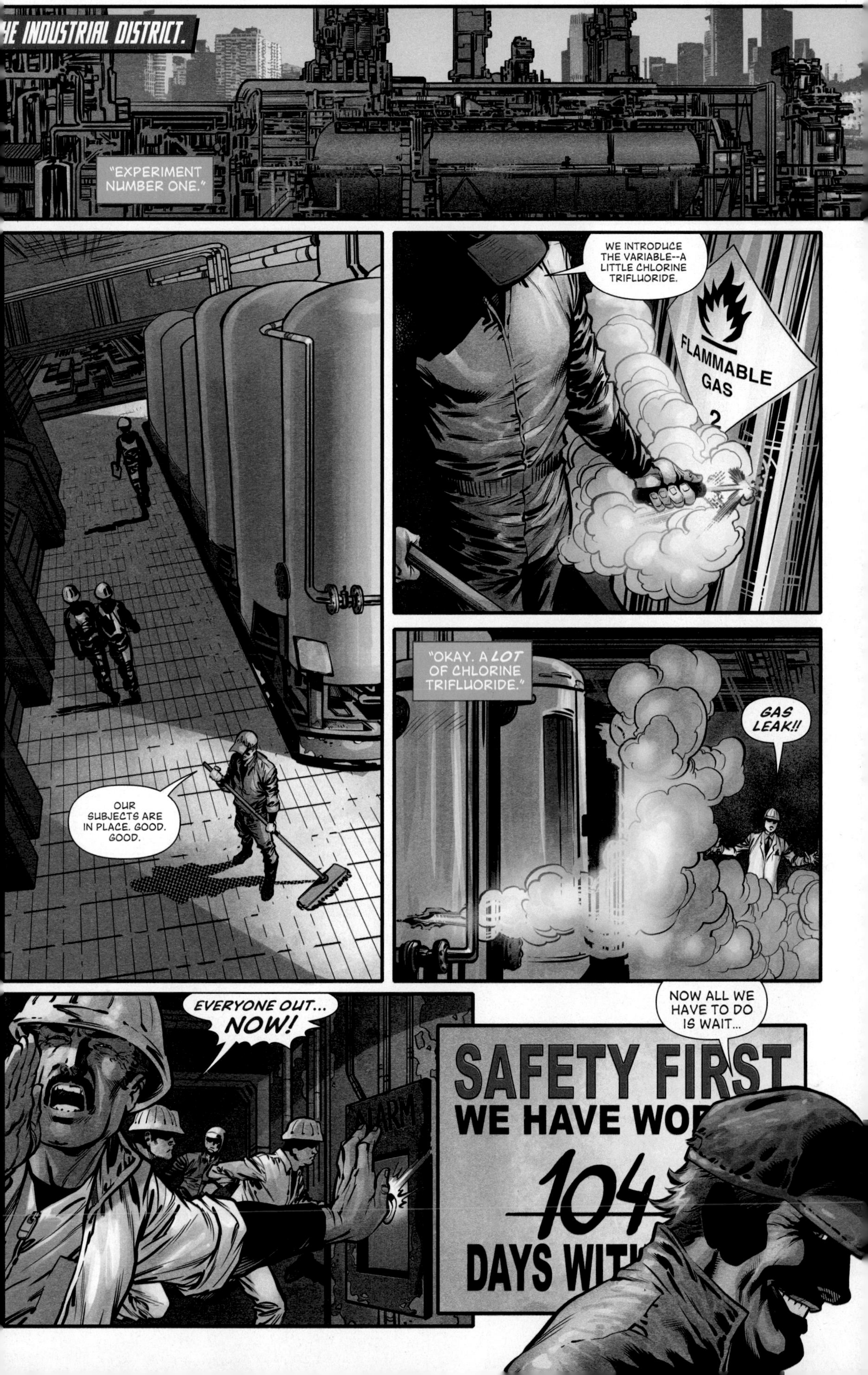

HE INDUSTRIAL DISTRICT.
"EXPERIMENT NUMBER ONE."
OUR SUBJECTS ARE IN PLACE. GOOD. GOOD.
WE INTRODUCE THE VARIABLE--A LITTLE CHLORINE TRIFLUORIDE.
FLAMMABLE GAS
2
"OKAY. A LOT OF CHLORINE TRIFLUORIDE."
GAS LEAK!!
EVERYONE OUT... NOW!
NOW ALL WE HAVE TO DO IS WAIT...
SAFETY FIRST
WE HAVE WO
104
DAYS WIT

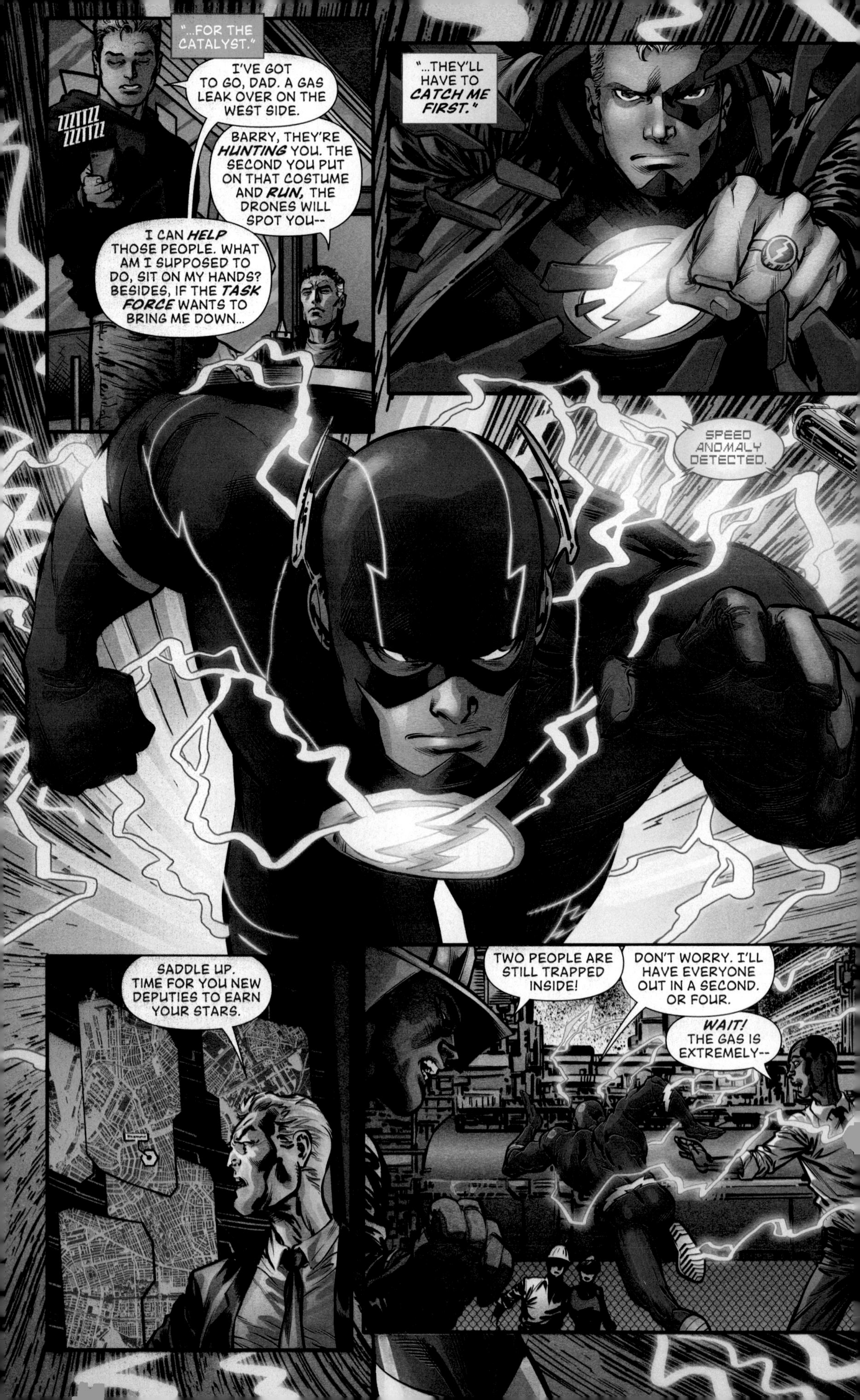
"...FOR THE CATALYST."
I'VE GOT TO GO, DAD. A GAS LEAK OVER ON THE WEST SIDE.
ZZZTTZZ ZZZTTZZ
BARRY, THEY'RE HUNTING YOU. THE SECOND YOU PUT ON THAT COSTUME AND RUN, THE DRONES WILL SPOT YOU--
I CAN HELP THOSE PEOPLE. WHAT AM I SUPPOSED TO DO, SIT ON MY HANDS? BESIDES, IF THE TASK FORCE WANTS TO BRING ME DOWN...
"...THEY'LL HAVE TO CATCH ME FIRST."
SPEED ANOMALY DETECTED.
SADDLE UP. TIME FOR YOU NEW DEPUTIES TO EARN YOUR STARS.
TWO PEOPLE ARE STILL TRAPPED INSIDE!
DON'T WORRY. I'LL HAVE EVERYONE OUT IN A SECOND. OR FOUR.
WAIT! THE GAS IS EXTREMELY--

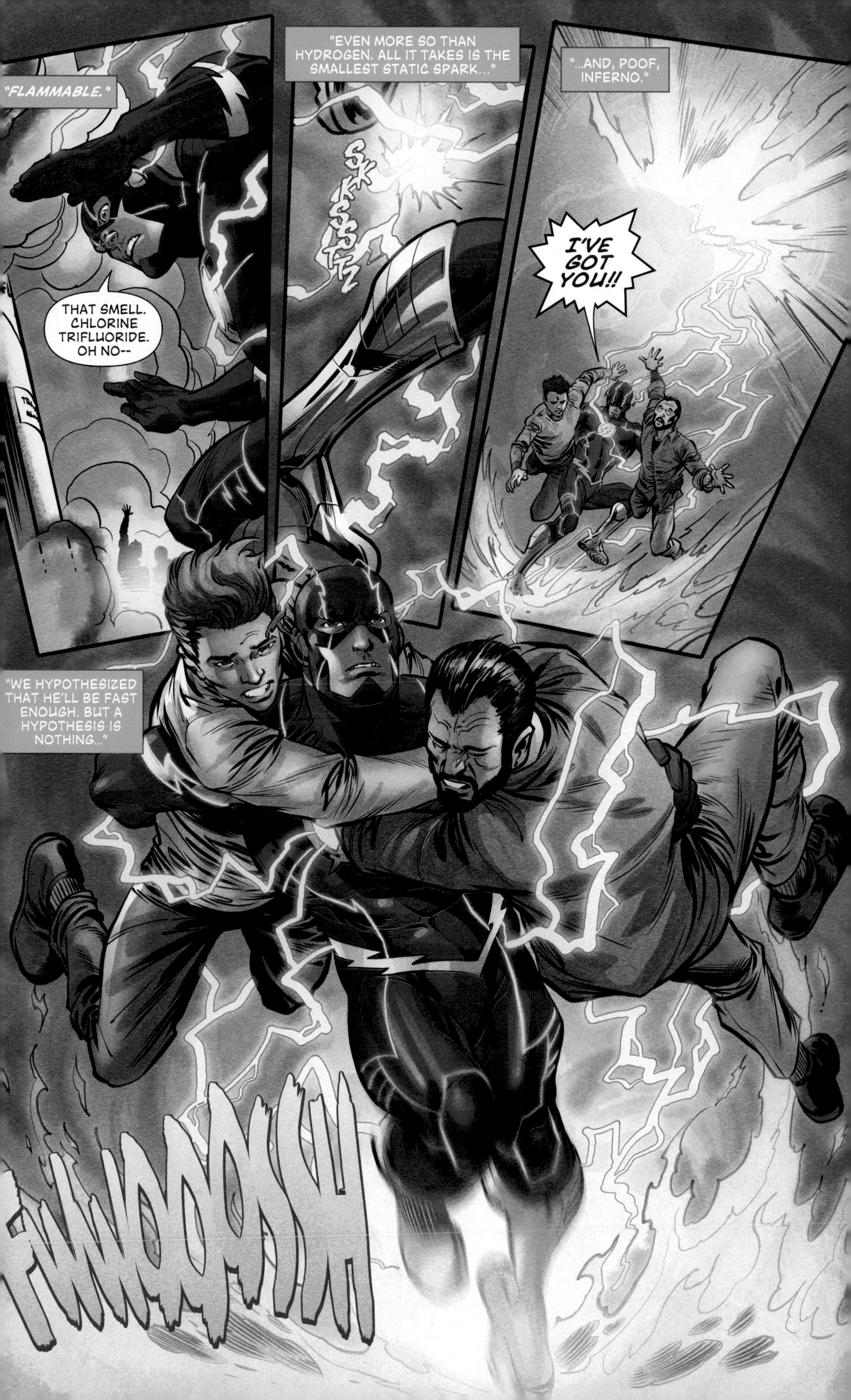
"FLAMMABLE."
THAT SMELL. CHLORINE TRIFLUORIDE. OH NO--
"EVEN MORE SO THAN HYDROGEN. ALL IT TAKES IS THE SMALLEST STATIC SPARK..."
SKKSSSTZ
"...AND, POOF, INFERNO."
I'VE GOT YOU!!
"WE HYPOTHESIZED THAT HE'LL BE FAST ENOUGH. BUT A HYPOTHESIS IS NOTHING..."
FWOOOSH

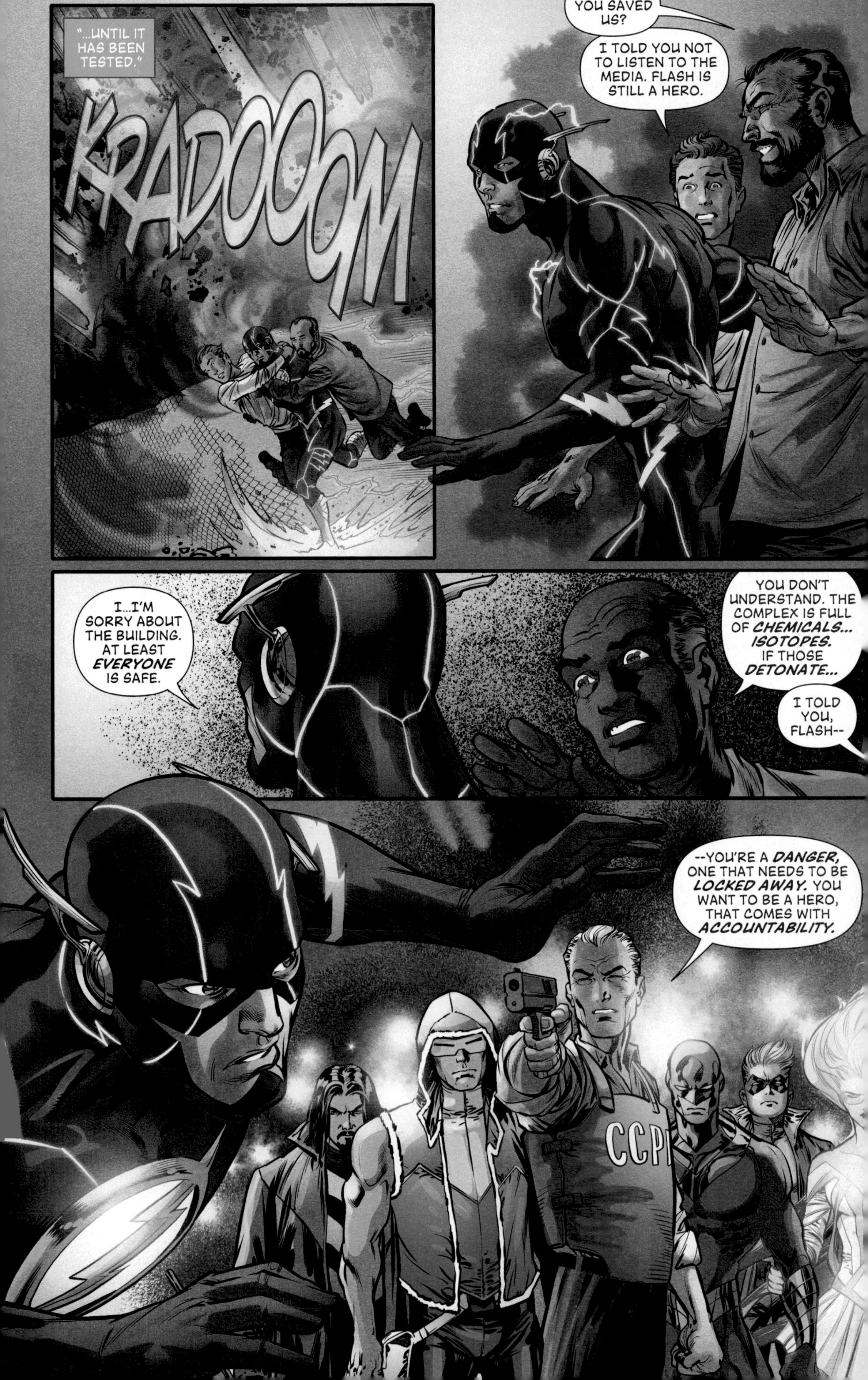
"...UNTIL IT HAS BEEN TESTED."
KRADOOOOM
YOU... YOU SAVED US?
I TOLD YOU NOT TO LISTEN TO THE MEDIA. FLASH IS STILL A HERO.
I...I'M SORRY ABOUT THE BUILDING. AT LEAST EVERYONE IS SAFE.
YOU DON'T UNDERSTAND. THE COMPLEX IS FULL OF CHEMICALS... ISOTOPES. IF THOSE DETONATE...
I TOLD YOU, FLASH--
--YOU'RE A DANGER, ONE THAT NEEDS TO BE LOCKED AWAY. YOU WANT TO BE A HERO, THAT COMES WITH ACCOUNTABILITY.
CCPD

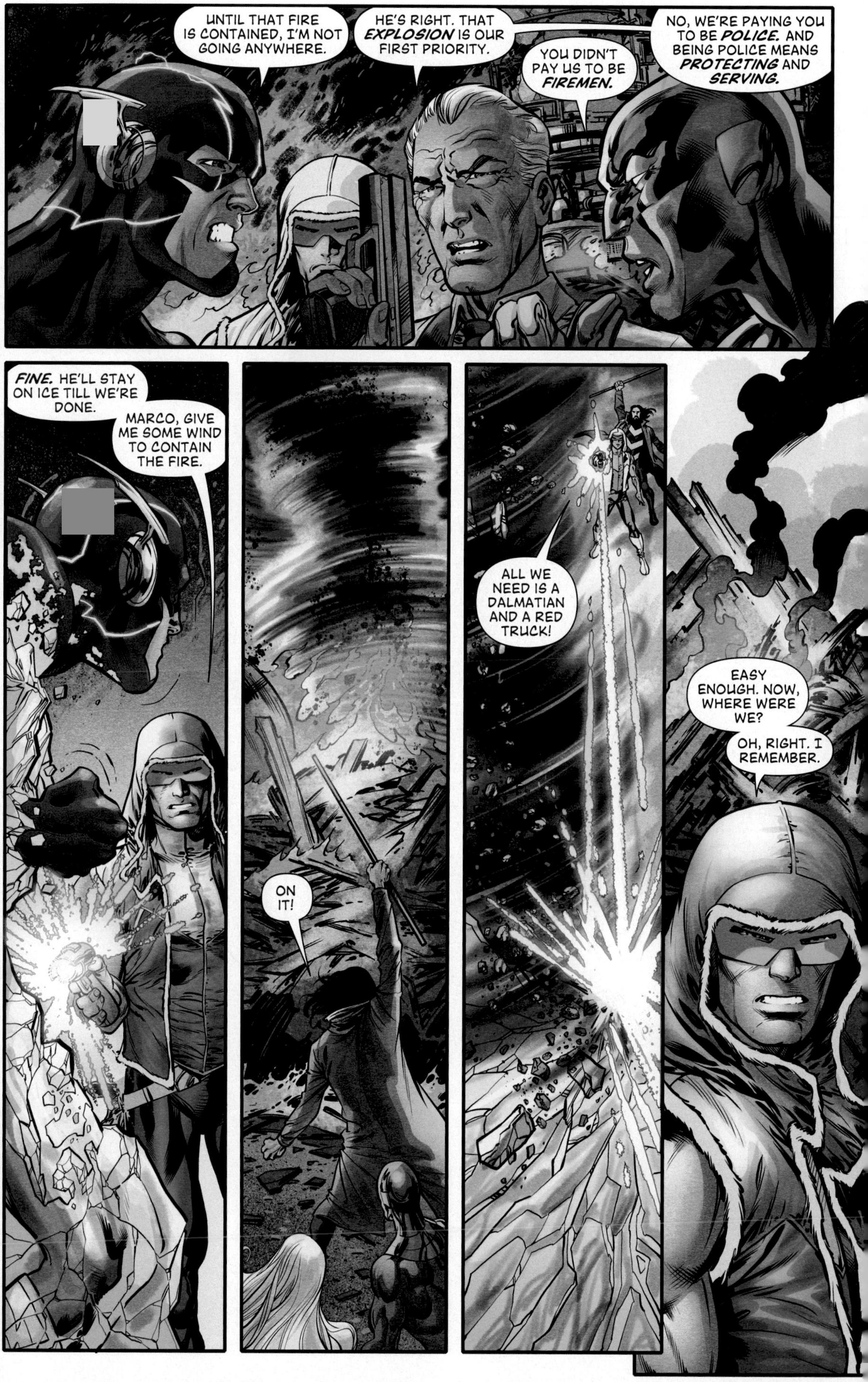
UNTIL THAT FIRE IS CONTAINED, I'M NOT GOING ANYWHERE.
HE'S RIGHT. THAT *EXPLOSION* IS OUR FIRST PRIORITY.
YOU DIDN'T PAY US TO BE *FIREMEN.*
NO, WE'RE PAYING YOU TO BE *POLICE.* AND BEING POLICE MEANS *PROTECTING* AND *SERVING.*
FINE. HE'LL STAY ON ICE TILL WE'RE DONE.
MARCO, GIVE ME SOME WIND TO CONTAIN THE FIRE.
ON IT!
ALL WE NEED IS A DALMATIAN AND A RED TRUCK!
EASY ENOUGH. NOW, WHERE WERE WE?
OH, RIGHT. I REMEMBER.

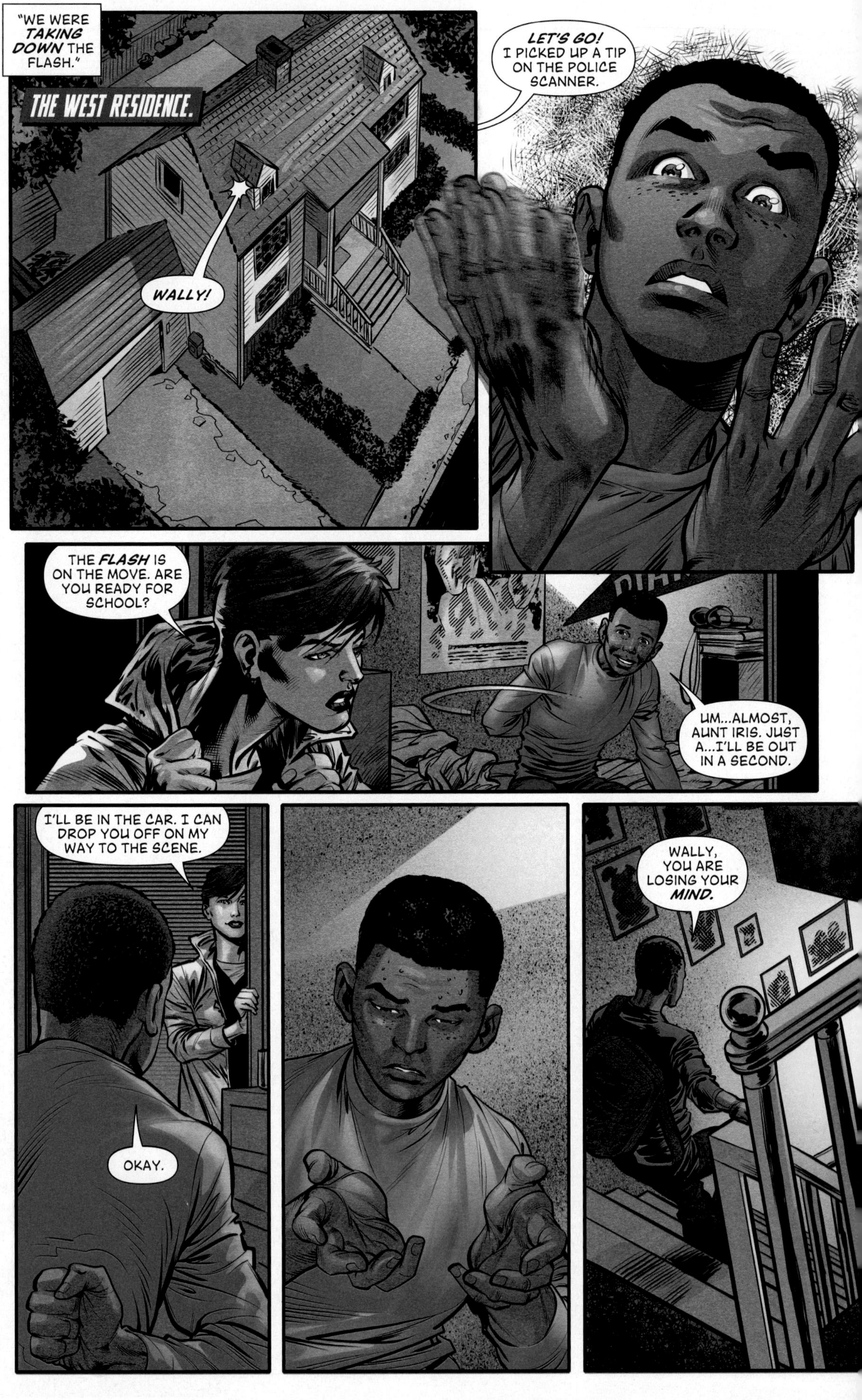
"WE WERE TAKING DOWN THE FLASH."
THE WEST RESIDENCE.
WALLY!
LET'S GO! I PICKED UP A TIP ON THE POLICE SCANNER.
THE FLASH IS ON THE MOVE. ARE YOU READY FOR SCHOOL?
UM...ALMOST, AUNT IRIS. JUST A...I'LL BE OUT IN A SECOND.
I'LL BE IN THE CAR. I CAN DROP YOU OFF ON MY WAY TO THE SCENE.
OKAY.
WALLY, YOU ARE LOSING YOUR MIND.

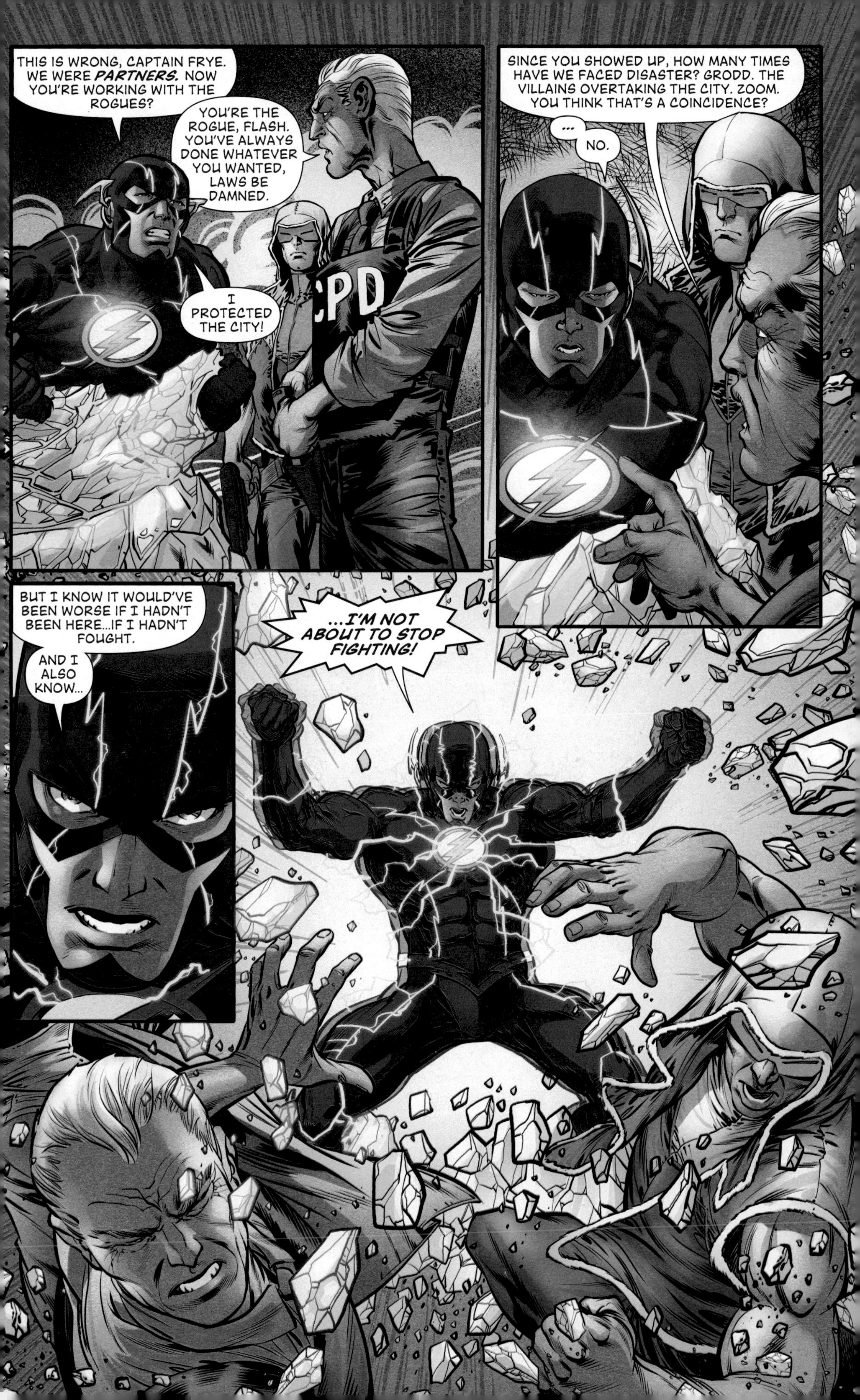
THIS IS WRONG, CAPTAIN FRYE. WE WERE **PARTNERS.** NOW YOU'RE WORKING WITH THE ROGUES?
YOU'RE THE ROGUE, FLASH. YOU'VE ALWAYS DONE WHATEVER YOU WANTED, LAWS BE DAMNED.
I PROTECTED THE CITY!
CPD
SINCE YOU SHOWED UP, HOW MANY TIMES HAVE WE FACED DISASTER? GRODD. THE VILLAINS OVERTAKING THE CITY. ZOOM. YOU THINK THAT'S A COINCIDENCE?
...
NO.
BUT I KNOW IT WOULD'VE BEEN WORSE IF I HADN'T BEEN HERE...IF I HADN'T FOUGHT.
AND I ALSO KNOW...
...I'M NOT ABOUT TO STOP FIGHTING!

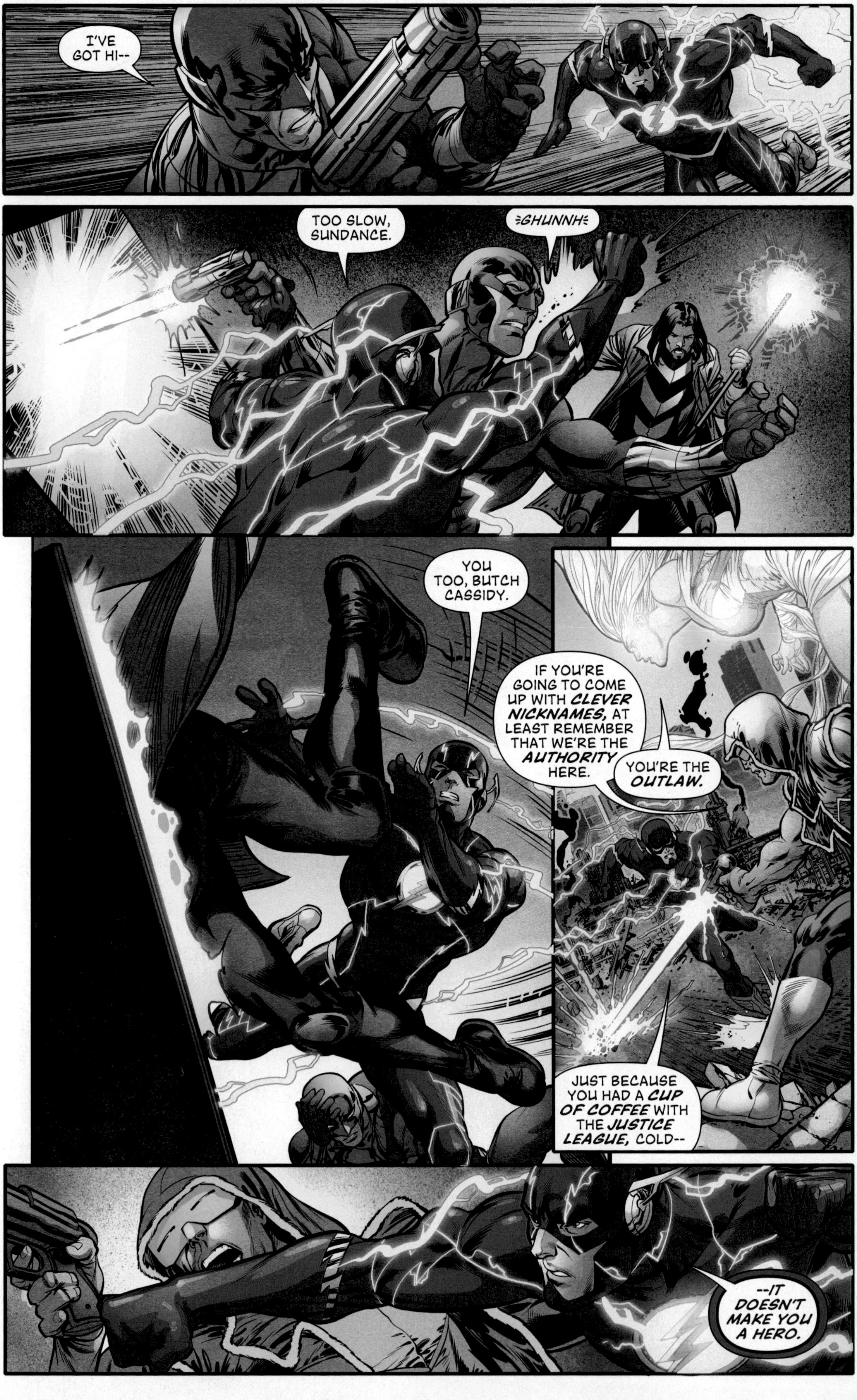
I'VE GOT HI--
TOO SLOW, SUNDANCE.
GHUNNH
YOU TOO, BUTCH CASSIDY.
IF YOU'RE GOING TO COME UP WITH CLEVER NICKNAMES, AT LEAST REMEMBER THAT WE'RE THE AUTHORITY HERE.
YOU'RE THE OUTLAW.
JUST BECAUSE YOU HAD A CUP OF COFFEE WITH THE JUSTICE LEAGUE, COLD--
--IT DOESN'T MAKE YOU A HERO.

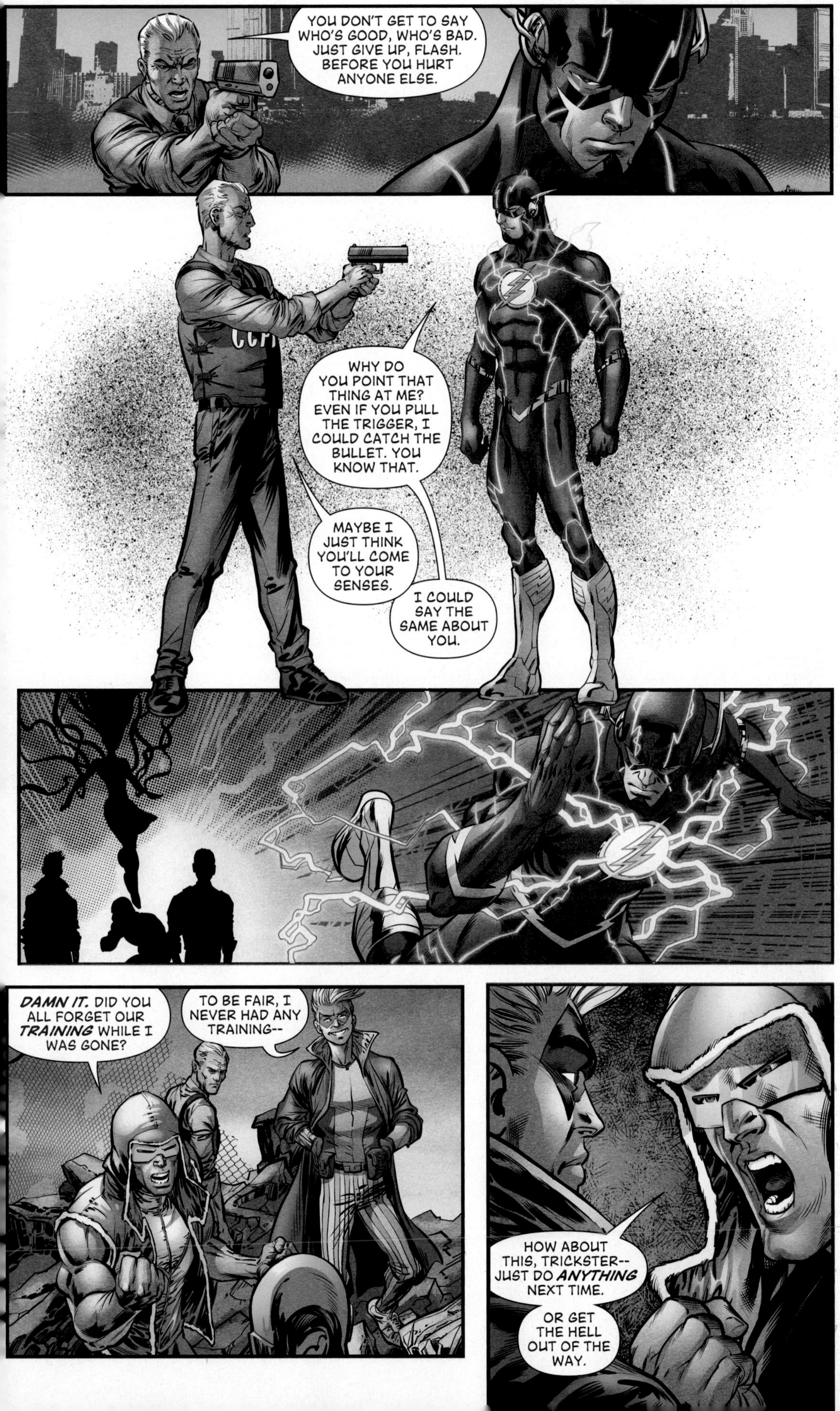
YOU DON'T GET TO SAY WHO'S GOOD, WHO'S BAD. JUST GIVE UP, FLASH. BEFORE YOU HURT ANYONE ELSE.
WHY DO YOU POINT THAT THING AT ME? EVEN IF YOU PULL THE TRIGGER, I COULD CATCH THE BULLET. YOU KNOW THAT.
MAYBE I JUST THINK YOU'LL COME TO YOUR SENSES.
I COULD SAY THE SAME ABOUT YOU.
DAMN IT. DID YOU ALL FORGET OUR TRAINING WHILE I WAS GONE?
TO BE FAIR, I NEVER HAD ANY TRAINING--
HOW ABOUT THIS, TRICKSTER-- JUST DO ANYTHING NEXT TIME.
OR GET THE HELL OUT OF THE WAY.

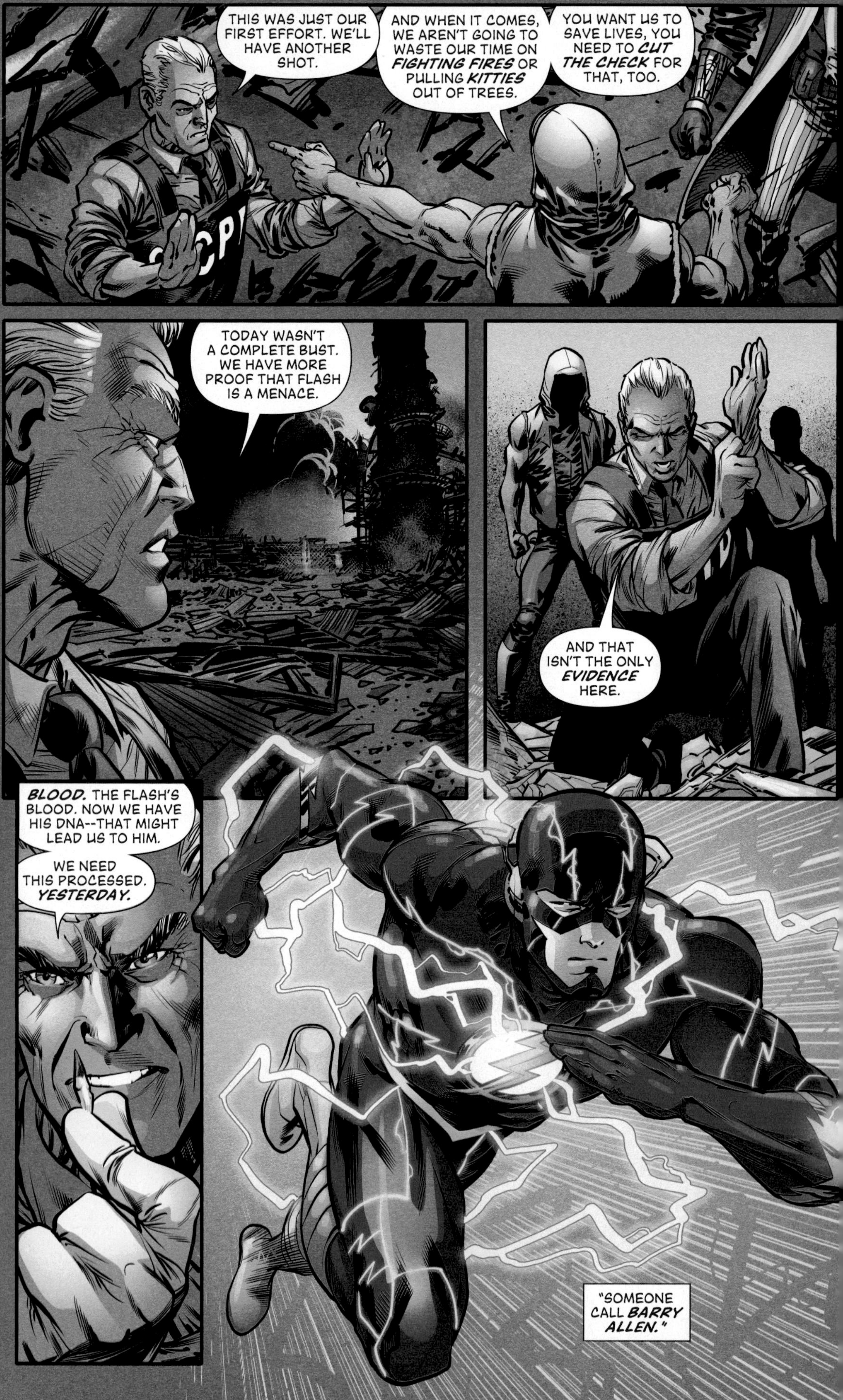
THIS WAS JUST OUR FIRST EFFORT. WE'LL HAVE ANOTHER SHOT.
AND WHEN IT COMES, WE AREN'T GOING TO WASTE OUR TIME ON *FIGHTING FIRES* OR PULLING *KITTIES* OUT OF TREES.
YOU WANT US TO SAVE LIVES, YOU NEED TO *CUT THE CHECK* FOR THAT, TOO.
TODAY WASN'T A COMPLETE BUST. WE HAVE MORE PROOF THAT FLASH IS A MENACE.
AND THAT ISN'T THE ONLY *EVIDENCE* HERE.
BLOOD. THE FLASH'S BLOOD. NOW WE HAVE HIS DNA--THAT MIGHT LEAD US TO HIM.
WE NEED THIS PROCESSED. *YESTERDAY.*
"SOMEONE CALL *BARRY ALLEN.*"

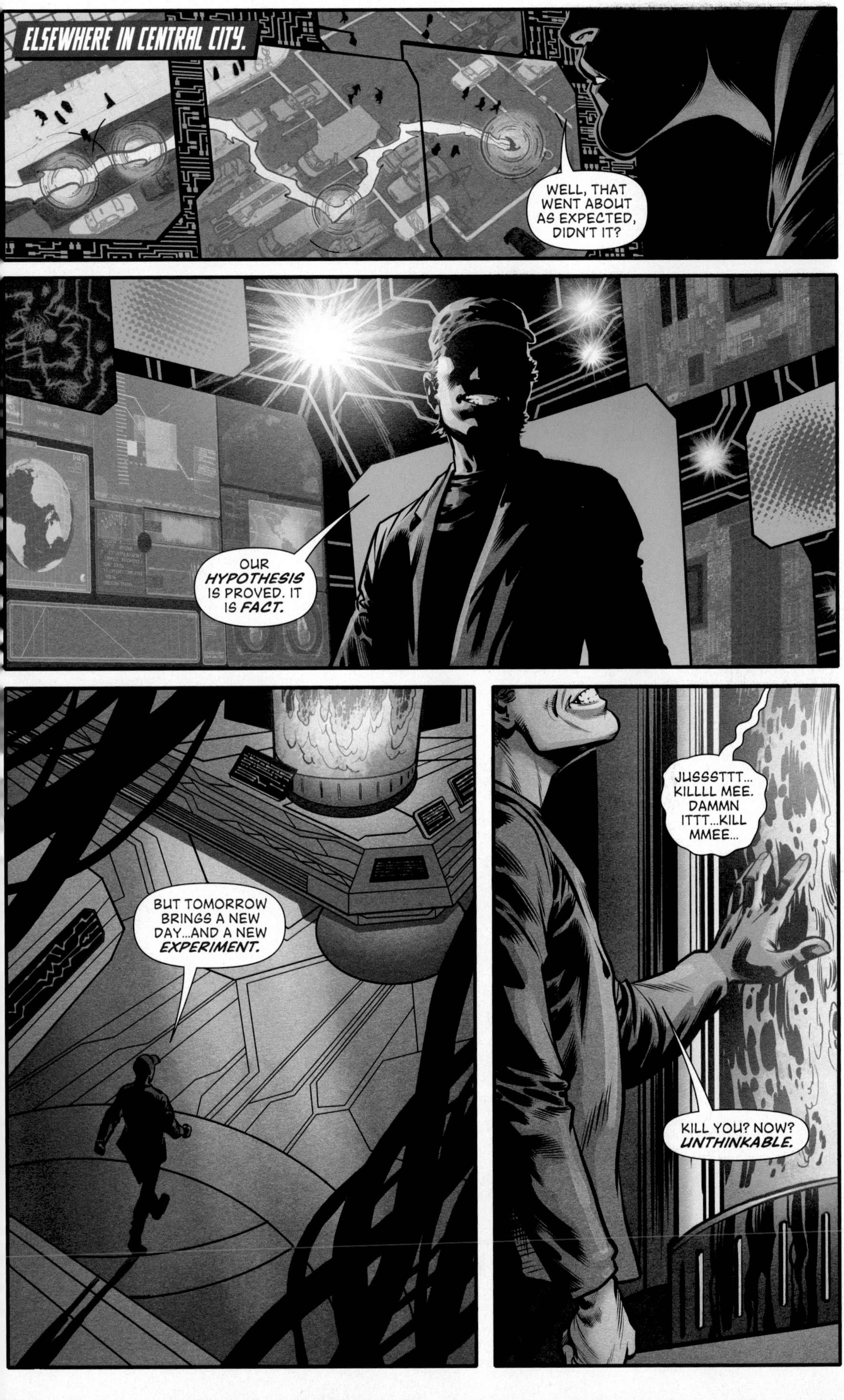
ELSEWHERE IN CENTRAL CITY.
WELL, THAT WENT ABOUT AS EXPECTED, DIDN'T IT?
OUR *HYPOTHESIS* IS PROVED. IT IS *FACT.*
BUT TOMORROW BRINGS A NEW DAY...AND A NEW *EXPERIMENT.*
JUSSSTTT... KILLLL MEE. DAMMN ITTT...KILL MMEE...
KILL YOU? NOW? ***UNTHINKABLE.***

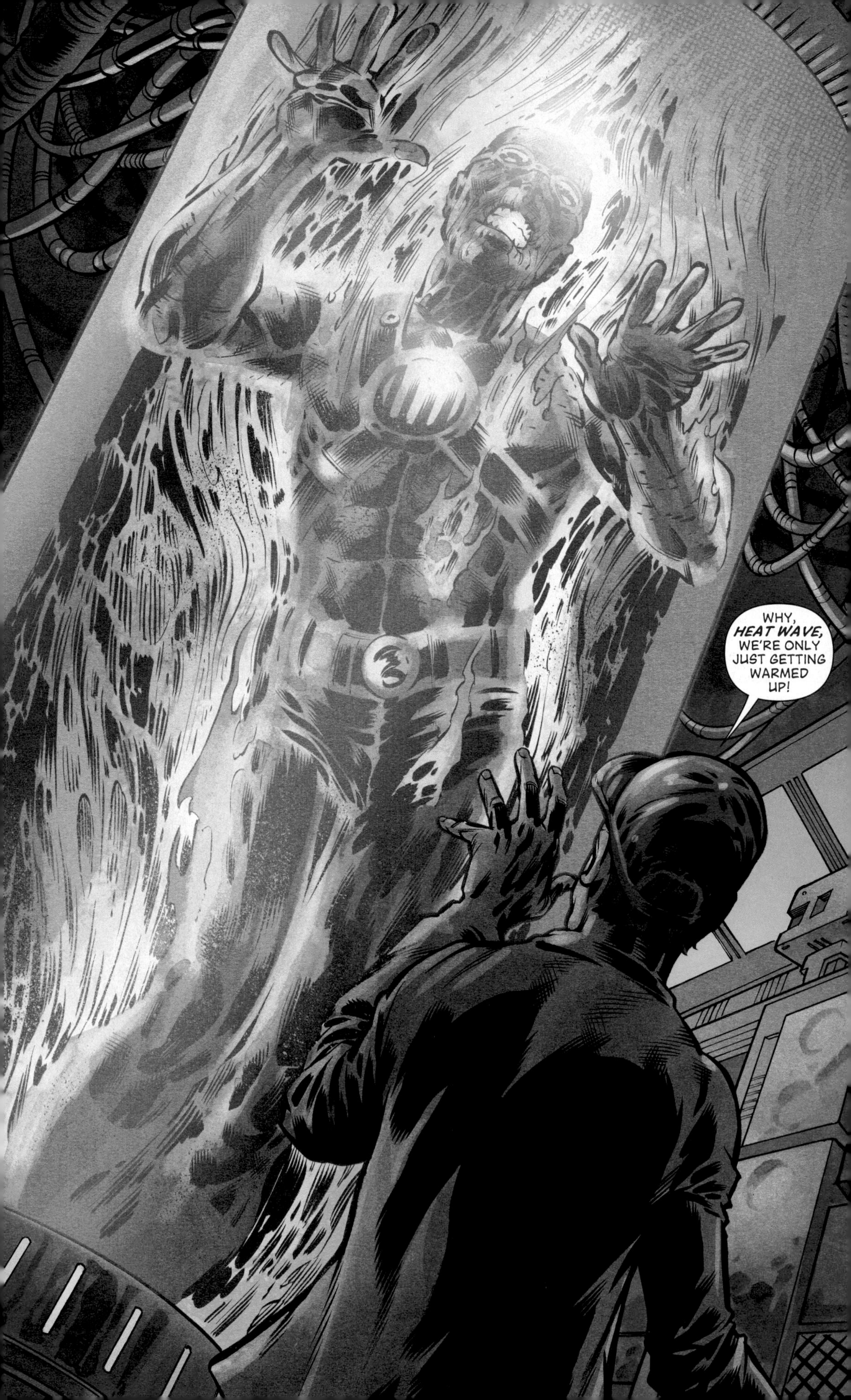
WHY, HEAT WAVE, WE'RE ONLY JUST GETTING WARMED UP!

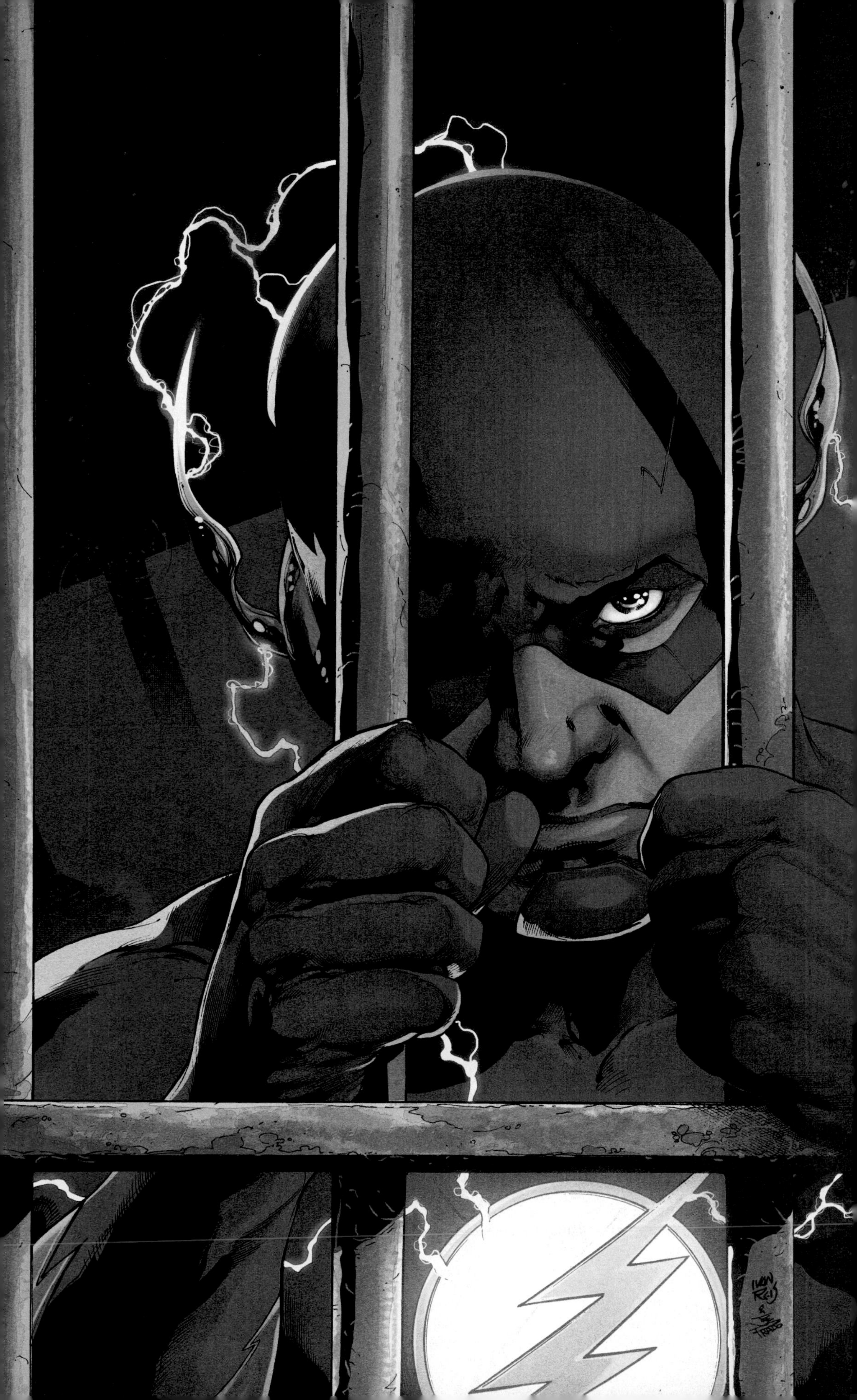

ROBERT VENDITTI VAN JENSEN writers PHIL BRIONES artist GUY MAJOR colorist PAT BROSSEAU letterer IVAN REIS JOE PRADO ADRIANO LUCAS cover

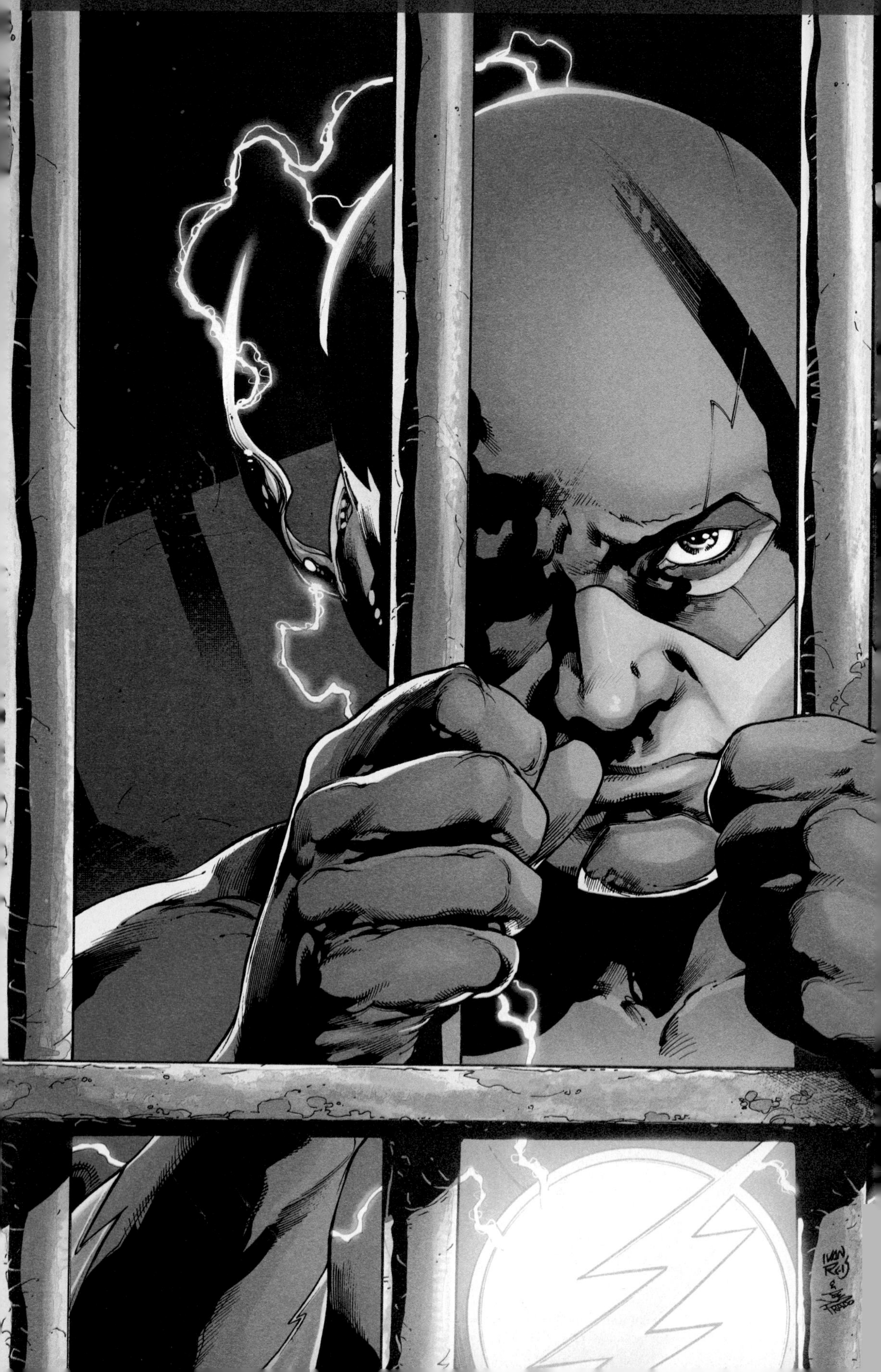

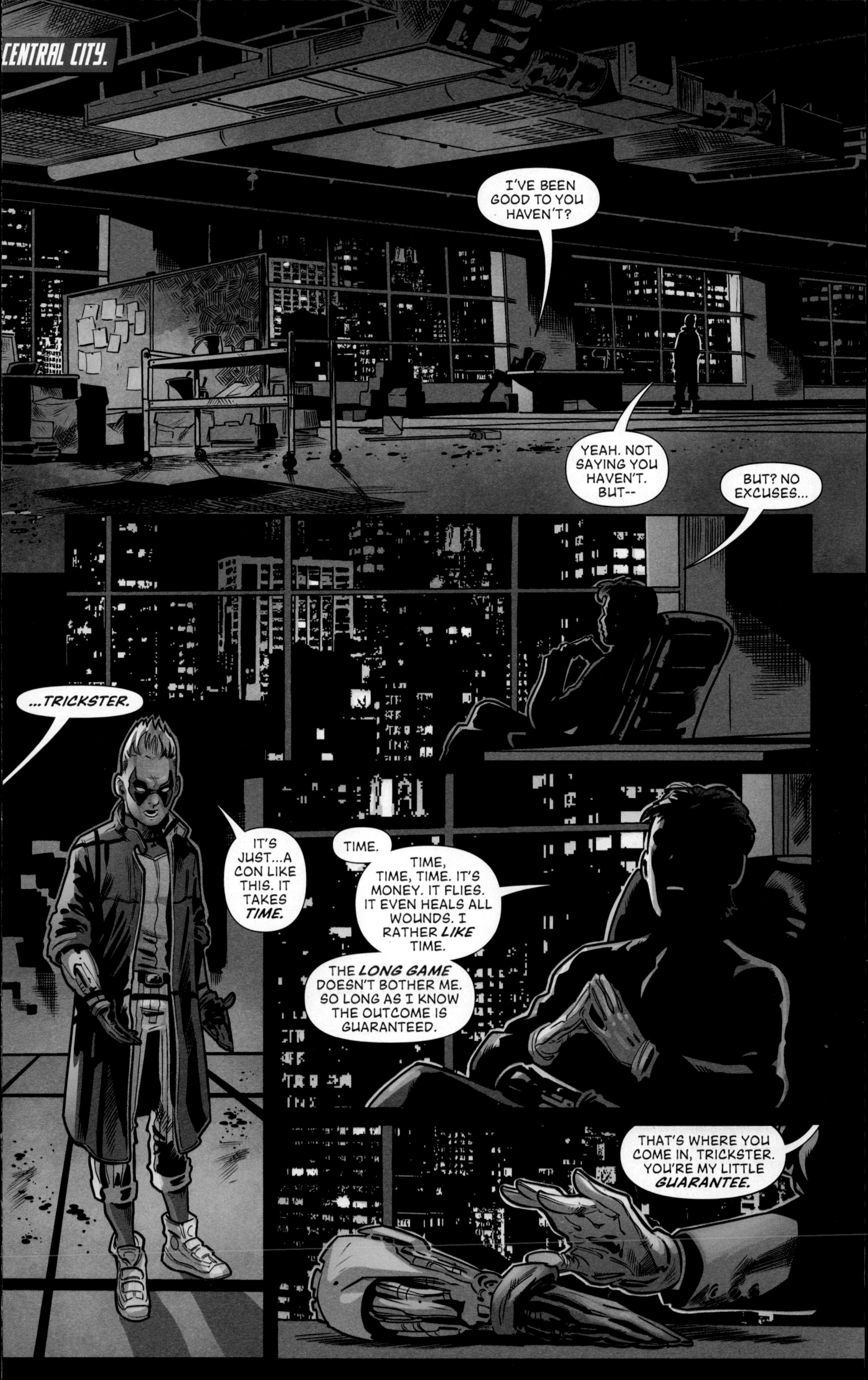
CENTRAL CITY.
I'VE BEEN GOOD TO YOU HAVEN'T?
YEAH. NOT SAYING YOU HAVEN'T. BUT--
BUT? NO EXCUSES...
...TRICKSTER.
IT'S JUST...A CON LIKE THIS. IT TAKES *TIME.*
TIME.
TIME, TIME, TIME. IT'S MONEY. IT FLIES. IT EVEN HEALS ALL WOUNDS. I RATHER *LIKE* TIME.
THE *LONG GAME* DOESN'T BOTHER ME. SO LONG AS I KNOW THE OUTCOME IS GUARANTEED.
THAT'S WHERE YOU COME IN, TRICKSTER. YOU'RE MY LITTLE *GUARANTEE.*

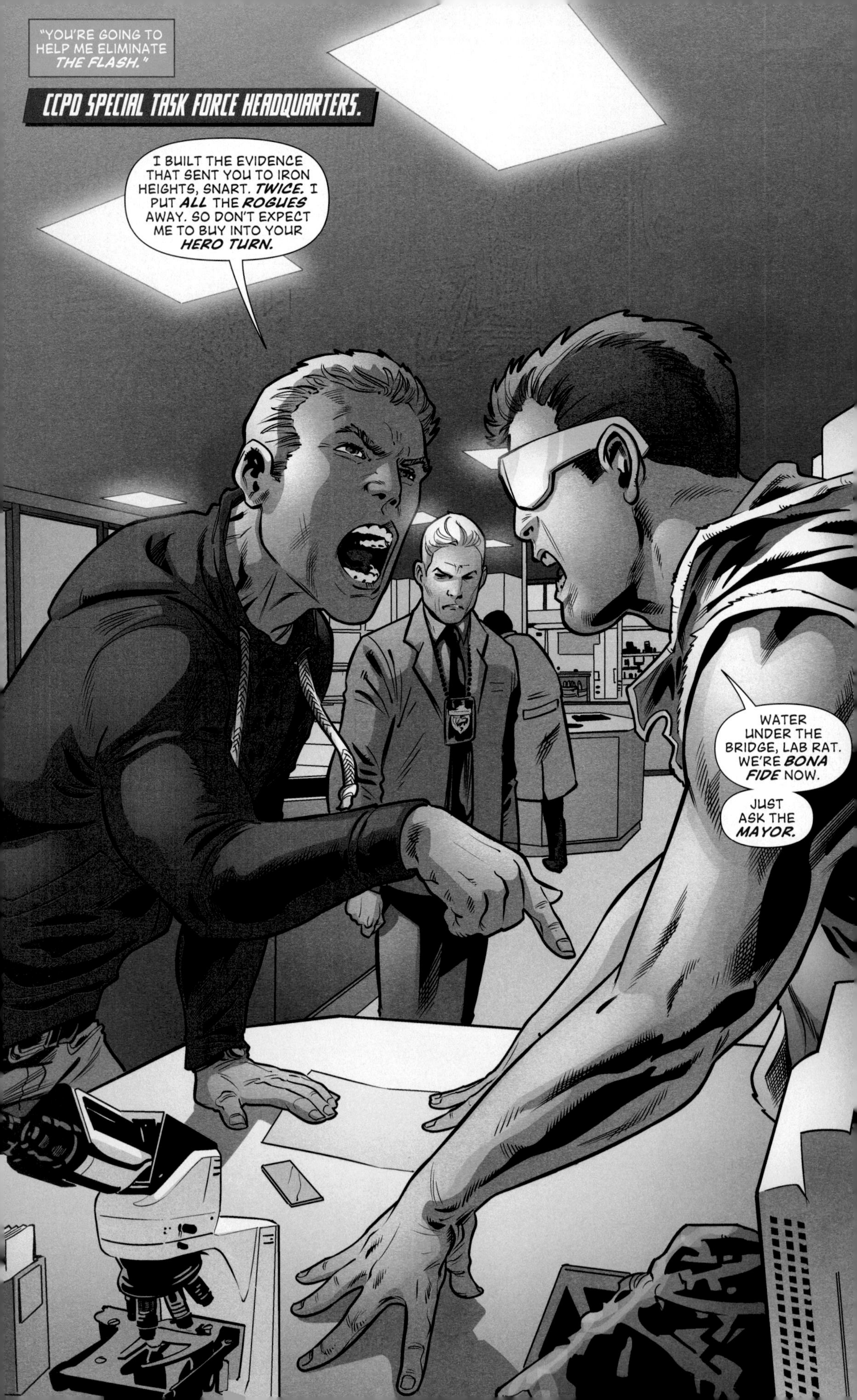
"YOU'RE GOING TO HELP ME ELIMINATE *THE FLASH.*"
CCPD SPECIAL TASK FORCE HEADQUARTERS.
I BUILT THE EVIDENCE THAT SENT YOU TO IRON HEIGHTS, SNART. *TWICE.* I PUT *ALL* THE *ROGUES* AWAY. SO DON'T EXPECT ME TO BUY INTO YOUR *HERO TURN.*
WATER UNDER THE BRIDGE, LAB RAT. WE'RE *BONA FIDE* NOW.
JUST ASK THE *MAYOR.*

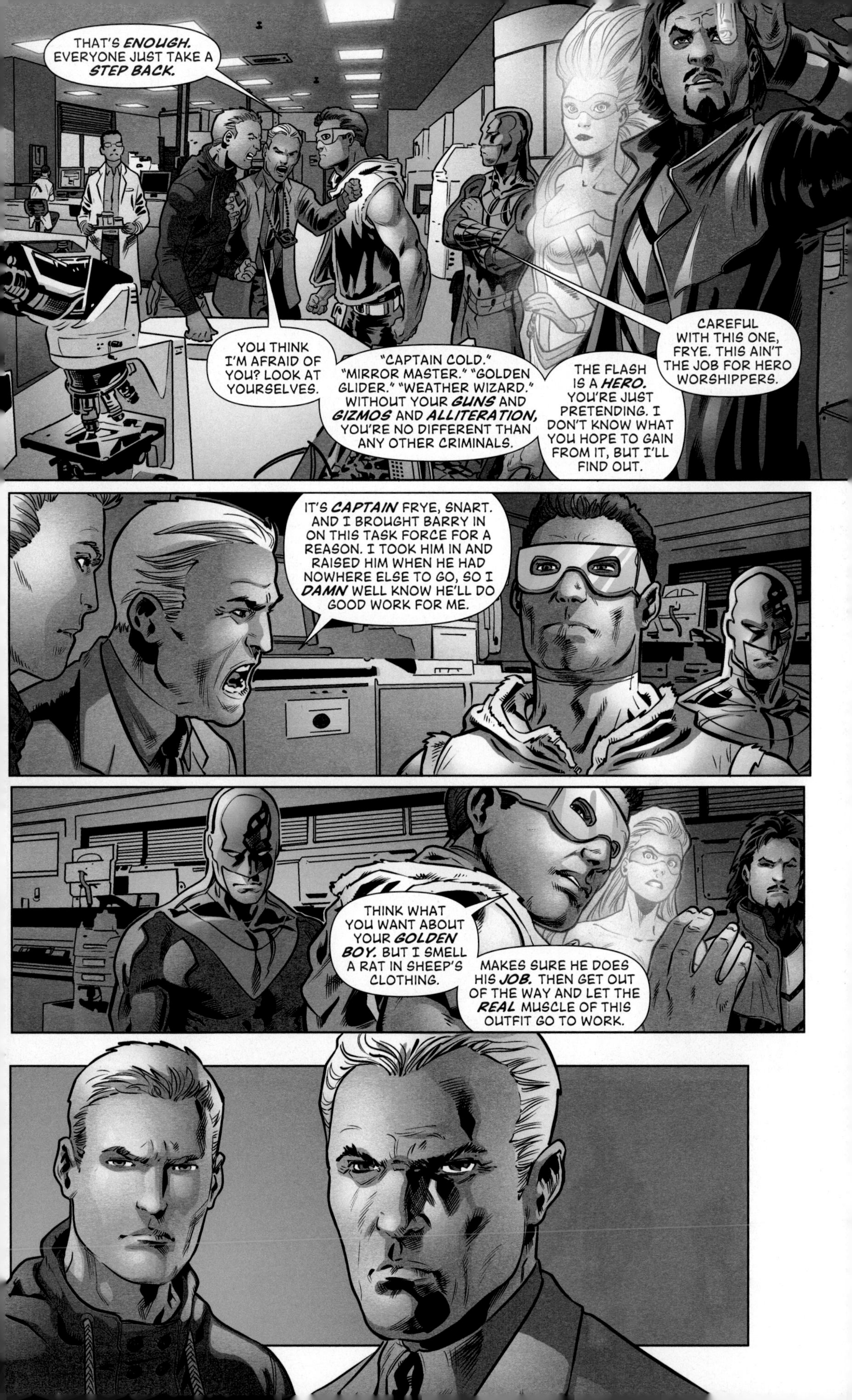
THAT'S ENOUGH. EVERYONE JUST TAKE A STEP BACK.
YOU THINK I'M AFRAID OF YOU? LOOK AT YOURSELVES.
"CAPTAIN COLD." "MIRROR MASTER." "GOLDEN GLIDER." "WEATHER WIZARD." WITHOUT YOUR GUNS AND GIZMOS AND ALLITERATION, YOU'RE NO DIFFERENT THAN ANY OTHER CRIMINALS.
THE FLASH IS A HERO. YOU'RE JUST PRETENDING. I DON'T KNOW WHAT YOU HOPE TO GAIN FROM IT, BUT I'LL FIND OUT.
CAREFUL WITH THIS ONE, FRYE. THIS AIN'T THE JOB FOR HERO WORSHIPPERS.
IT'S CAPTAIN FRYE, SNART. AND I BROUGHT BARRY IN ON THIS TASK FORCE FOR A REASON. I TOOK HIM IN AND RAISED HIM WHEN HE HAD NOWHERE ELSE TO GO, SO I DAMN WELL KNOW HE'LL DO GOOD WORK FOR ME.
THINK WHAT YOU WANT ABOUT YOUR GOLDEN BOY. BUT I SMELL A RAT IN SHEEP'S CLOTHING.
MAKES SURE HE DOES HIS JOB. THEN GET OUT OF THE WAY AND LET THE REAL MUSCLE OF THIS OUTFIT GO TO WORK.

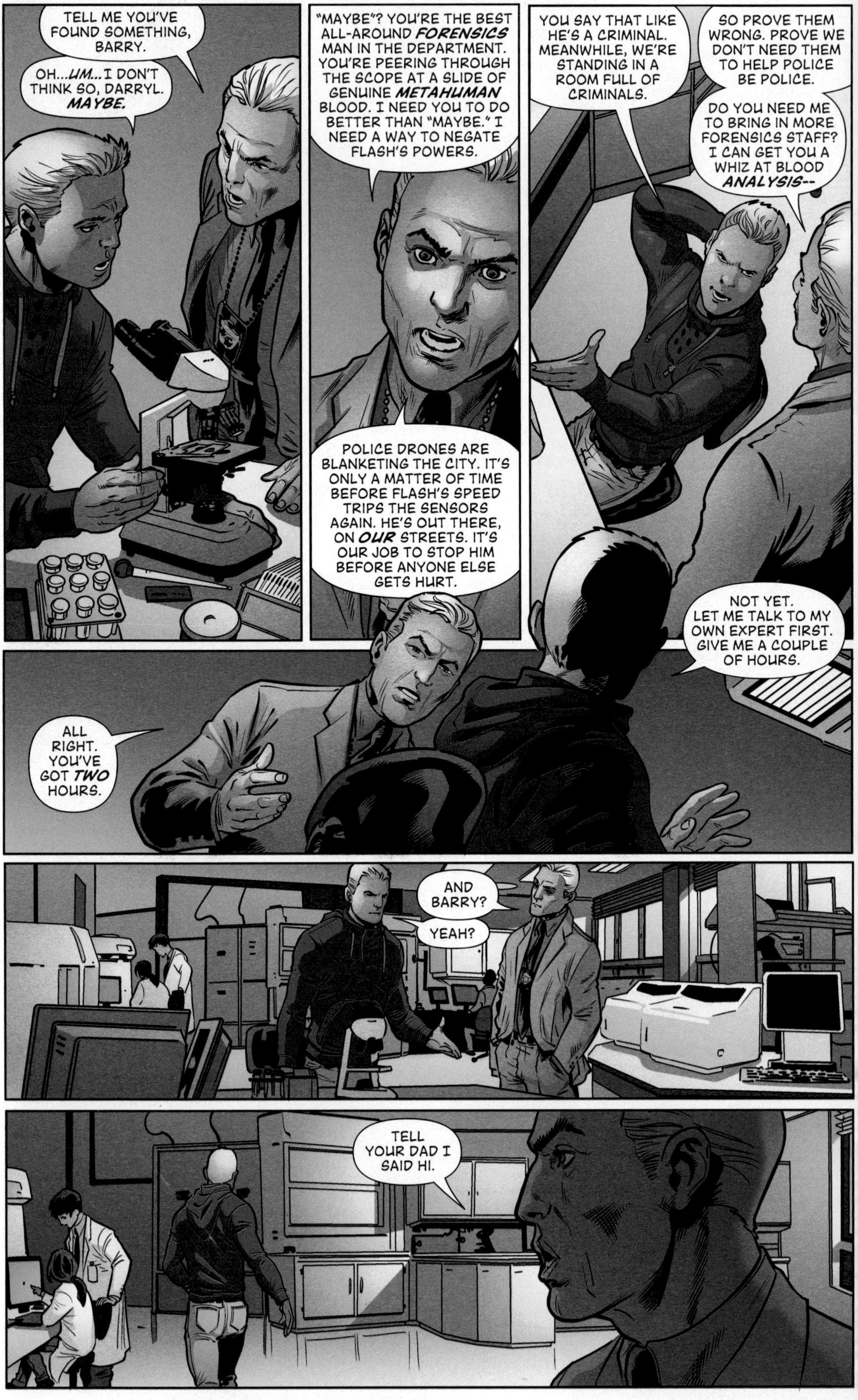
TELL ME YOU'VE FOUND SOMETHING, BARRY.
OH...UM...I DON'T THINK SO, DARRYL. MAYBE.
"MAYBE"? YOU'RE THE BEST ALL-AROUND FORENSICS MAN IN THE DEPARTMENT. YOU'RE PEERING THROUGH THE SCOPE AT A SLIDE OF GENUINE METAHUMAN BLOOD. I NEED YOU TO DO BETTER THAN "MAYBE." I NEED A WAY TO NEGATE FLASH'S POWERS.
POLICE DRONES ARE BLANKETING THE CITY. IT'S ONLY A MATTER OF TIME BEFORE FLASH'S SPEED TRIPS THE SENSORS AGAIN. HE'S OUT THERE, ON OUR STREETS. IT'S OUR JOB TO STOP HIM BEFORE ANYONE ELSE GETS HURT.
YOU SAY THAT LIKE HE'S A CRIMINAL. MEANWHILE, WE'RE STANDING IN A ROOM FULL OF CRIMINALS.
SO PROVE THEM WRONG. PROVE WE DON'T NEED THEM TO HELP POLICE BE POLICE.
DO YOU NEED ME TO BRING IN MORE FORENSICS STAFF? I CAN GET YOU A WHIZ AT BLOOD ANALYSIS--
NOT YET. LET ME TALK TO MY OWN EXPERT FIRST. GIVE ME A COUPLE OF HOURS.
ALL RIGHT. YOU'VE GOT TWO HOURS.
AND BARRY?
YEAH?
TELL YOUR DAD I SAID HI.

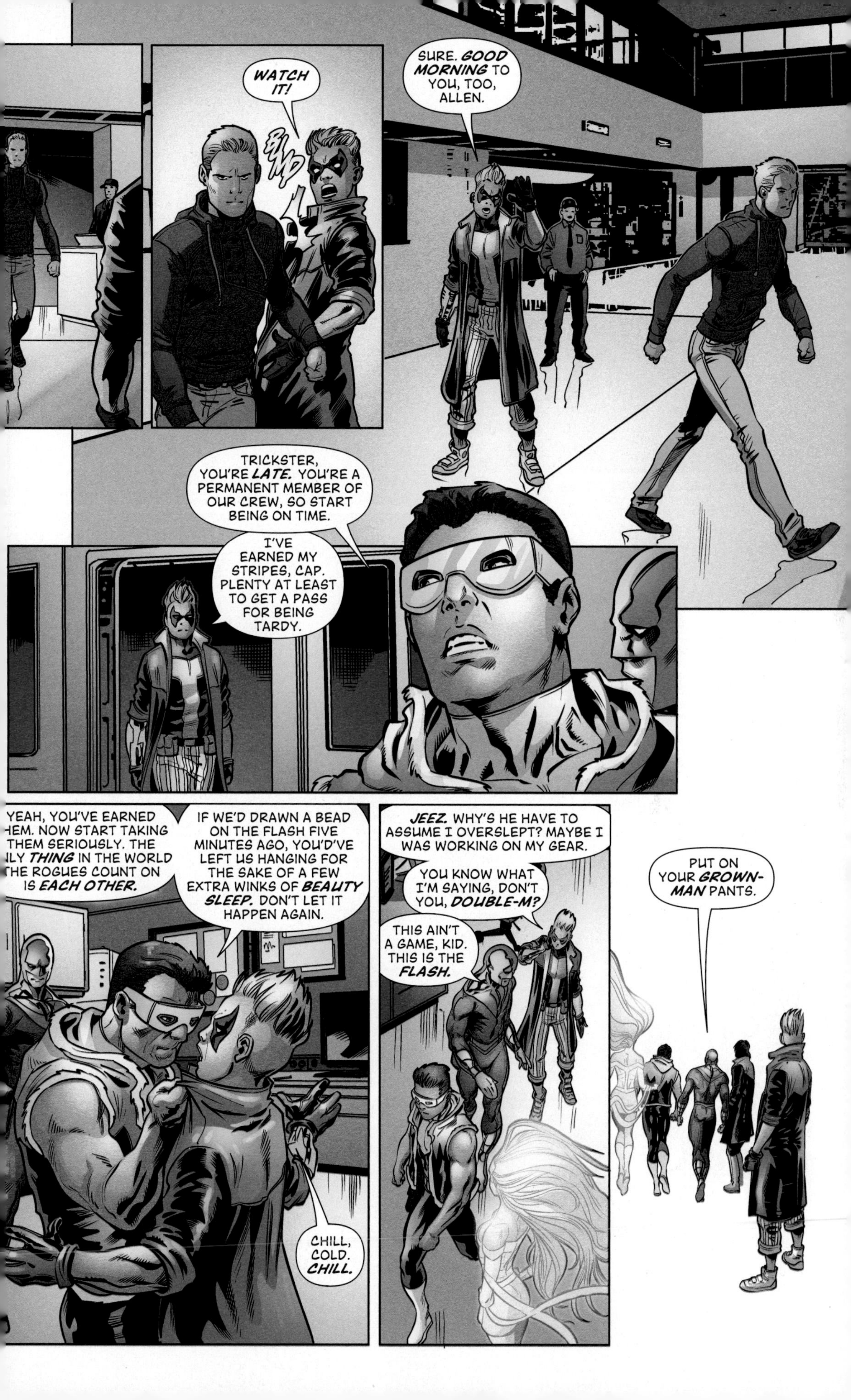
WATCH IT!
SURE. GOOD MORNING TO YOU, TOO, ALLEN.
TRICKSTER, YOU'RE LATE. YOU'RE A PERMANENT MEMBER OF OUR CREW, SO START BEING ON TIME.
I'VE EARNED MY STRIPES, CAP. PLENTY AT LEAST TO GET A PASS FOR BEING TARDY.
YEAH, YOU'VE EARNED HEM. NOW START TAKING THEM SERIOUSLY. THE ILY THING IN THE WORLD THE ROGUES COUNT ON IS EACH OTHER.
IF WE'D DRAWN A BEAD ON THE FLASH FIVE MINUTES AGO, YOU'D'VE LEFT US HANGING FOR THE SAKE OF A FEW EXTRA WINKS OF BEAUTY SLEEP. DON'T LET IT HAPPEN AGAIN.
CHILL, COLD. CHILL.
JEEZ. WHY'S HE HAVE TO ASSUME I OVERSLEPT? MAYBE I WAS WORKING ON MY GEAR.
YOU KNOW WHAT I'M SAYING, DON'T YOU, DOUBLE-M?
THIS AIN'T A GAME, KID. THIS IS THE FLASH.
PUT ON YOUR GROWN-MAN PANTS.

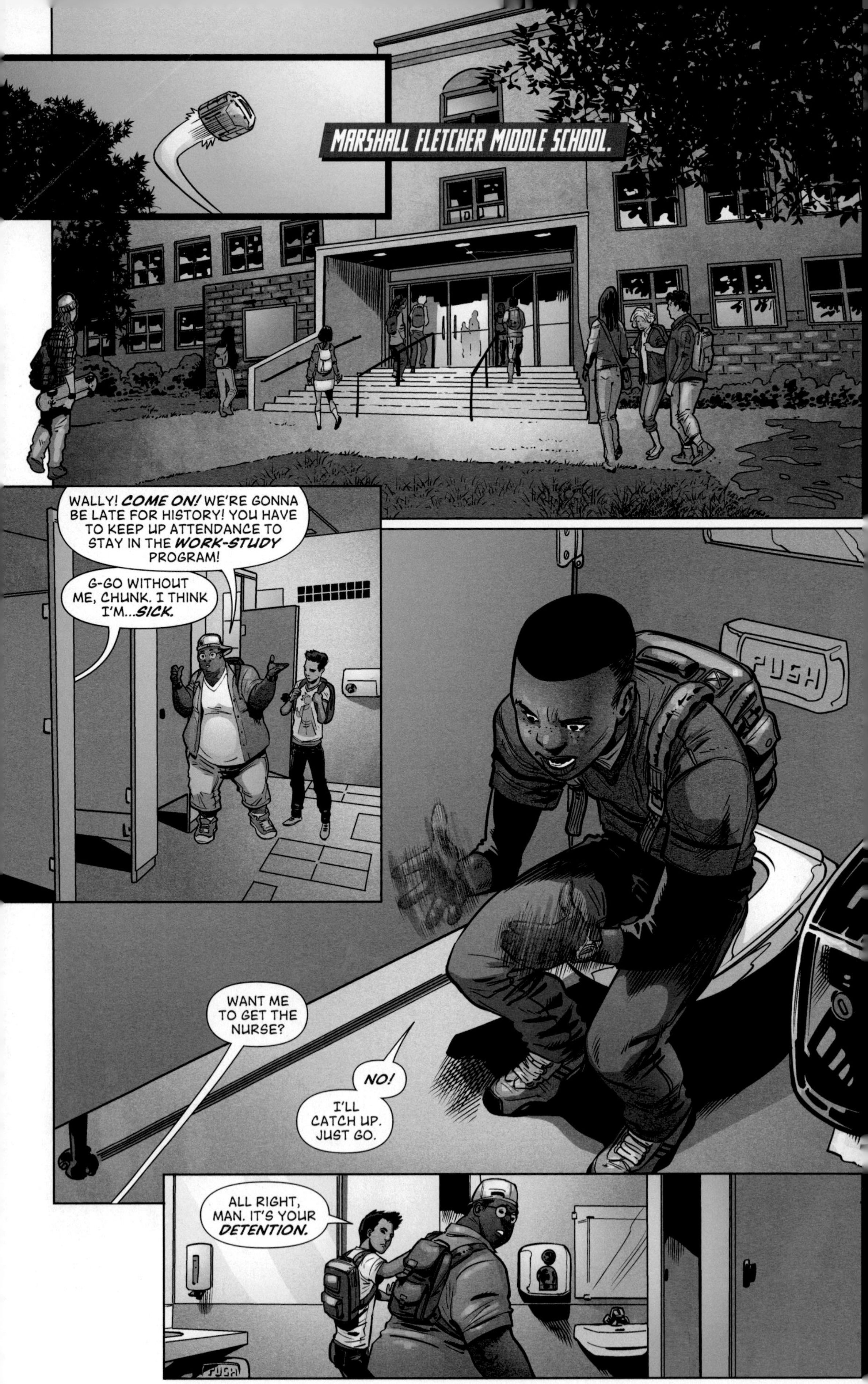
MARSHALL FLETCHER MIDDLE SCHOOL.
WALLY! COME ON! WE'RE GONNA BE LATE FOR HISTORY! YOU HAVE TO KEEP UP ATTENDANCE TO STAY IN THE WORK-STUDY PROGRAM!
G-GO WITHOUT ME, CHUNK. I THINK I'M...SICK.
PUSH
WANT ME TO GET THE NURSE?
NO!
I'LL CATCH UP. JUST GO.
ALL RIGHT, MAN. IT'S YOUR DETENTION.

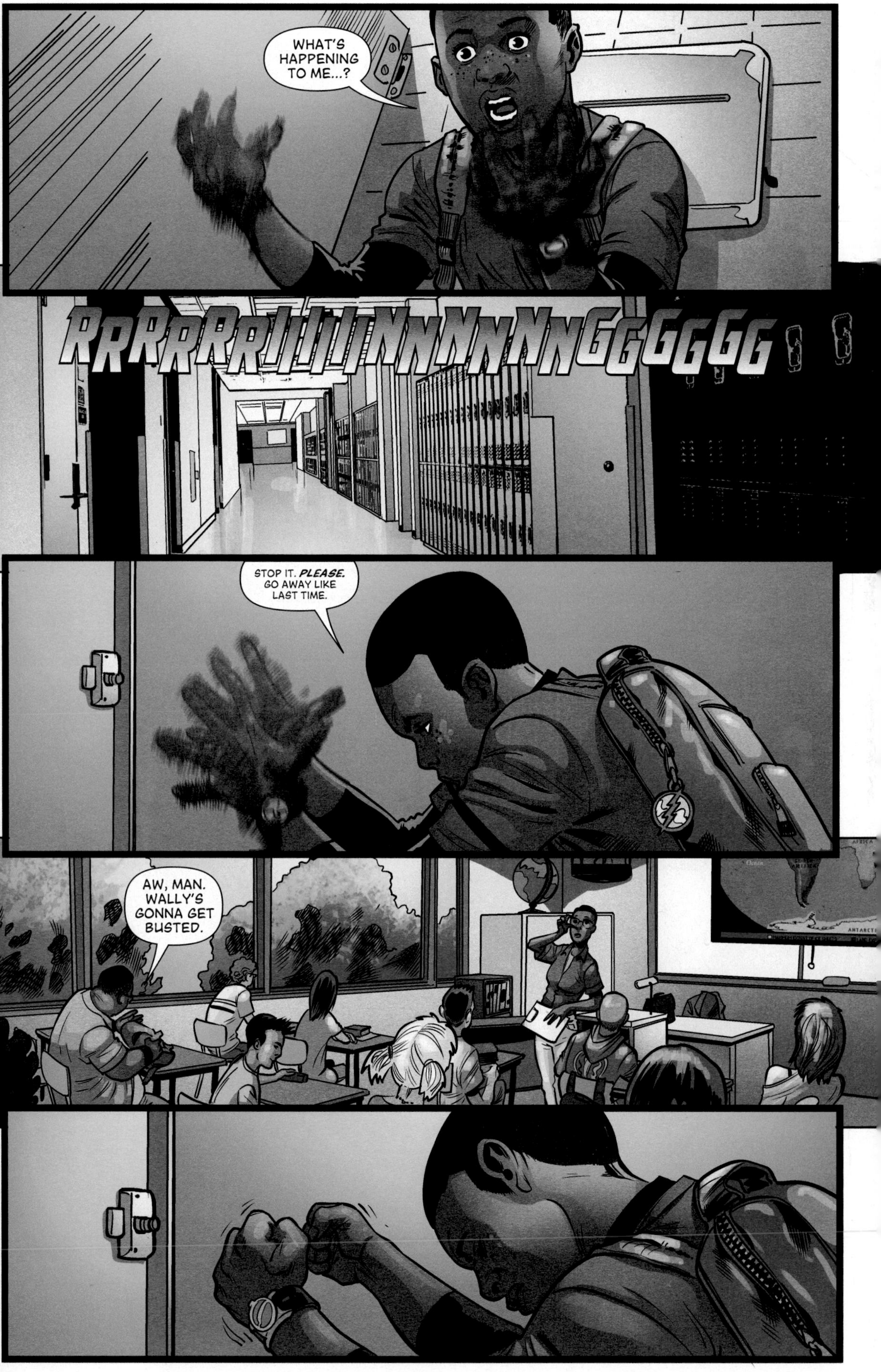
WHAT'S HAPPENING TO ME...?
RRRRRRIIIIIINNNNNNGGGGGG
STOP IT. PLEASE. GO AWAY LIKE LAST TIME.
AW, MAN. WALLY'S GONNA GET BUSTED.

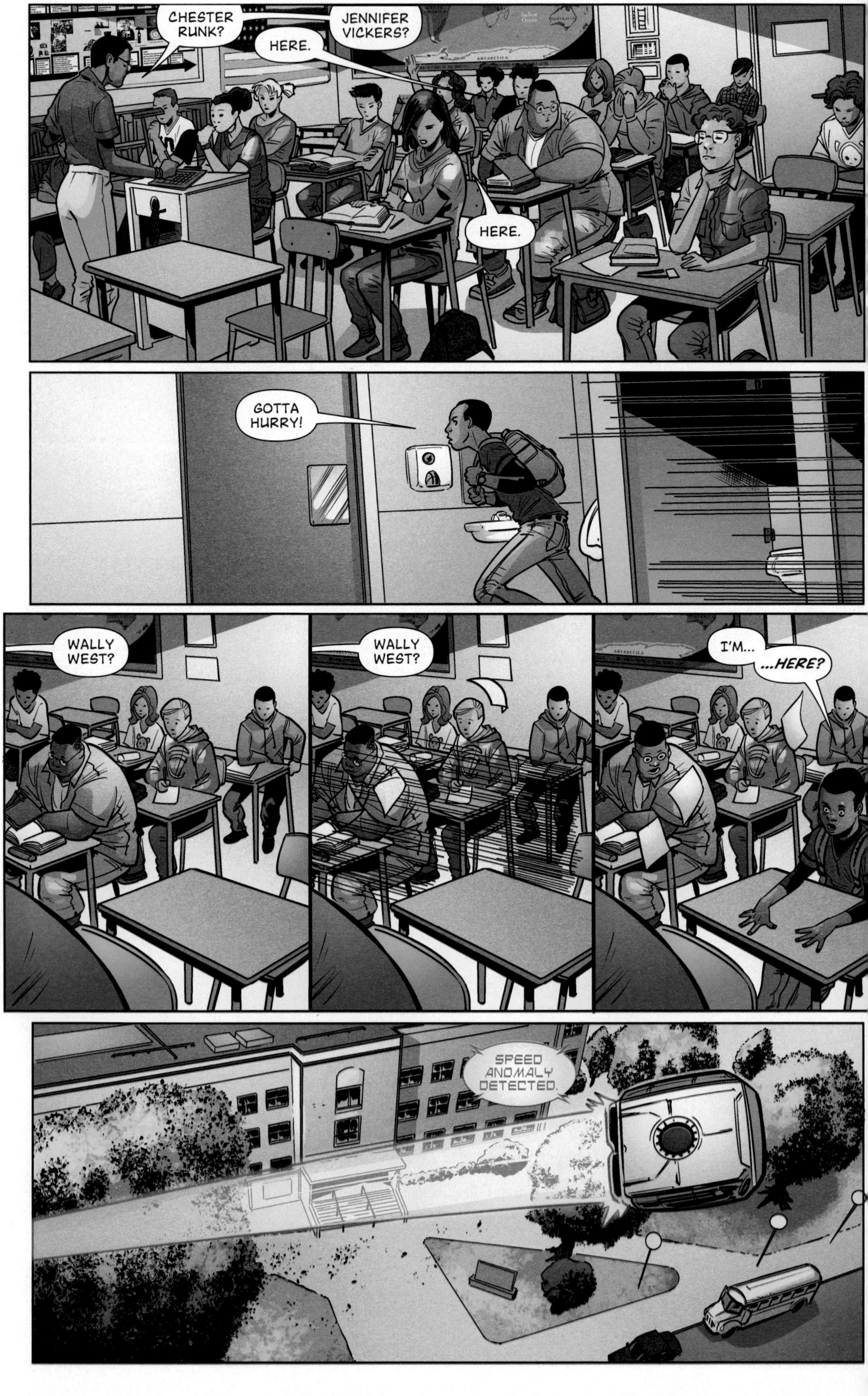
CHESTER RUNK?
JENNIFER VICKERS?
HERE.
HERE.
GOTTA HURRY!
WALLY WEST?
WALLY WEST?
I'M...
...HERE?
SPEED ANOMALY DETECTED.

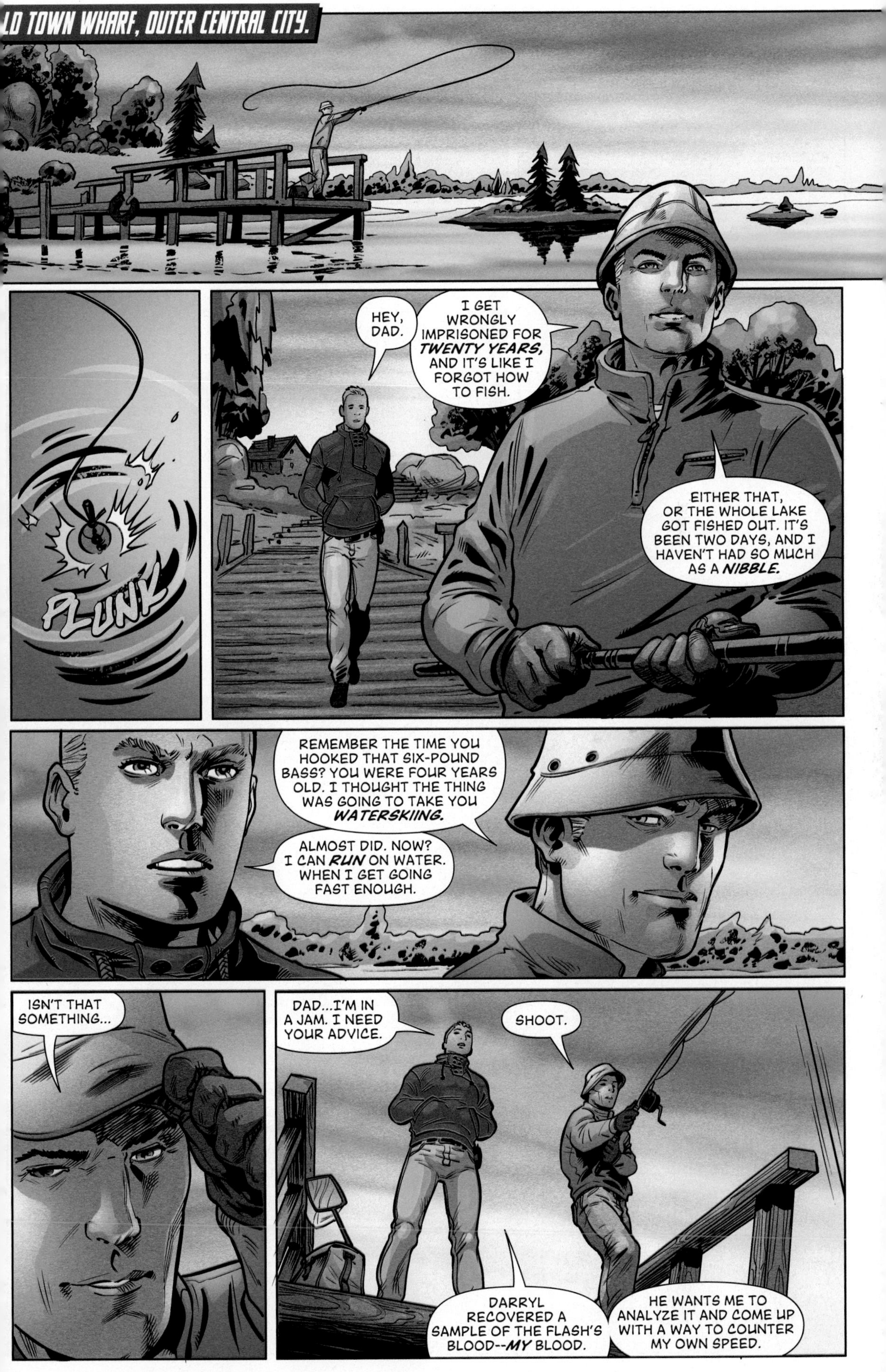
LD TOWN WHARF, OUTER CENTRAL CITY.
PLUNK
HEY, DAD.
I GET WRONGLY IMPRISONED FOR TWENTY YEARS, AND IT'S LIKE I FORGOT HOW TO FISH.
EITHER THAT, OR THE WHOLE LAKE GOT FISHED OUT. IT'S BEEN TWO DAYS, AND I HAVEN'T HAD SO MUCH AS A NIBBLE.
REMEMBER THE TIME YOU HOOKED THAT SIX-POUND BASS? YOU WERE FOUR YEARS OLD. I THOUGHT THE THING WAS GOING TO TAKE YOU WATERSKIING.
ALMOST DID. NOW? I CAN RUN ON WATER. WHEN I GET GOING FAST ENOUGH.
ISN'T THAT SOMETHING...
DAD...I'M IN A JAM. I NEED YOUR ADVICE.
SHOOT.
DARRYL RECOVERED A SAMPLE OF THE FLASH'S BLOOD--MY BLOOD.
HE WANTS ME TO ANALYZE IT AND COME UP WITH A WAY TO COUNTER MY OWN SPEED.

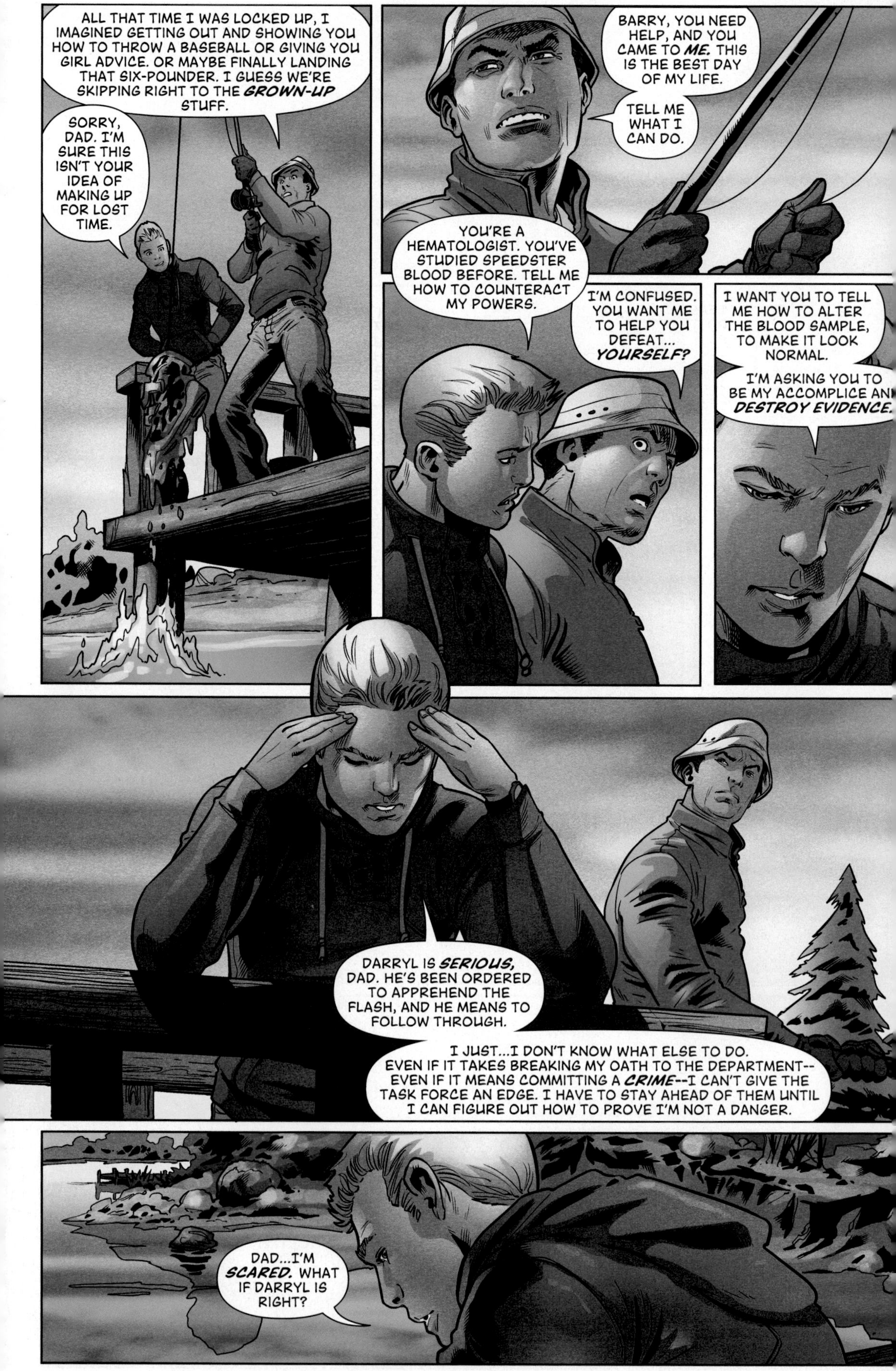
ALL THAT TIME I WAS LOCKED UP, I IMAGINED GETTING OUT AND SHOWING YOU HOW TO THROW A BASEBALL OR GIVING YOU GIRL ADVICE. OR MAYBE FINALLY LANDING THAT SIX-POUNDER. I GUESS WE'RE SKIPPING RIGHT TO THE *GROWN-UP* STUFF.
SORRY, DAD. I'M SURE THIS ISN'T YOUR IDEA OF MAKING UP FOR LOST TIME.
BARRY, YOU NEED HELP, AND YOU CAME TO *ME.* THIS IS THE BEST DAY OF MY LIFE.
TELL ME WHAT I CAN DO.
YOU'RE A HEMATOLOGIST. YOU'VE STUDIED SPEEDSTER BLOOD BEFORE. TELL ME HOW TO COUNTERACT MY POWERS.
I'M CONFUSED. YOU WANT ME TO HELP YOU DEFEAT... *YOURSELF?*
I WANT YOU TO TELL ME HOW TO ALTER THE BLOOD SAMPLE, TO MAKE IT LOOK NORMAL.
I'M ASKING YOU TO BE MY ACCOMPLICE AN *DESTROY EVIDENCE.*
DARRYL IS *SERIOUS,* DAD. HE'S BEEN ORDERED TO APPREHEND THE FLASH, AND HE MEANS TO FOLLOW THROUGH.
I JUST...I DON'T KNOW WHAT ELSE TO DO. EVEN IF IT TAKES BREAKING MY OATH TO THE DEPARTMENT-- EVEN IF IT MEANS COMMITTING A *CRIME*--I CAN'T GIVE THE TASK FORCE AN EDGE. I HAVE TO STAY AHEAD OF THEM UNTIL I CAN FIGURE OUT HOW TO PROVE I'M NOT A DANGER.
DAD...I'M *SCARED.* WHAT IF DARRYL IS RIGHT?

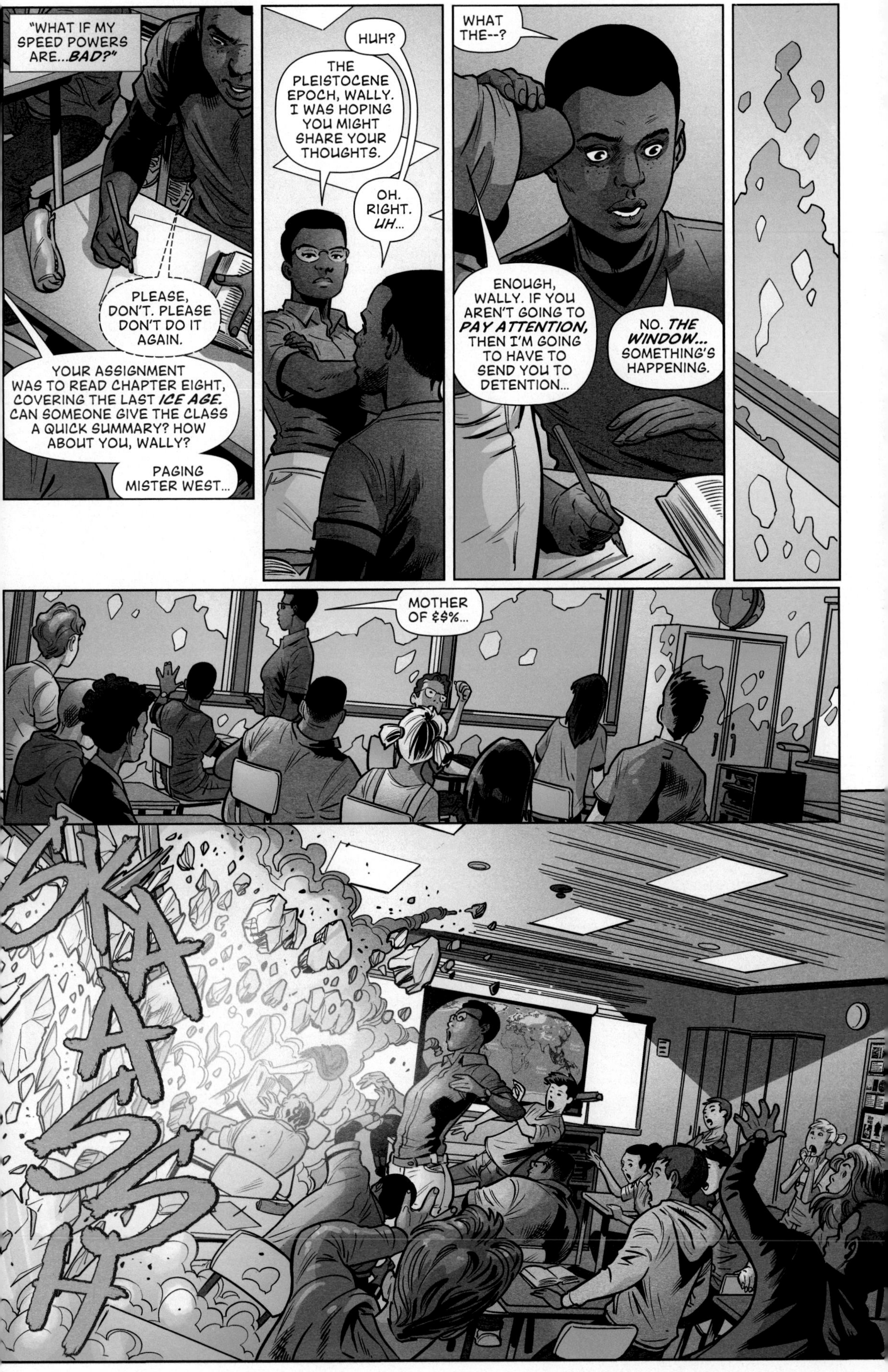
"WHAT IF MY SPEED POWERS ARE...BAD?"
PLEASE, DON'T. PLEASE DON'T DO IT AGAIN.
YOUR ASSIGNMENT WAS TO READ CHAPTER EIGHT, COVERING THE LAST ICE AGE. CAN SOMEONE GIVE THE CLASS A QUICK SUMMARY? HOW ABOUT YOU, WALLY?
PAGING MISTER WEST...
HUH?
THE PLEISTOCENE EPOCH, WALLY. I WAS HOPING YOU MIGHT SHARE YOUR THOUGHTS.
OH. RIGHT. UH...
WHAT THE--?
ENOUGH, WALLY. IF YOU AREN'T GOING TO PAY ATTENTION, THEN I'M GOING TO HAVE TO SEND YOU TO DETENTION...
NO. THE WINDOW... SOMETHING'S HAPPENING.
MOTHER OF $$%...
SKAASSH

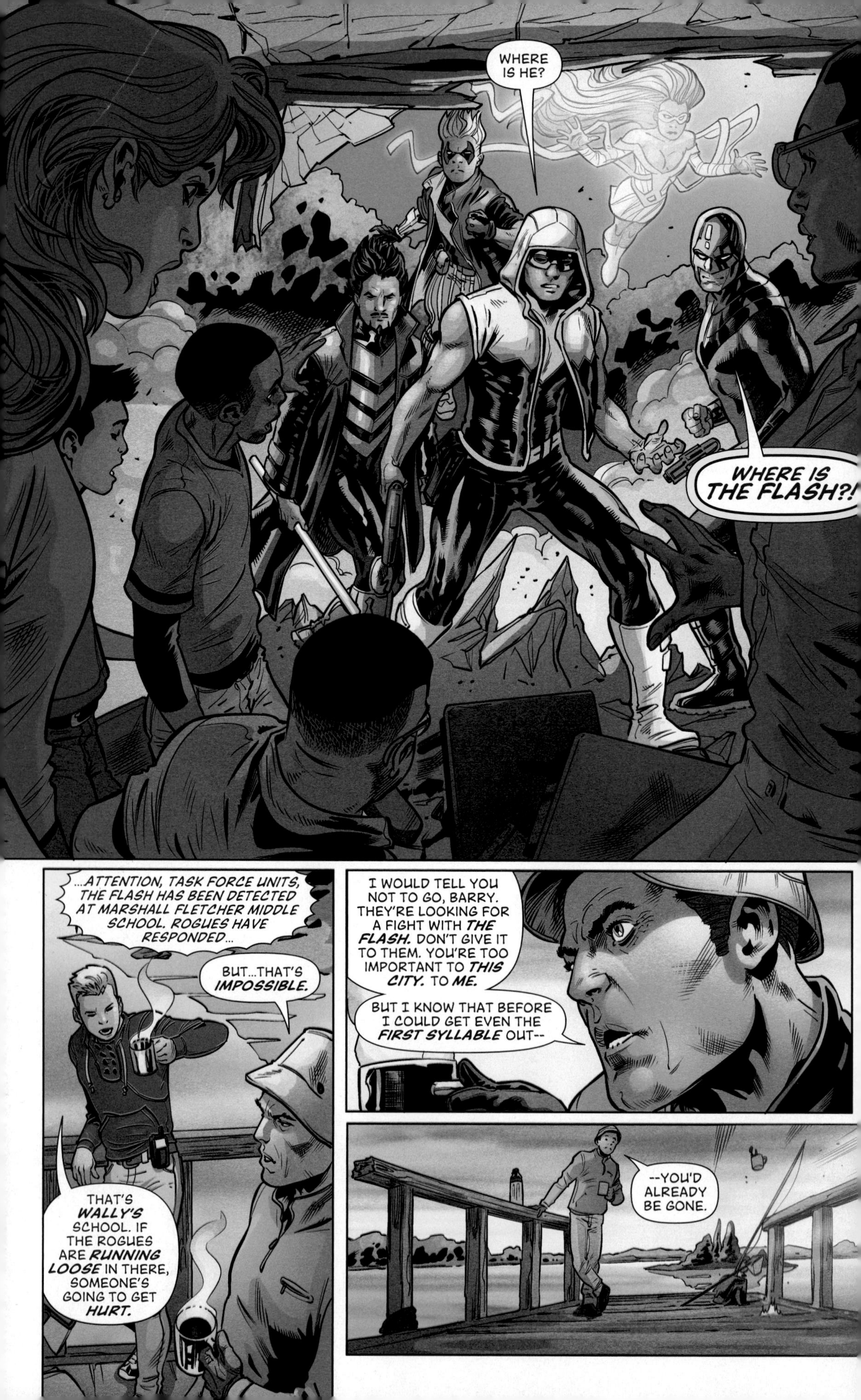
WHERE IS HE?
WHERE IS THE FLASH?!
...ATTENTION, TASK FORCE UNITS, THE FLASH HAS BEEN DETECTED AT MARSHALL FLETCHER MIDDLE SCHOOL. ROGUES HAVE RESPONDED...
BUT...THAT'S IMPOSSIBLE.
THAT'S WALLY'S SCHOOL. IF THE ROGUES ARE RUNNING LOOSE IN THERE, SOMEONE'S GOING TO GET HURT.
I WOULD TELL YOU NOT TO GO, BARRY. THEY'RE LOOKING FOR A FIGHT WITH THE FLASH. DON'T GIVE IT TO THEM. YOU'RE TOO IMPORTANT TO THIS CITY. TO ME.
BUT I KNOW THAT BEFORE I COULD GET EVEN THE FIRST SYLLABLE OUT--
--YOU'D ALREADY BE GONE.

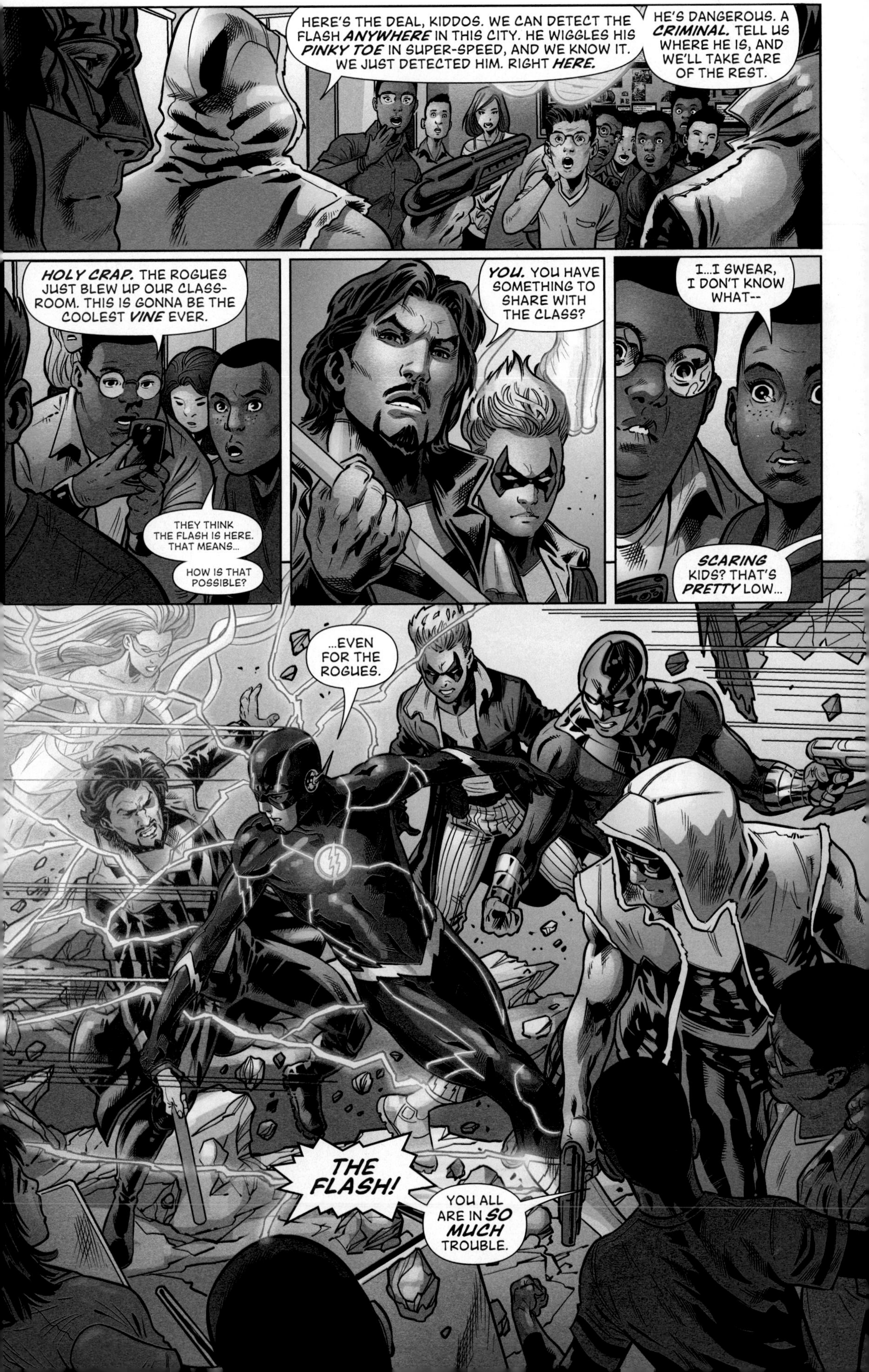
HERE'S THE DEAL, KIDDOS. WE CAN DETECT THE FLASH ANYWHERE IN THIS CITY. HE WIGGLES HIS PINKY TOE IN SUPER-SPEED, AND WE KNOW IT. WE JUST DETECTED HIM. RIGHT HERE.
HE'S DANGEROUS. A CRIMINAL. TELL US WHERE HE IS, AND WE'LL TAKE CARE OF THE REST.
HOLY CRAP. THE ROGUES JUST BLEW UP OUR CLASS-ROOM. THIS IS GONNA BE THE COOLEST VINE EVER.
THEY THINK THE FLASH IS HERE. THAT MEANS...
HOW IS THAT POSSIBLE?
YOU. YOU HAVE SOMETHING TO SHARE WITH THE CLASS?
I...I SWEAR, I DON'T KNOW WHAT--
SCARING KIDS? THAT'S PRETTY LOW...
...EVEN FOR THE ROGUES.
THE FLASH!
YOU ALL ARE IN SO MUCH TROUBLE.

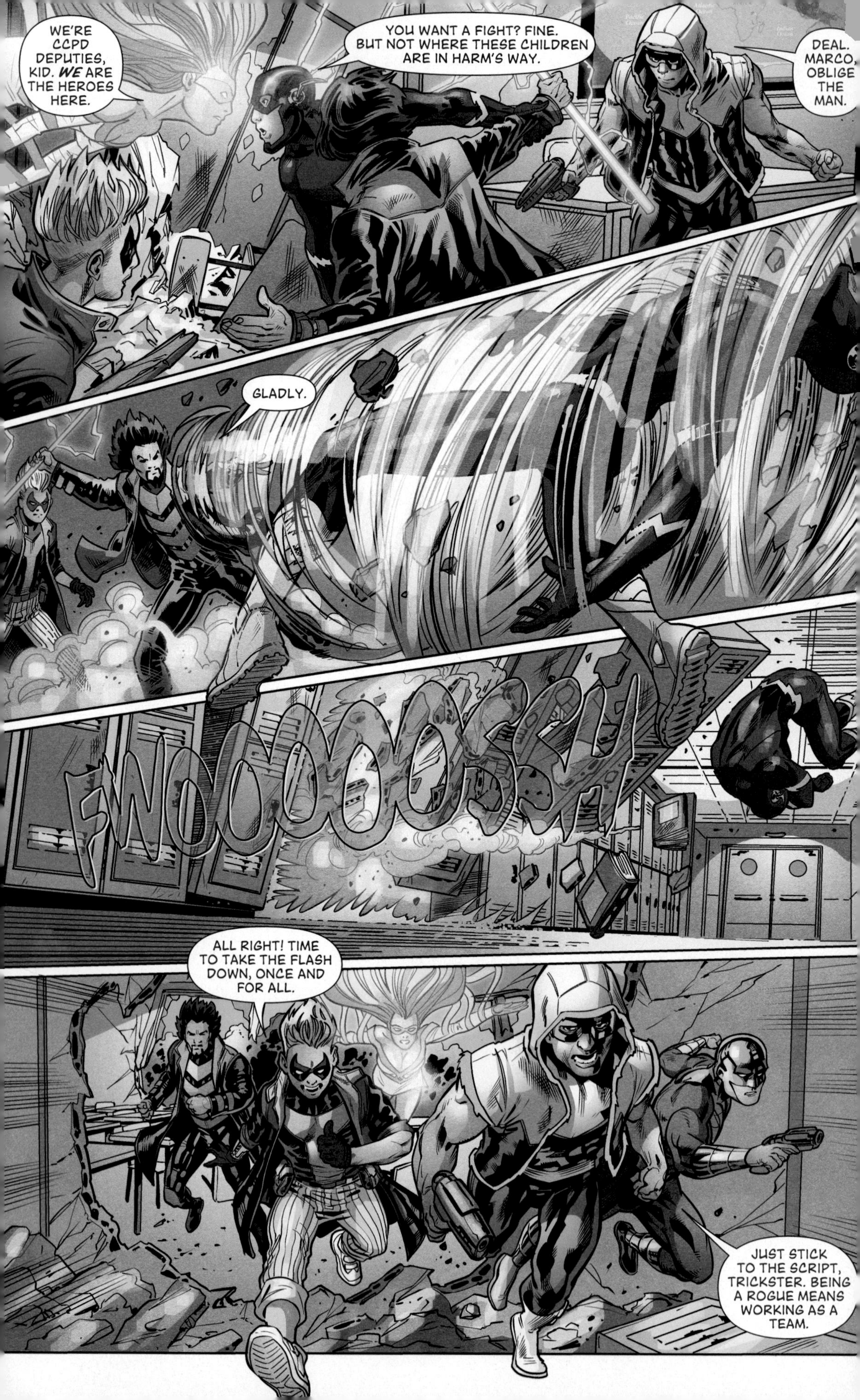
WE'RE CCPD DEPUTIES, KID. *WE* ARE THE HEROES HERE.
YOU WANT A FIGHT? FINE. BUT NOT WHERE THESE CHILDREN ARE IN HARM'S WAY.
DEAL. MARCO, OBLIGE THE MAN.
GLADLY.
FWOOOOOSH
ALL RIGHT! TIME TO TAKE THE FLASH DOWN, ONCE AND FOR ALL.
JUST STICK TO THE SCRIPT, TRICKSTER. BEING A ROGUE MEANS WORKING AS A TEAM.

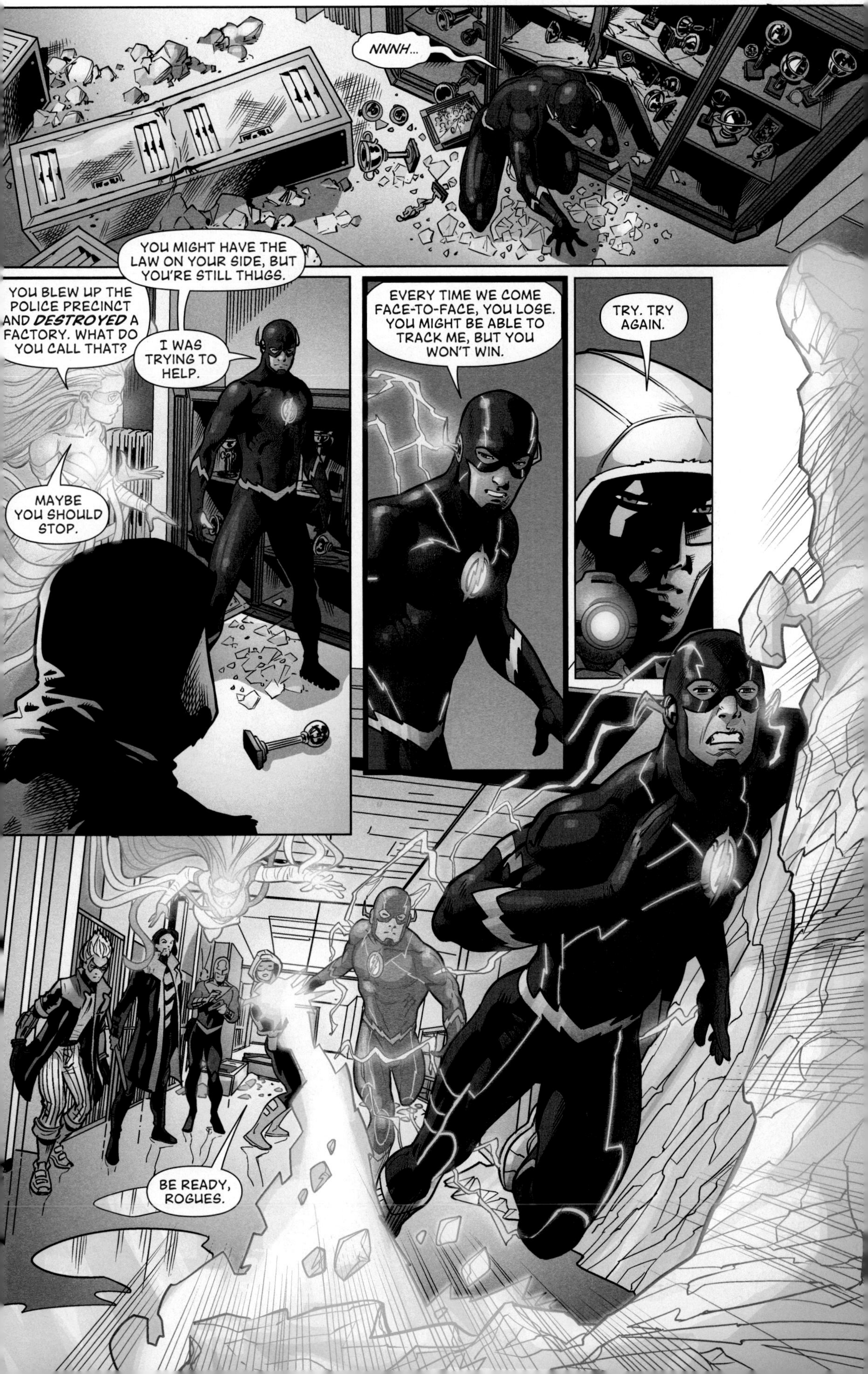
NNNH...
YOU MIGHT HAVE THE LAW ON YOUR SIDE, BUT YOU'RE STILL THUGS.
YOU BLEW UP THE POLICE PRECINCT AND *DESTROYED* A FACTORY. WHAT DO YOU CALL THAT?
I WAS TRYING TO HELP.
MAYBE YOU SHOULD STOP.
EVERY TIME WE COME FACE-TO-FACE, YOU LOSE. YOU MIGHT BE ABLE TO TRACK ME, BUT YOU WON'T WIN.
TRY. TRY AGAIN.
BE READY, ROGUES.

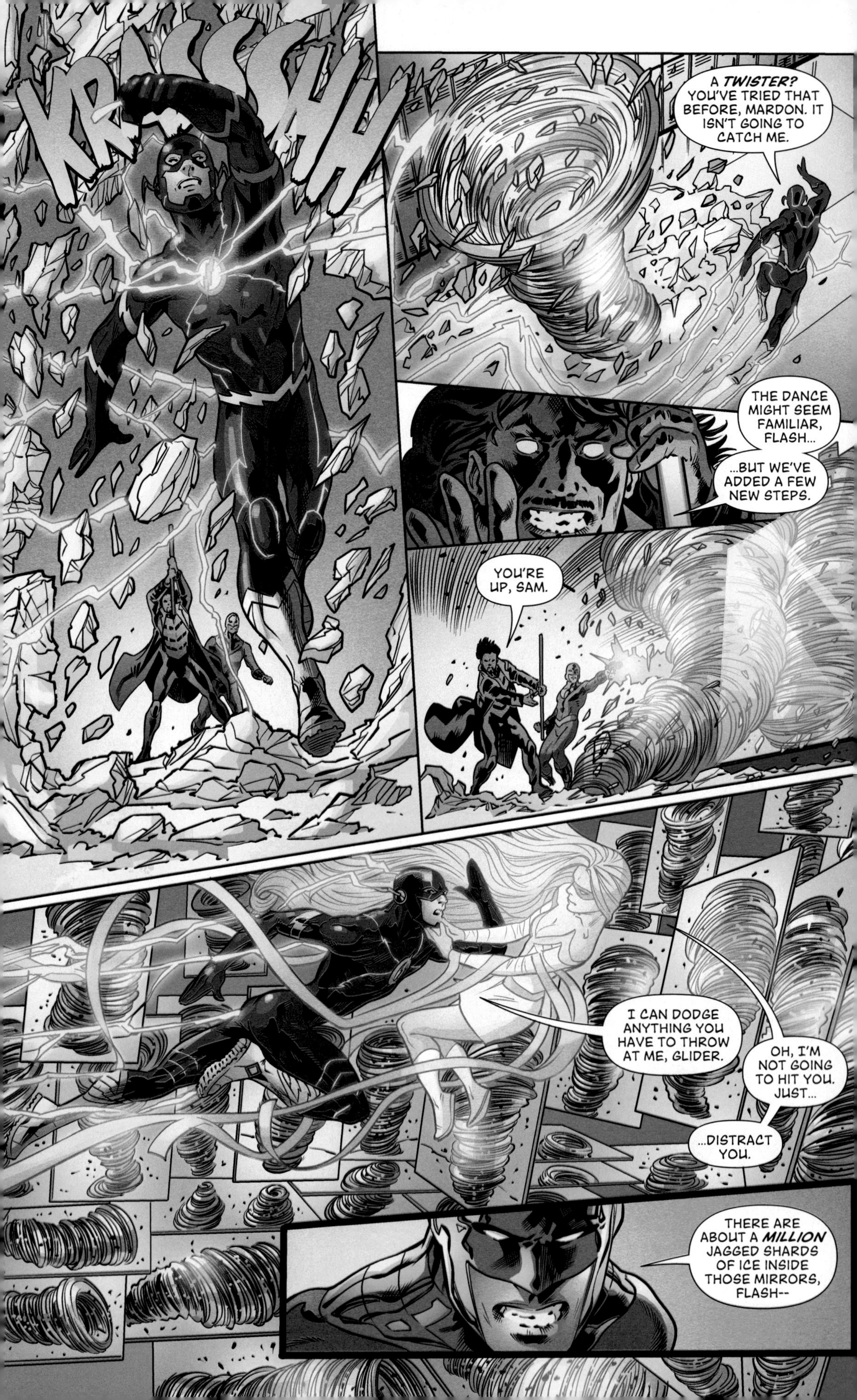
KRSSSHH
A TWISTER? YOU'VE TRIED THAT BEFORE, MARDON. IT ISN'T GOING TO CATCH ME.
THE DANCE MIGHT SEEM FAMILIAR, FLASH...
...BUT WE'VE ADDED A FEW NEW STEPS.
YOU'RE UP, SAM.
I CAN DODGE ANYTHING YOU HAVE TO THROW AT ME, GLIDER.
OH, I'M NOT GOING TO HIT YOU. JUST...
...DISTRACT YOU.
THERE ARE ABOUT A MILLION JAGGED SHARDS OF ICE INSIDE THOSE MIRRORS, FLASH--

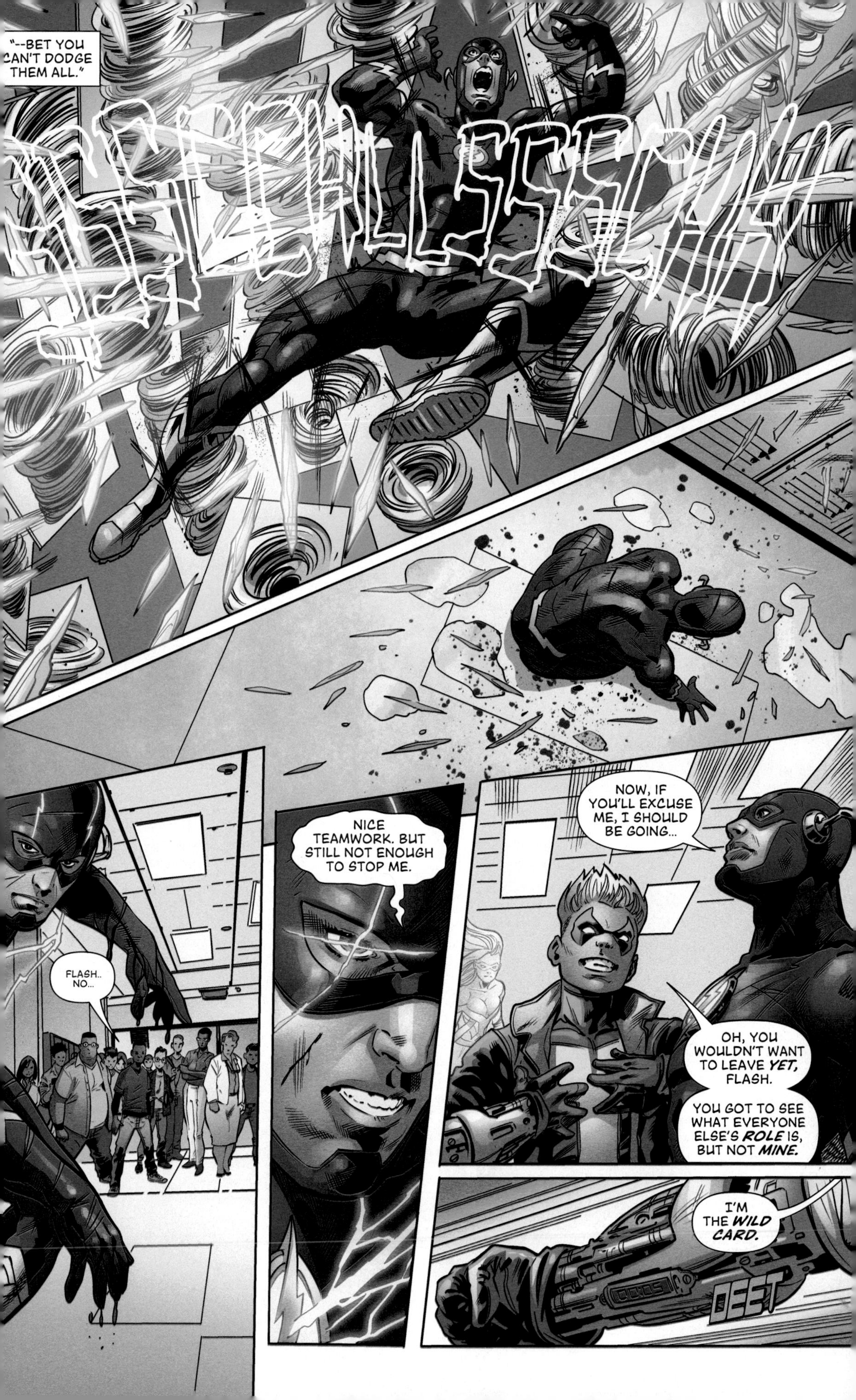
"--BET YOU CAN'T DODGE THEM ALL."
SSPCHLSSSCHH
FLASH.. NO...
NICE TEAMWORK. BUT STILL NOT ENOUGH TO STOP ME.
NOW, IF YOU'LL EXCUSE ME, I SHOULD BE GOING...
OH, YOU WOULDN'T WANT TO LEAVE *YET,* FLASH.
YOU GOT TO SEE WHAT EVERYONE ELSE'S *ROLE* IS, BUT NOT *MINE.*
I'M THE *WILD CARD.*
DEET

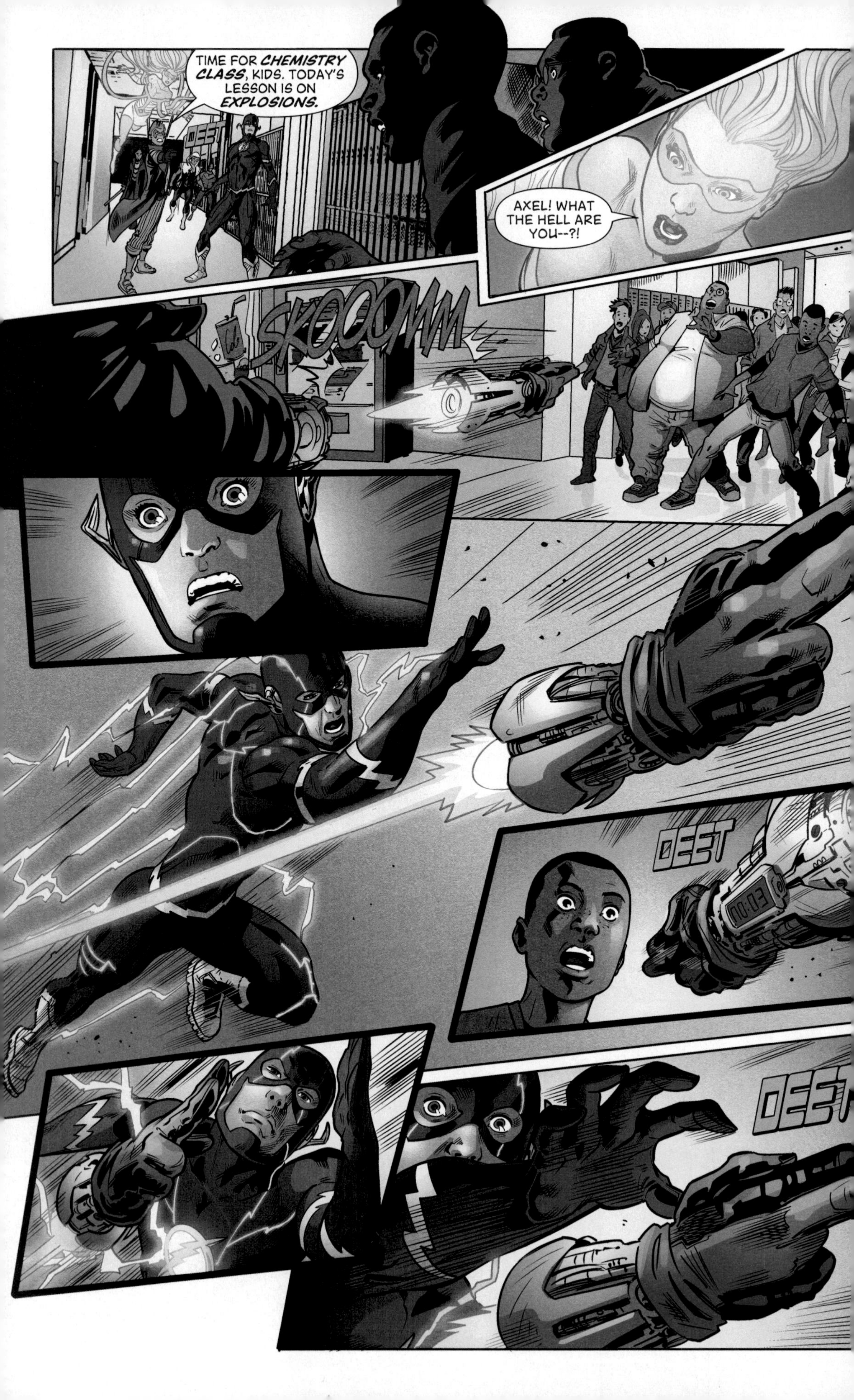

TIME FOR CHEMISTRY CLASS, KIDS. TODAY'S LESSON IS ON EXPLOSIONS.
DEET
AXEL! WHAT THE HELL ARE YOU--?!
SKOOOMM
DEET
DEET

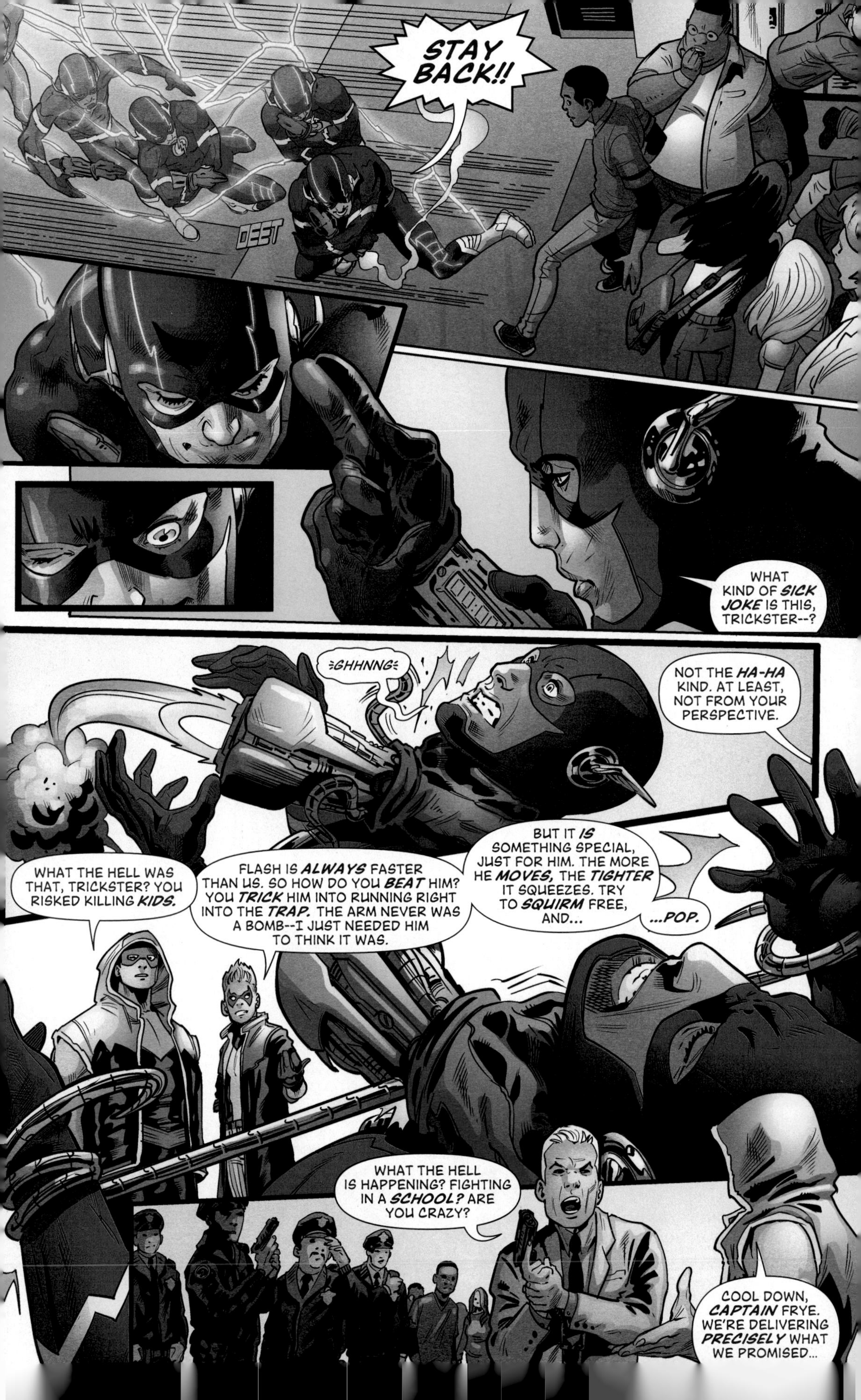
STAY BACK!!
DEET
WHAT KIND OF SICK JOKE IS THIS, TRICKSTER--?
GHHNNG
NOT THE HA-HA KIND. AT LEAST, NOT FROM YOUR PERSPECTIVE.
WHAT THE HELL WAS THAT, TRICKSTER? YOU RISKED KILLING KIDS.
FLASH IS ALWAYS FASTER THAN US. SO HOW DO YOU BEAT HIM? YOU TRICK HIM INTO RUNNING RIGHT INTO THE TRAP. THE ARM NEVER WAS A BOMB--I JUST NEEDED HIM TO THINK IT WAS.
BUT IT IS SOMETHING SPECIAL, JUST FOR HIM. THE MORE HE MOVES, THE TIGHTER IT SQUEEZES. TRY TO SQUIRM FREE, AND...
...POP.
WHAT THE HELL IS HAPPENING? FIGHTING IN A SCHOOL? ARE YOU CRAZY?
COOL DOWN, CAPTAIN FRYE. WE'RE DELIVERING PRECISELY WHAT WE PROMISED...

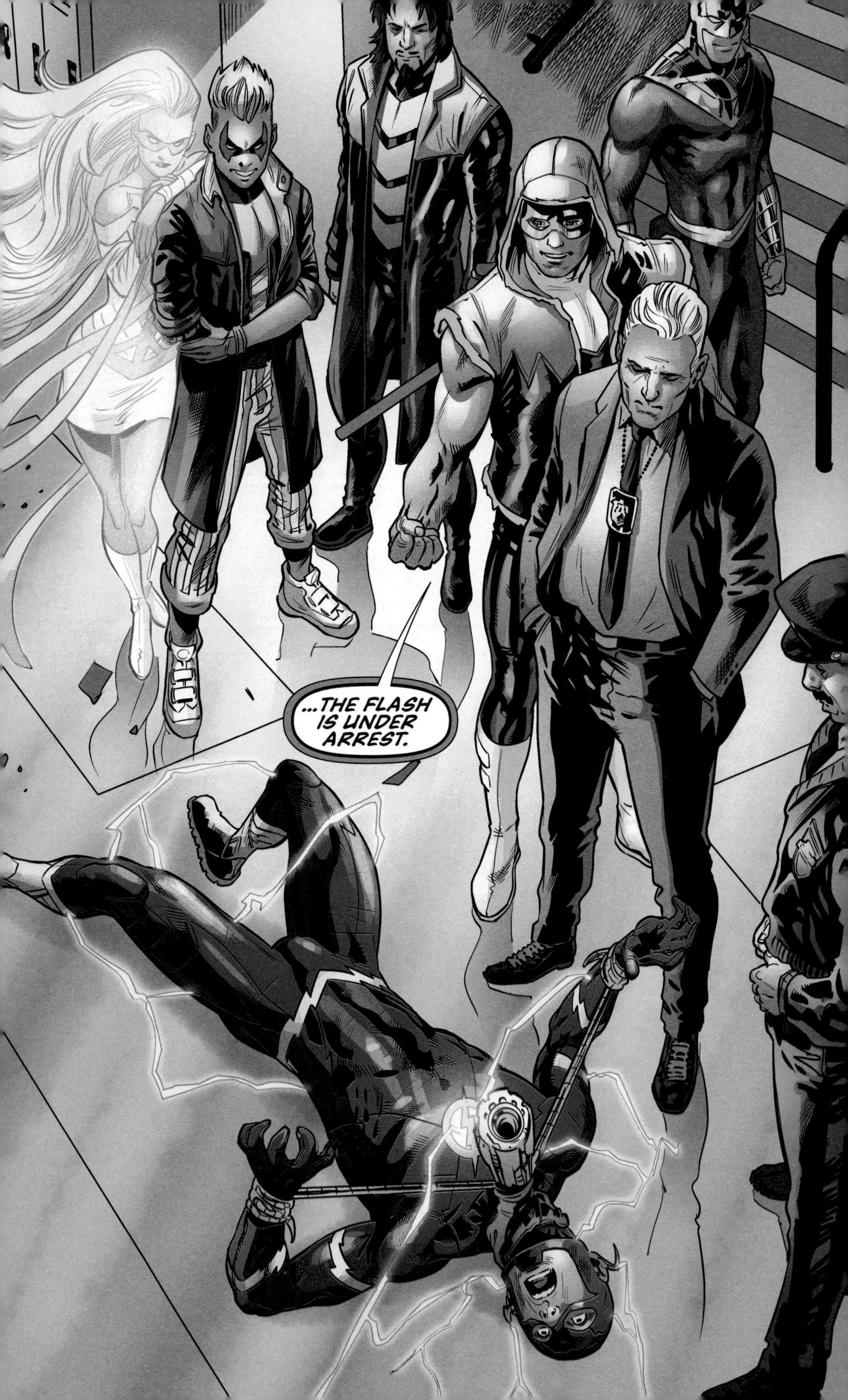
...THE FLASH IS UNDER ARREST.

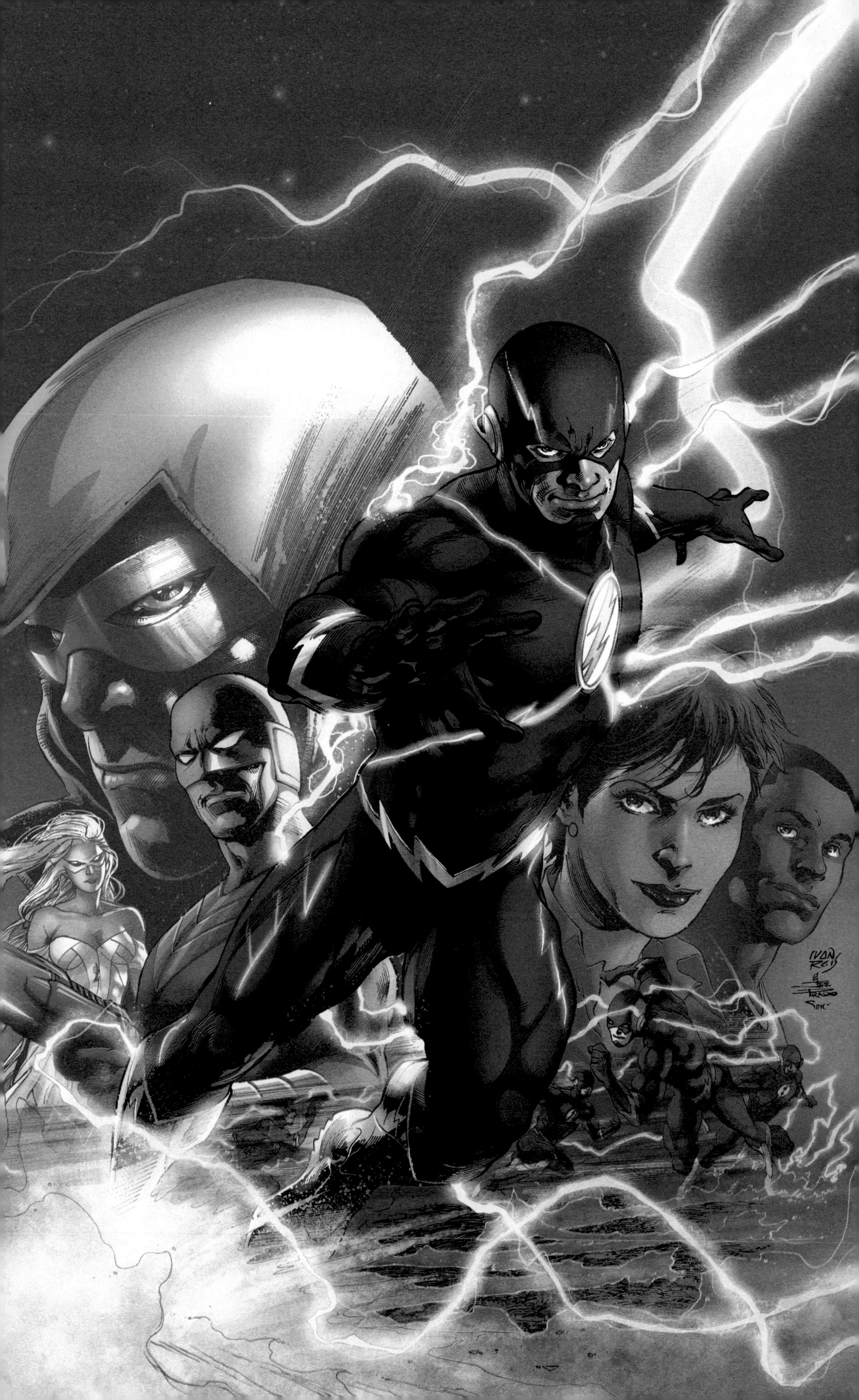

YOU'RE UNDER ARREST

VAN JENSEN writer **JESÚS MERINO PAUL PELLETIER** pencillers **JESÚS MERINO SCOTT HANNA TONY KORDOS WAYNE FAUCHER** inkers **GUY MAJOR PETE PANTAZIS** colorists **PAT BROSSEAU** letterer **IVAN REIS JOE PRADO ALEX SINCLAIR** cover

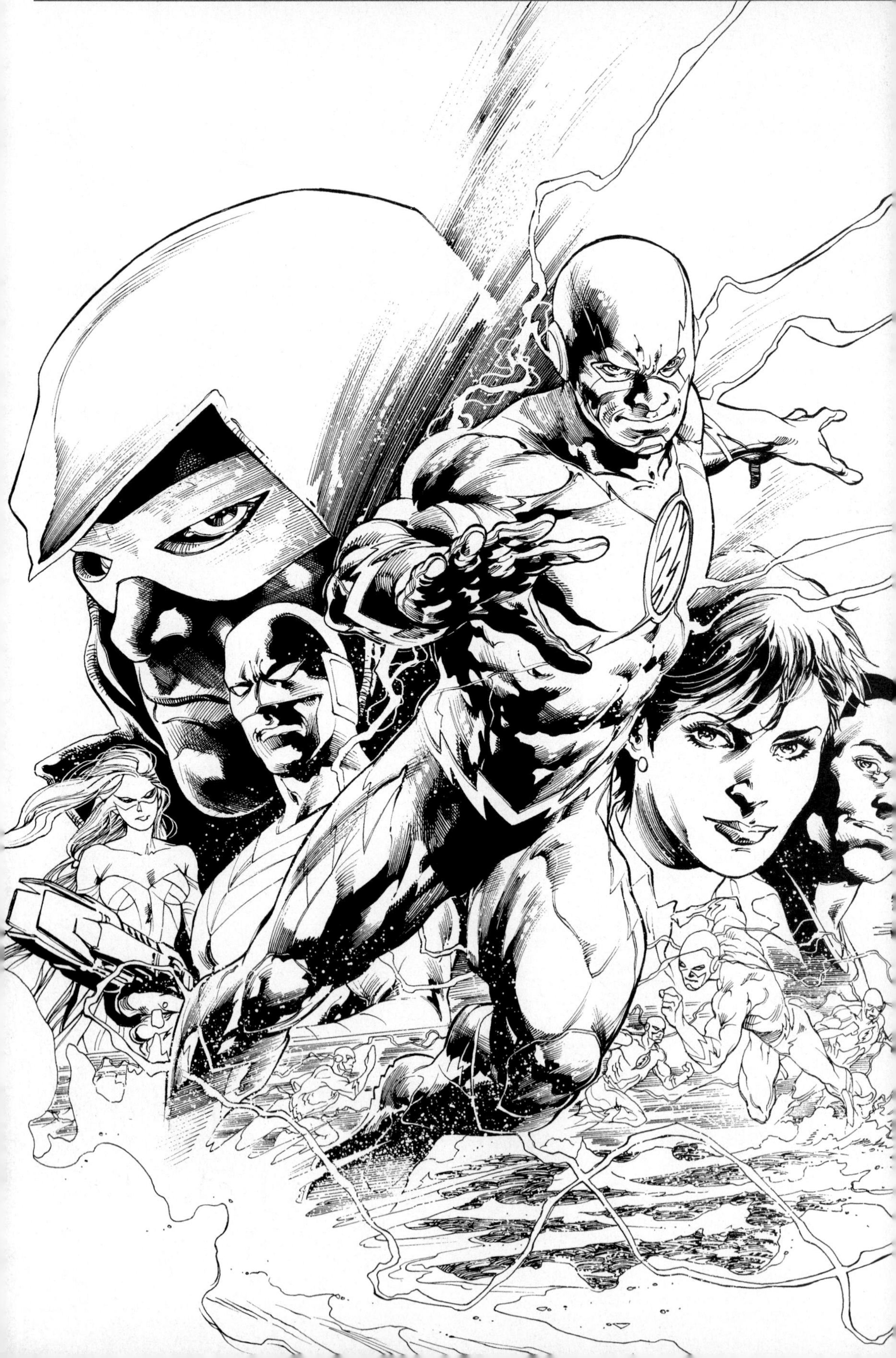

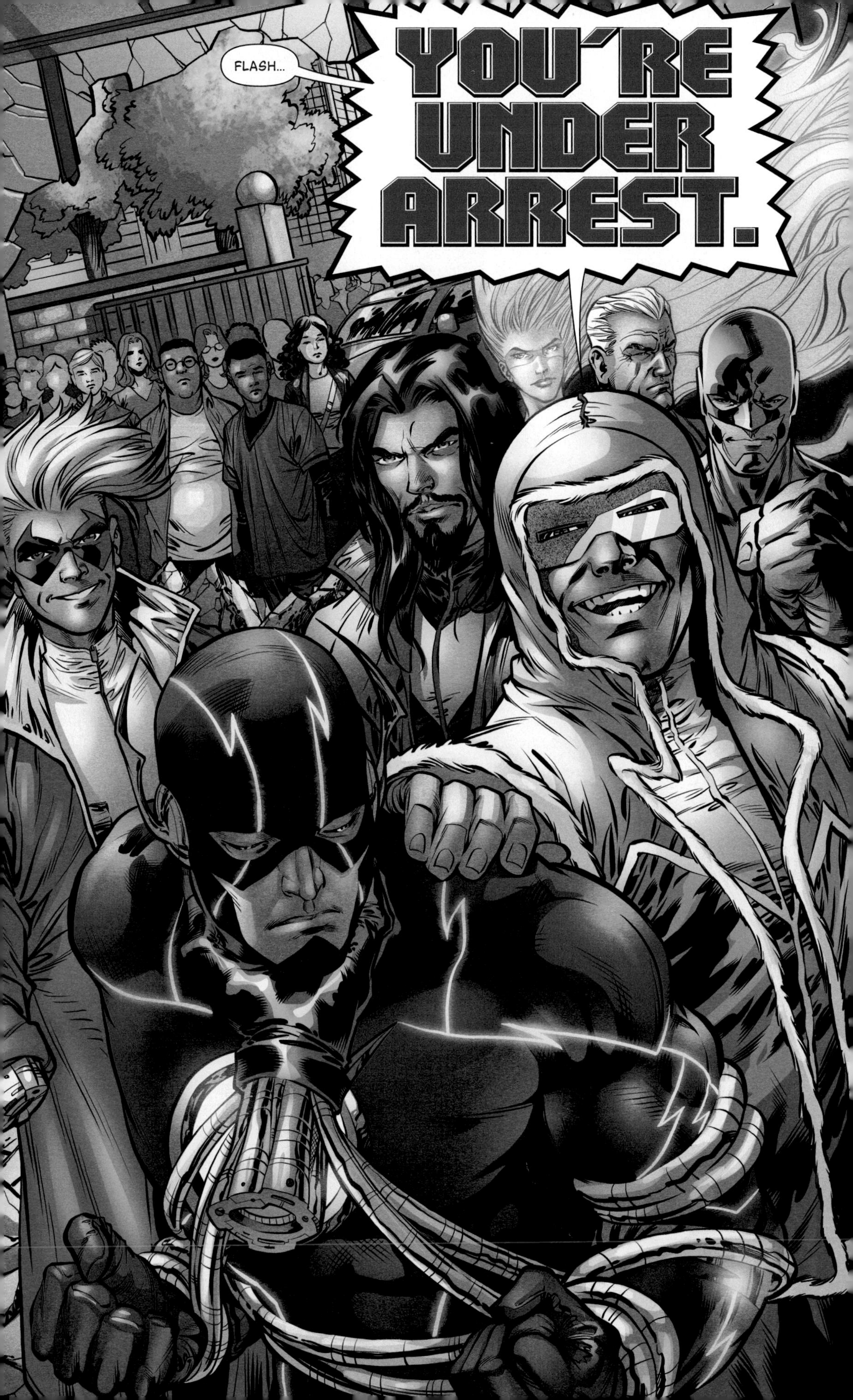
FLASH...
YOU'RE UNDER ARREST.

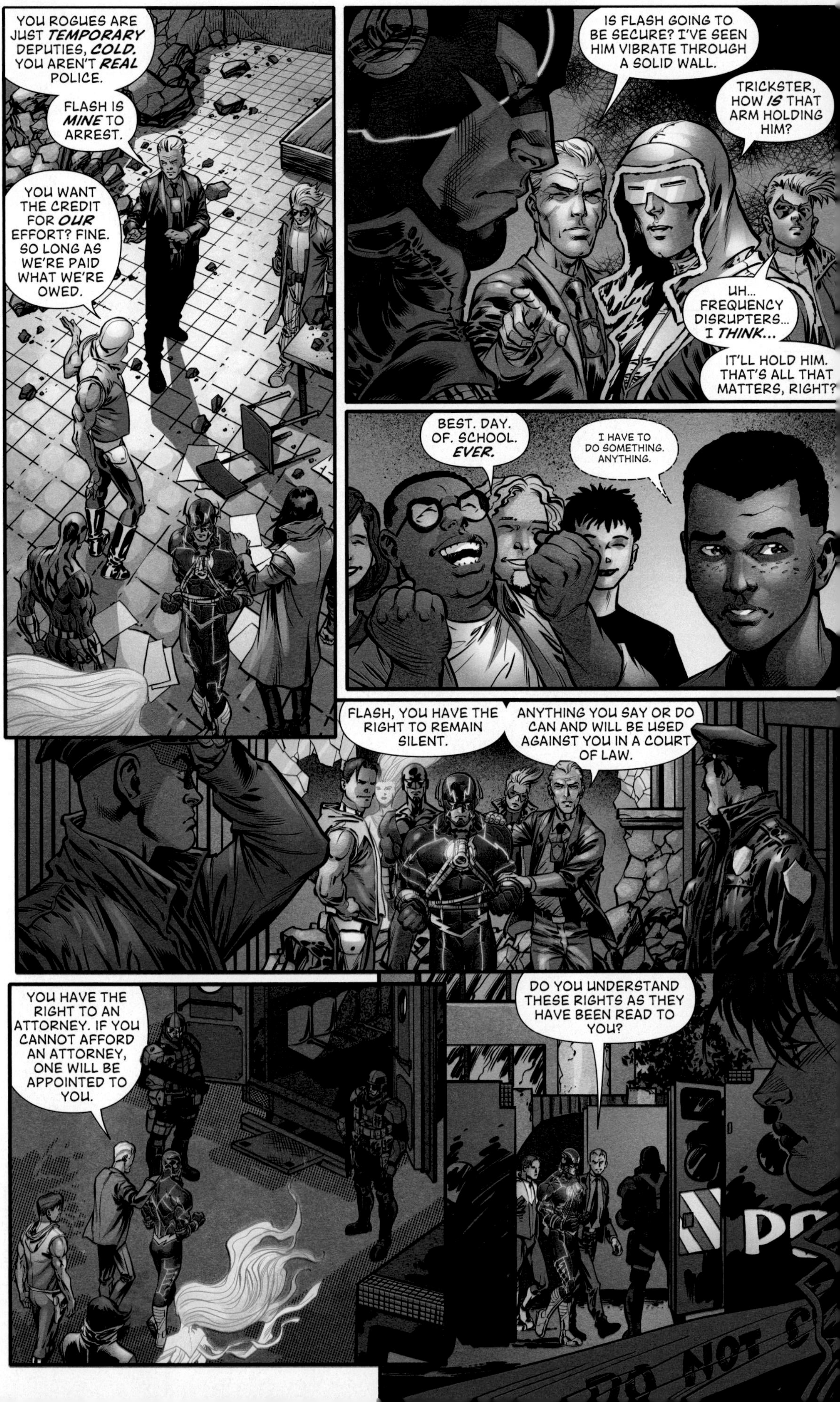
YOU ROGUES ARE JUST TEMPORARY DEPUTIES, COLD. YOU AREN'T REAL POLICE.
FLASH IS MINE TO ARREST.
YOU WANT THE CREDIT FOR OUR EFFORT? FINE. SO LONG AS WE'RE PAID WHAT WE'RE OWED.
IS FLASH GOING TO BE SECURE? I'VE SEEN HIM VIBRATE THROUGH A SOLID WALL.
TRICKSTER, HOW IS THAT ARM HOLDING HIM?
UH... FREQUENCY DISRUPTERS... I THINK...
IT'LL HOLD HIM. THAT'S ALL THAT MATTERS, RIGHT?
BEST. DAY. OF. SCHOOL. EVER.
I HAVE TO DO SOMETHING. ANYTHING.
FLASH, YOU HAVE THE RIGHT TO REMAIN SILENT.
ANYTHING YOU SAY OR DO CAN AND WILL BE USED AGAINST YOU IN A COURT OF LAW.
YOU HAVE THE RIGHT TO AN ATTORNEY. IF YOU CANNOT AFFORD AN ATTORNEY, ONE WILL BE APPOINTED TO YOU.
DO YOU UNDERSTAND THESE RIGHTS AS THEY HAVE BEEN READ TO YOU?

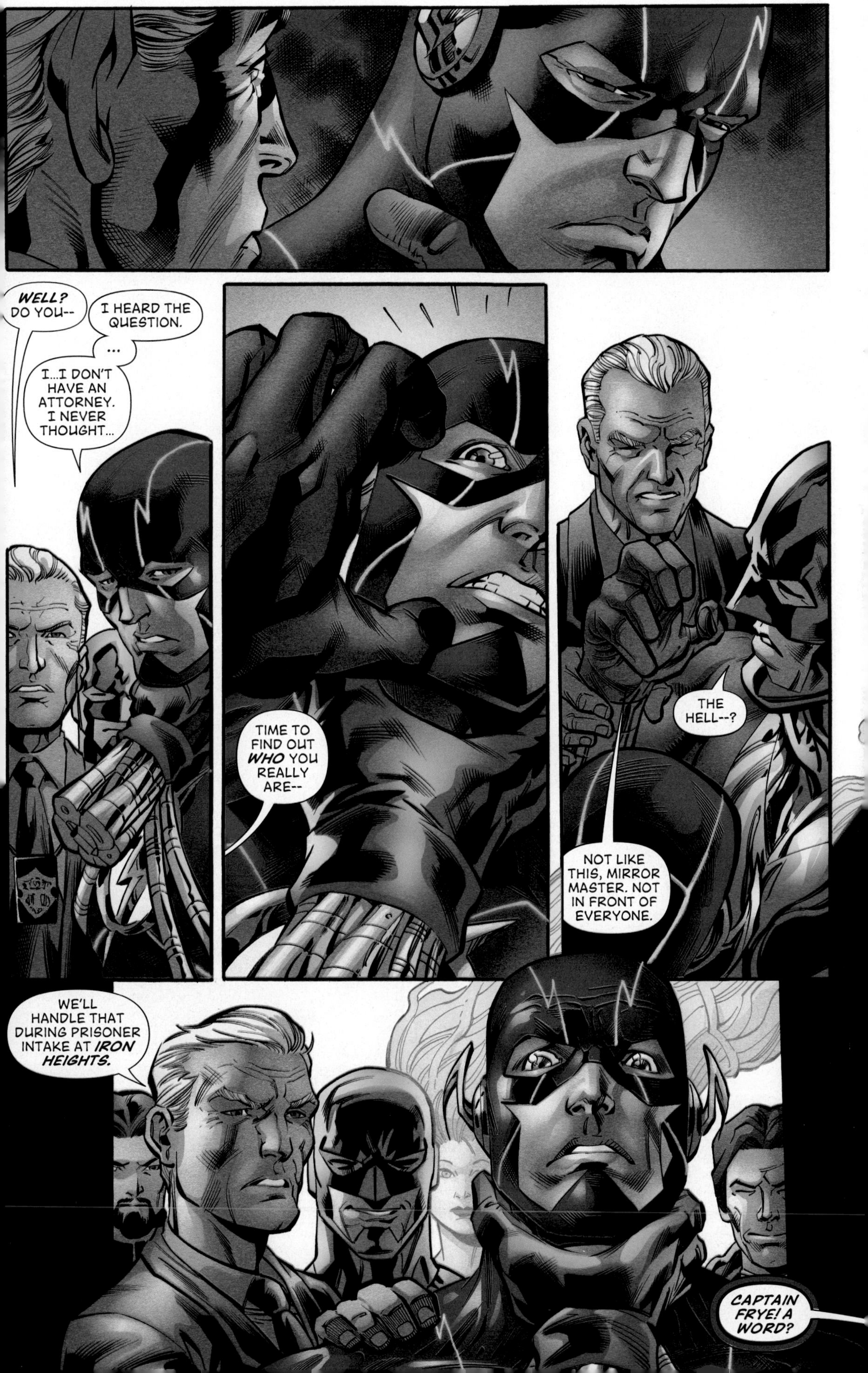

WELL? DO YOU--
I HEARD THE QUESTION.
...
I...I DON'T HAVE AN ATTORNEY. I NEVER THOUGHT...
TIME TO FIND OUT WHO YOU REALLY ARE--
THE HELL--?
NOT LIKE THIS, MIRROR MASTER. NOT IN FRONT OF EVERYONE.
WE'LL HANDLE THAT DURING PRISONER INTAKE AT IRON HEIGHTS.
CAPTAIN FRYE! A WORD?

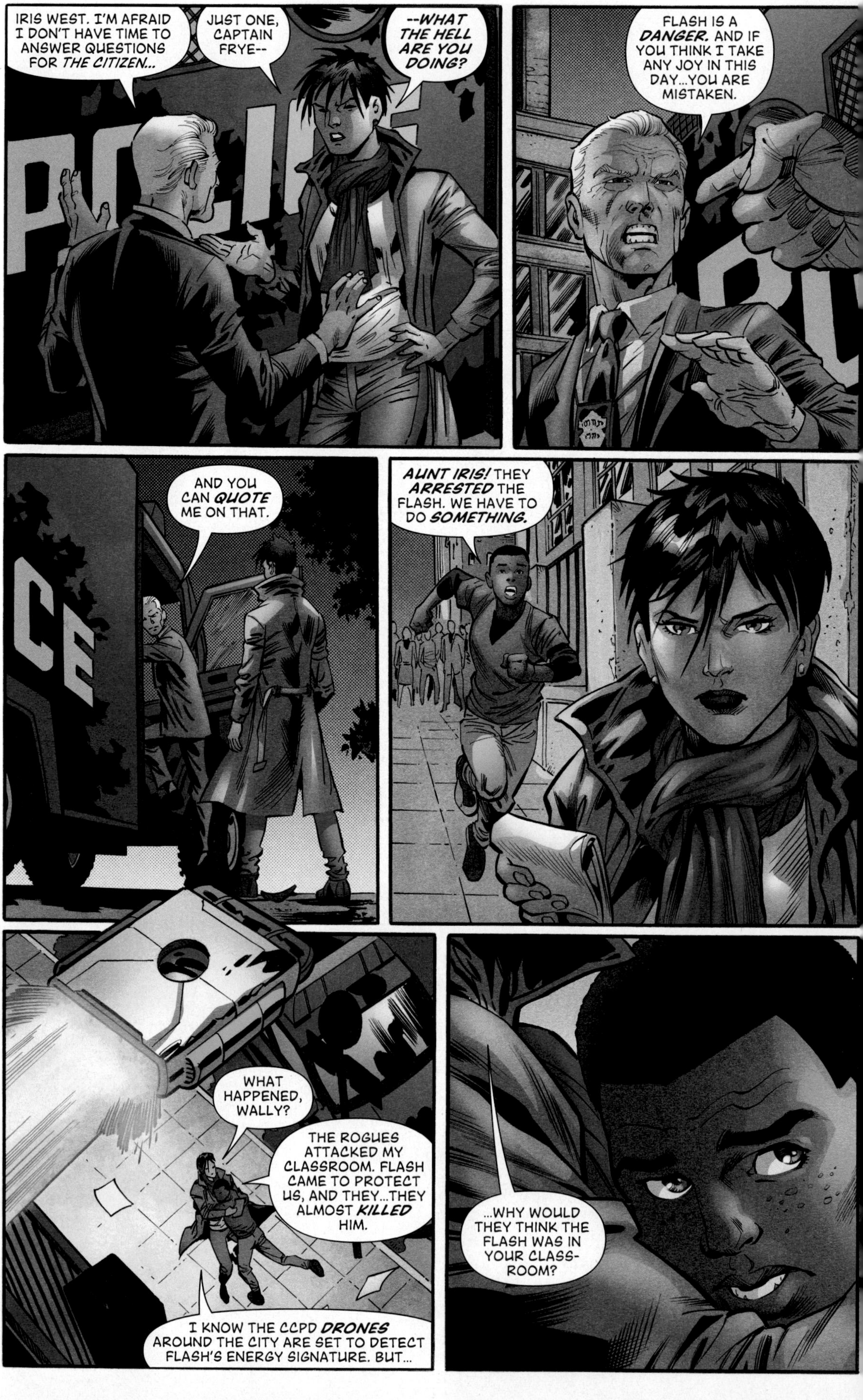
IRIS WEST. I'M AFRAID I DON'T HAVE TIME TO ANSWER QUESTIONS FOR THE CITIZEN...
JUST ONE, CAPTAIN FRYE--
--WHAT THE HELL ARE YOU DOING?
FLASH IS A DANGER. AND IF YOU THINK I TAKE ANY JOY IN THIS DAY...YOU ARE MISTAKEN.
AND YOU CAN QUOTE ME ON THAT.
AUNT IRIS! THEY ARRESTED THE FLASH. WE HAVE TO DO SOMETHING.
WHAT HAPPENED, WALLY?
THE ROGUES ATTACKED MY CLASSROOM. FLASH CAME TO PROTECT US, AND THEY...THEY ALMOST KILLED HIM.
I KNOW THE CCPD DRONES AROUND THE CITY ARE SET TO DETECT FLASH'S ENERGY SIGNATURE. BUT...
...WHY WOULD THEY THINK THE FLASH WAS IN YOUR CLASS-ROOM?

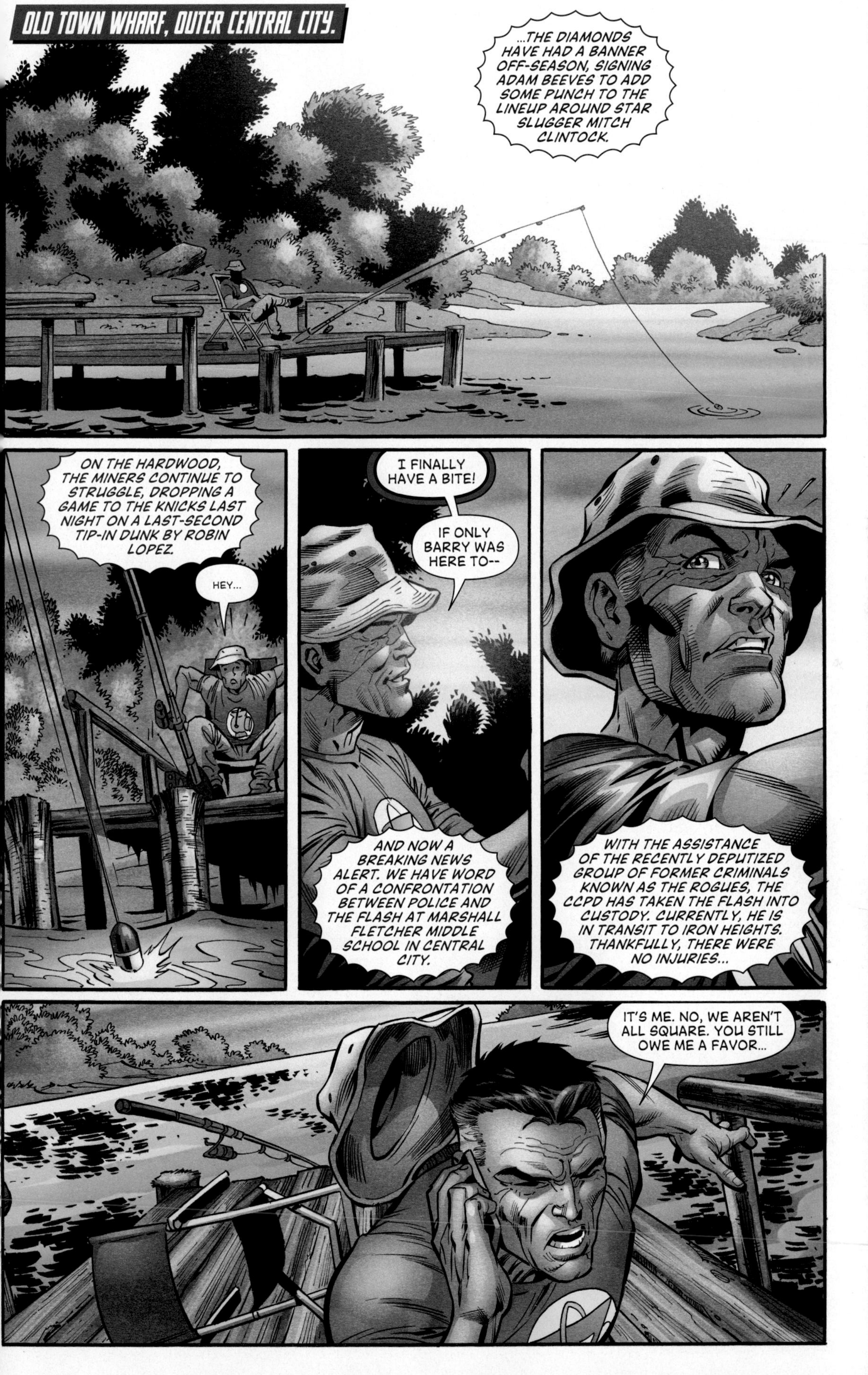
OLD TOWN WHARF, OUTER CENTRAL CITY.
...THE DIAMONDS HAVE HAD A BANNER OFF-SEASON, SIGNING ADAM BEEVES TO ADD SOME PUNCH TO THE LINEUP AROUND STAR SLUGGER MITCH CLINTOCK.
ON THE HARDWOOD, THE MINERS CONTINUE TO STRUGGLE, DROPPING A GAME TO THE KNICKS LAST NIGHT ON A LAST-SECOND TIP-IN DUNK BY ROBIN LOPEZ.
HEY...
I FINALLY HAVE A BITE!
IF ONLY BARRY WAS HERE TO--
AND NOW A BREAKING NEWS ALERT. WE HAVE WORD OF A CONFRONTATION BETWEEN POLICE AND THE FLASH AT MARSHALL FLETCHER MIDDLE SCHOOL IN CENTRAL CITY.
WITH THE ASSISTANCE OF THE RECENTLY DEPUTIZED GROUP OF FORMER CRIMINALS KNOWN AS THE ROGUES, THE CCPD HAS TAKEN THE FLASH INTO CUSTODY. CURRENTLY, HE IS IN TRANSIT TO IRON HEIGHTS. THANKFULLY, THERE WERE NO INJURIES...
IT'S ME. NO, WE AREN'T ALL SQUARE. YOU STILL OWE ME A FAVOR...

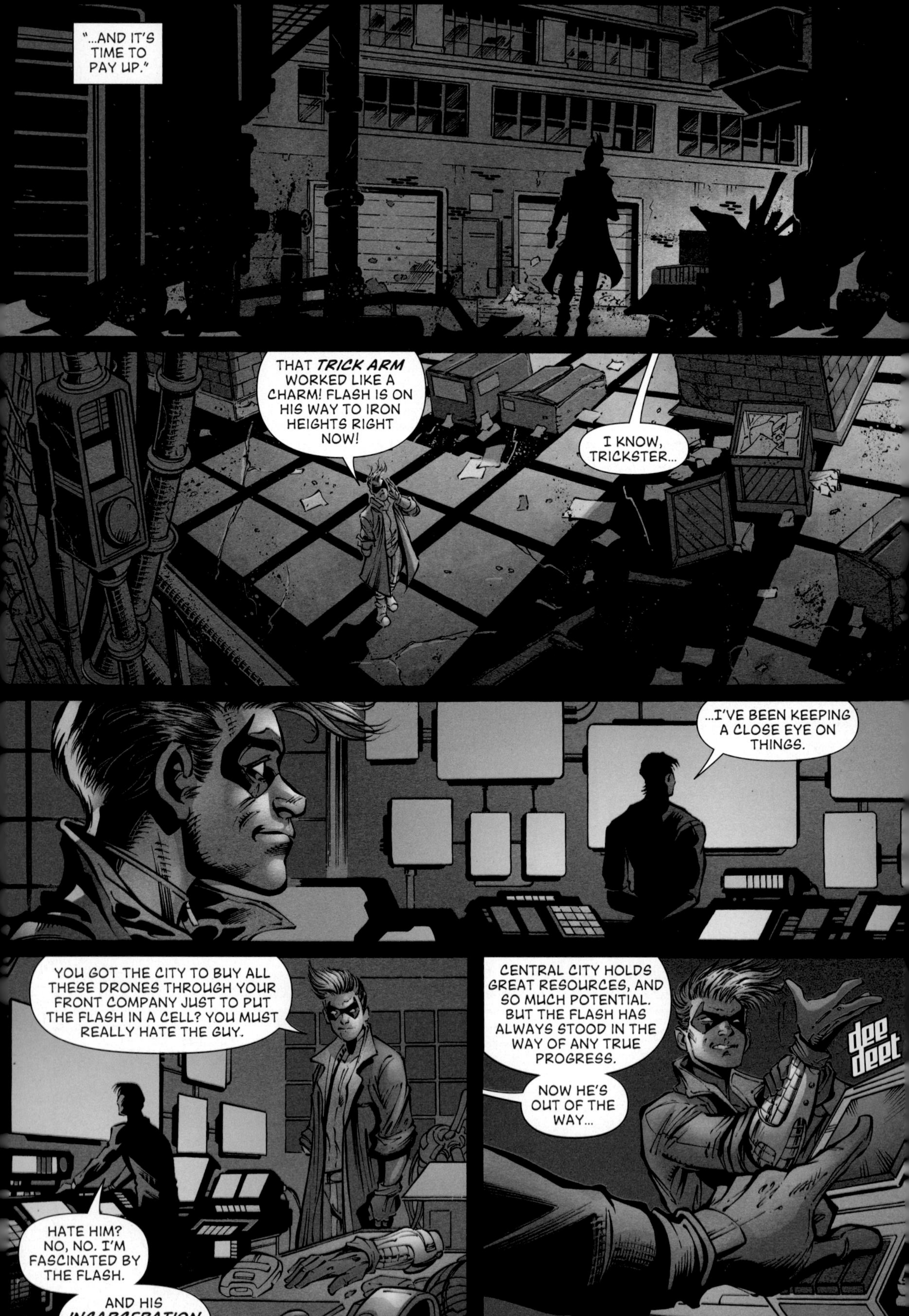
"...AND IT'S TIME TO PAY UP."
THAT TRICK ARM WORKED LIKE A CHARM! FLASH IS ON HIS WAY TO IRON HEIGHTS RIGHT NOW!
I KNOW, TRICKSTER...
...I'VE BEEN KEEPING A CLOSE EYE ON THINGS.
YOU GOT THE CITY TO BUY ALL THESE DRONES THROUGH YOUR FRONT COMPANY JUST TO PUT THE FLASH IN A CELL? YOU MUST REALLY HATE THE GUY.
HATE HIM? NO, NO. I'M FASCINATED BY THE FLASH.
AND HIS INCARCERATION ALONE ISN'T THE END GAME.
CENTRAL CITY HOLDS GREAT RESOURCES, AND SO MUCH POTENTIAL. BUT THE FLASH HAS ALWAYS STOOD IN THE WAY OF ANY TRUE PROGRESS.
NOW HE'S OUT OF THE WAY...
dee deet

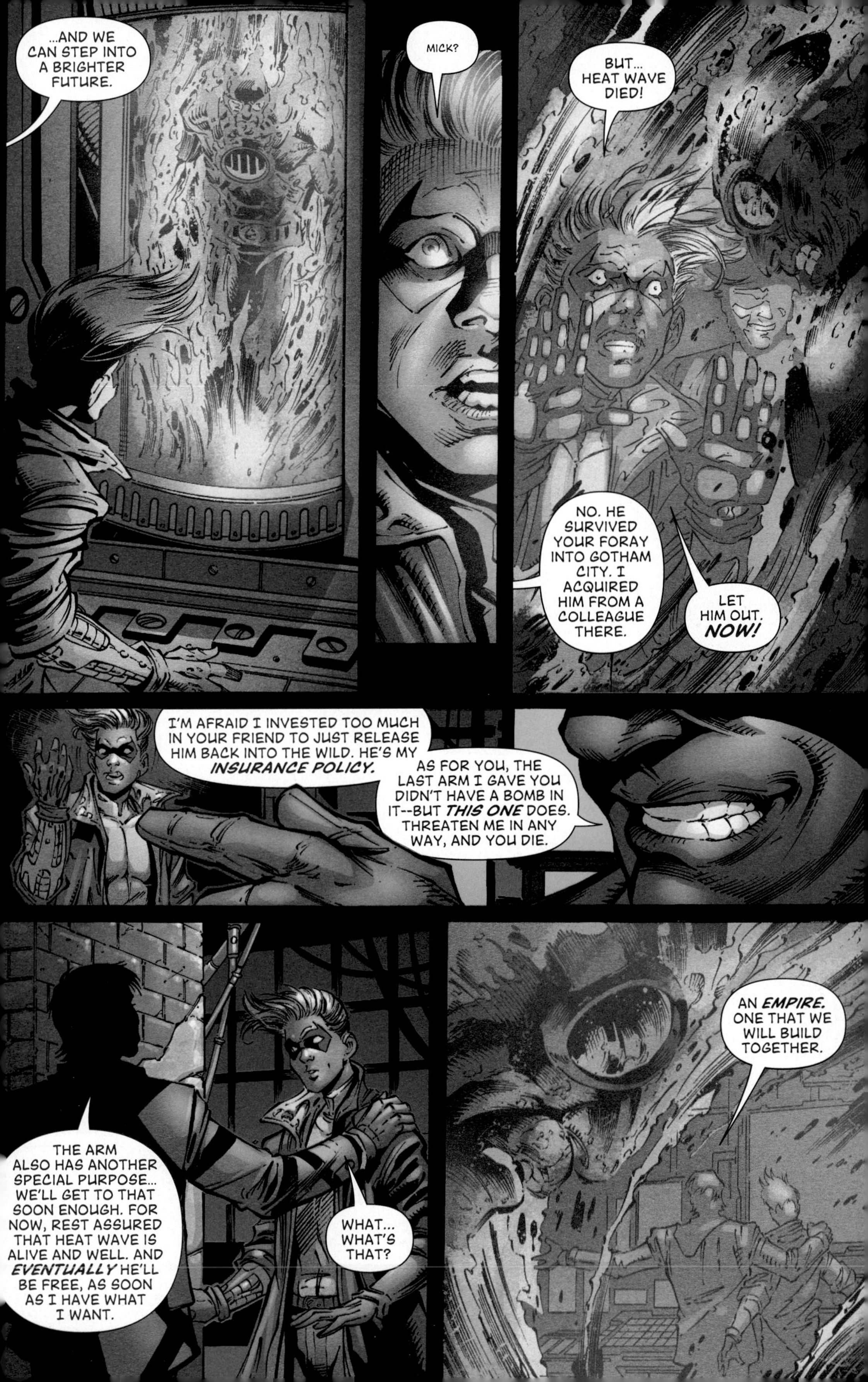
...AND WE CAN STEP INTO A BRIGHTER FUTURE.
MICK?
BUT... HEAT WAVE DIED!
NO. HE SURVIVED YOUR FORAY INTO GOTHAM CITY. I ACQUIRED HIM FROM A COLLEAGUE THERE.
LET HIM OUT. NOW!
I'M AFRAID I INVESTED TOO MUCH IN YOUR FRIEND TO JUST RELEASE HIM BACK INTO THE WILD. HE'S MY INSURANCE POLICY.
AS FOR YOU, THE LAST ARM I GAVE YOU DIDN'T HAVE A BOMB IN IT--BUT THIS ONE DOES. THREATEN ME IN ANY WAY, AND YOU DIE.
THE ARM ALSO HAS ANOTHER SPECIAL PURPOSE... WE'LL GET TO THAT SOON ENOUGH. FOR NOW, REST ASSURED THAT HEAT WAVE IS ALIVE AND WELL. AND EVENTUALLY HE'LL BE FREE, AS SOON AS I HAVE WHAT I WANT.
WHAT... WHAT'S THAT?
AN EMPIRE. ONE THAT WE WILL BUILD TOGETHER.

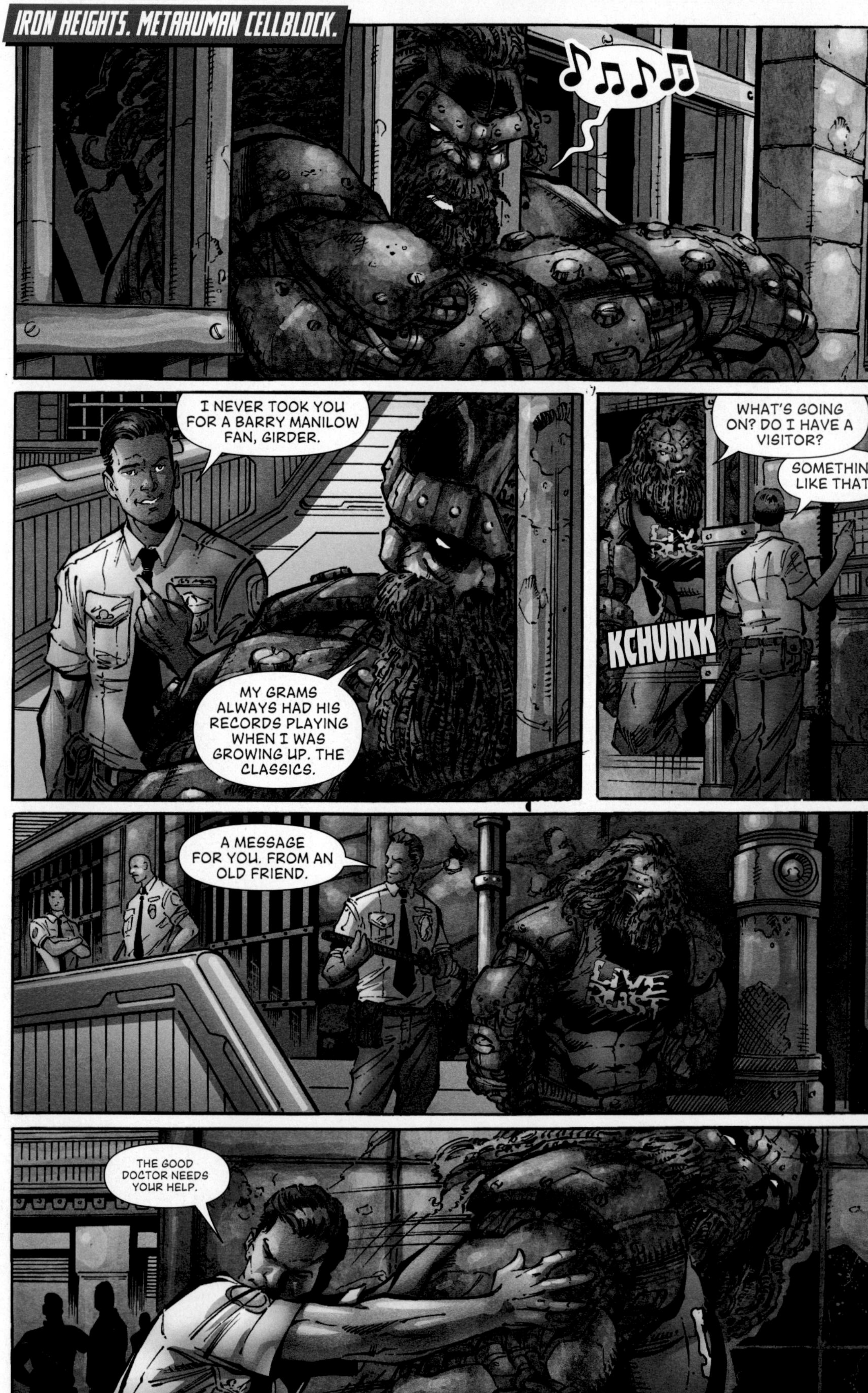
IRON HEIGHTS. METAHUMAN CELLBLOCK.
♪♫♪♫
I NEVER TOOK YOU FOR A BARRY MANILOW FAN, GIRDER.
MY GRAMS ALWAYS HAD HIS RECORDS PLAYING WHEN I WAS GROWING UP. THE CLASSICS.
WHAT'S GOING ON? DO I HAVE A VISITOR?
SOMETHING LIKE THAT.
KCHUNKK
A MESSAGE FOR YOU. FROM AN OLD FRIEND.
THE GOOD DOCTOR NEEDS YOUR HELP.

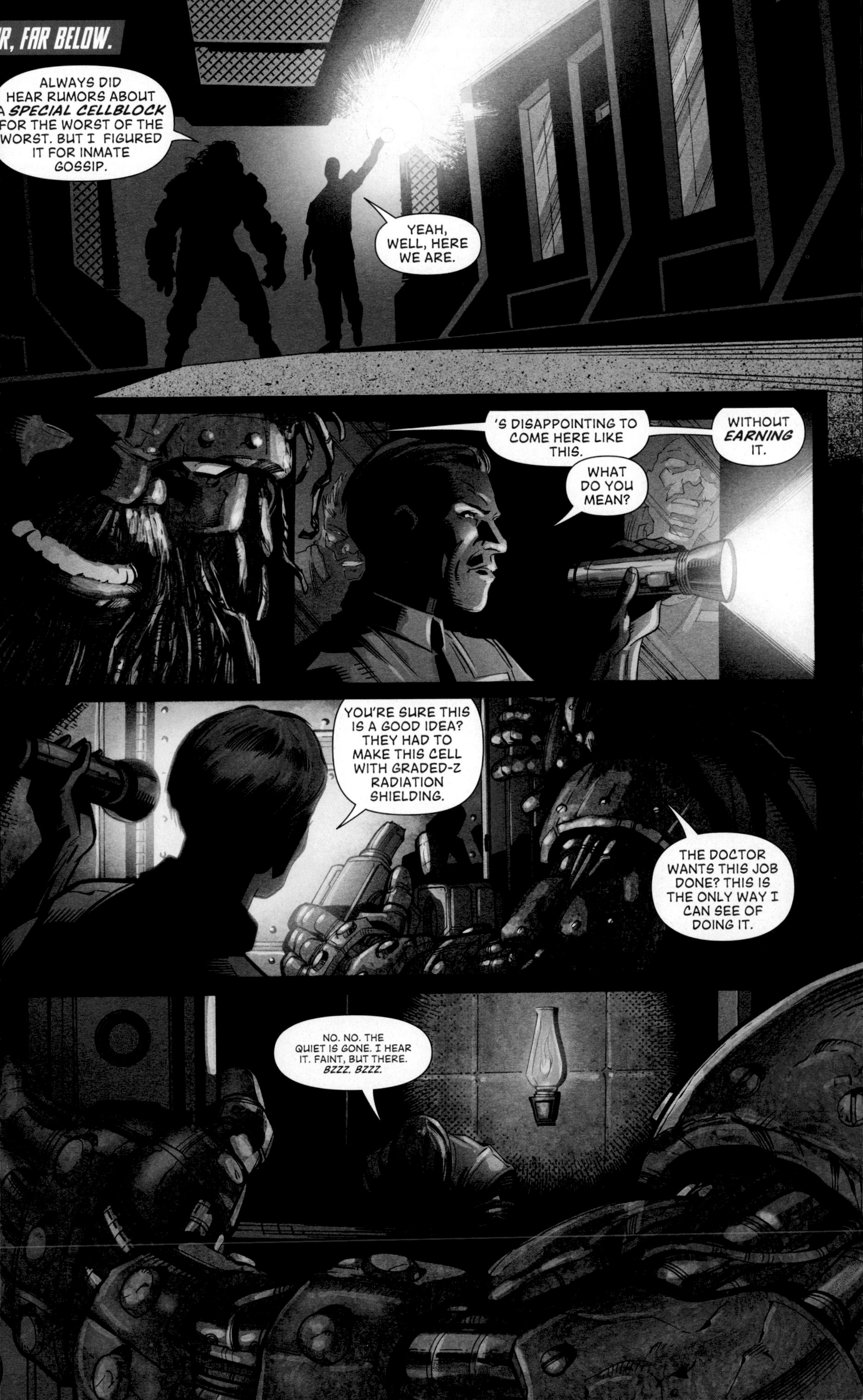
R, FAR BELOW.
ALWAYS DID HEAR RUMORS ABOUT A SPECIAL CELLBLOCK FOR THE WORST OF THE WORST. BUT I FIGURED IT FOR INMATE GOSSIP.
YEAH, WELL, HERE WE ARE.
'S DISAPPOINTING TO COME HERE LIKE THIS.
WITHOUT EARNING IT.
WHAT DO YOU MEAN?
YOU'RE SURE THIS IS A GOOD IDEA? THEY HAD TO MAKE THIS CELL WITH GRADED-Z RADIATION SHIELDING.
THE DOCTOR WANTS THIS JOB DONE? THIS IS THE ONLY WAY I CAN SEE OF DOING IT.
NO. NO. THE QUIET IS GONE. I HEAR IT. FAINT, BUT THERE. BZZZ. BZZZ.

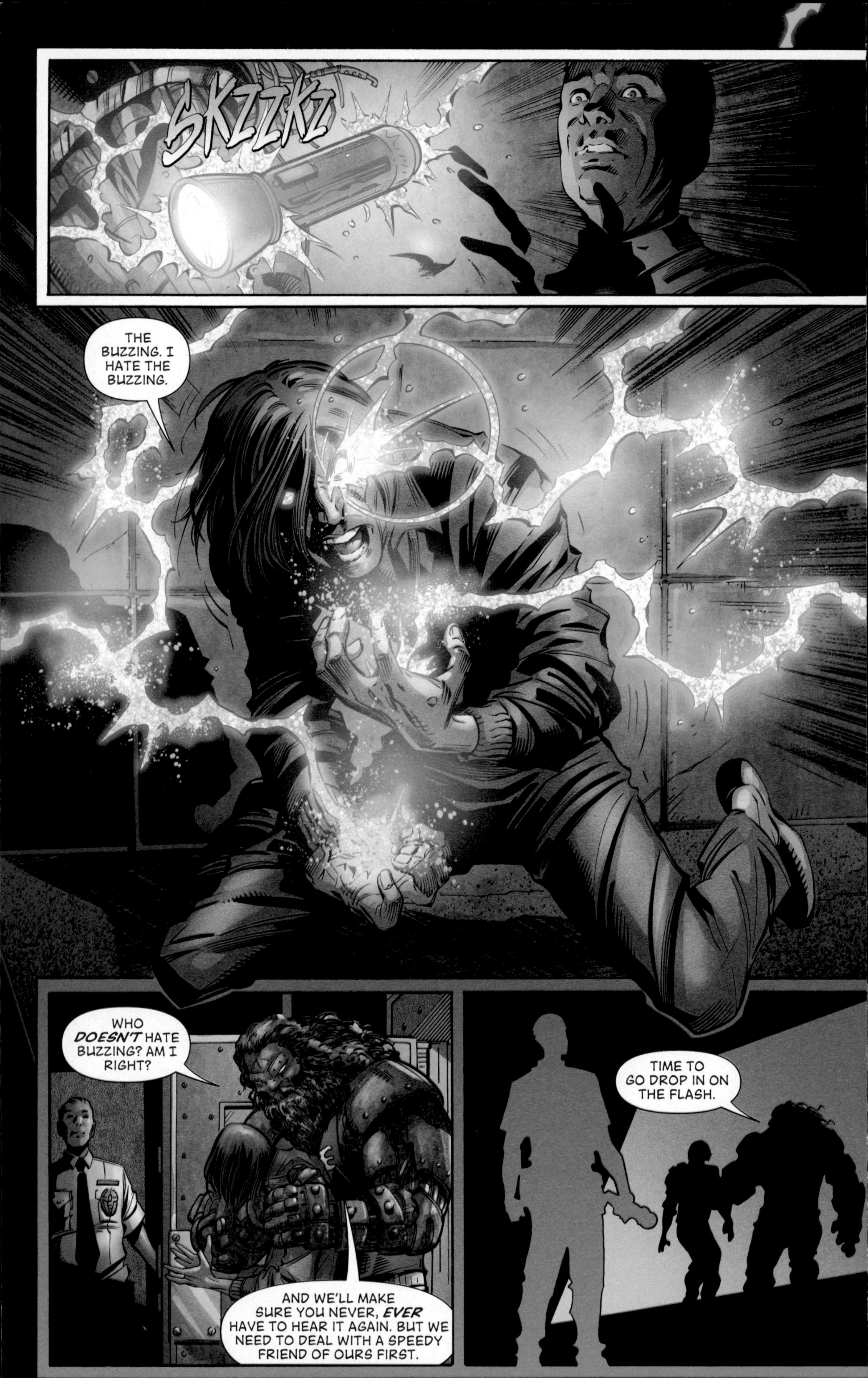
SKZZKZ
THE BUZZING. I HATE THE BUZZING.
WHO *DOESN'T* HATE BUZZING? AM I RIGHT?
AND WE'LL MAKE SURE YOU NEVER, *EVER* HAVE TO HEAR IT AGAIN. BUT WE NEED TO DEAL WITH A SPEEDY FRIEND OF OURS FIRST.
TIME TO GO DROP IN ON THE FLASH.

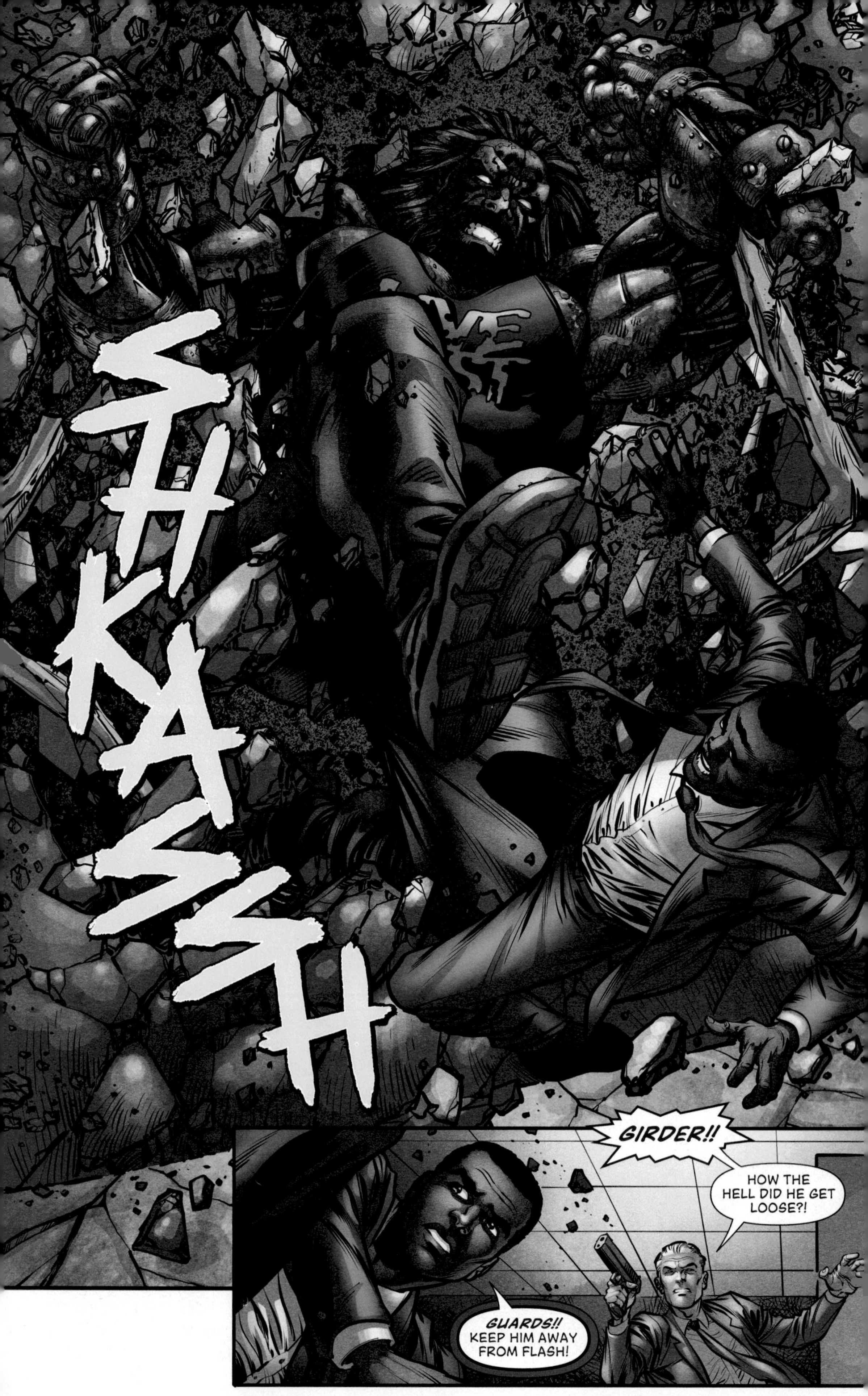
SHKASH
GIRDER!!
HOW THE HELL DID HE GET LOOSE?!
GUARDS!! KEEP HIM AWAY FROM FLASH!

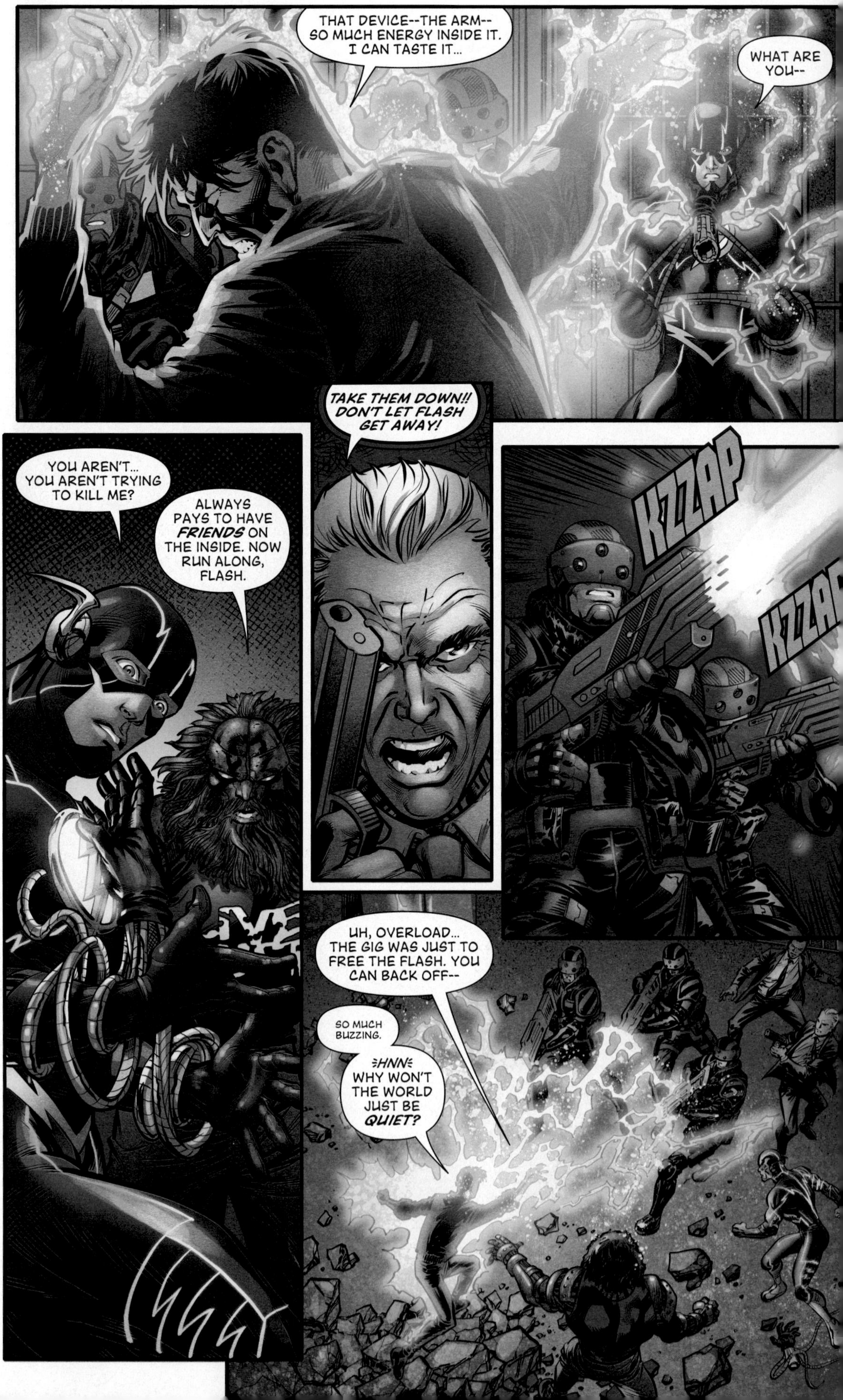
THAT DEVICE--THE ARM--
SO MUCH ENERGY INSIDE IT.
I CAN TASTE IT...
WHAT ARE YOU--
YOU AREN'T... YOU AREN'T TRYING TO KILL ME?
ALWAYS PAYS TO HAVE *FRIENDS* ON THE INSIDE. NOW RUN ALONG, FLASH.
TAKE THEM DOWN!! DON'T LET FLASH GET AWAY!
KZZAP
KZZAP
UH, OVERLOAD... THE GIG WAS JUST TO FREE THE FLASH. YOU CAN BACK OFF--
SO MUCH BUZZING.
HNN
WHY WON'T THE WORLD JUST BE *QUIET?*

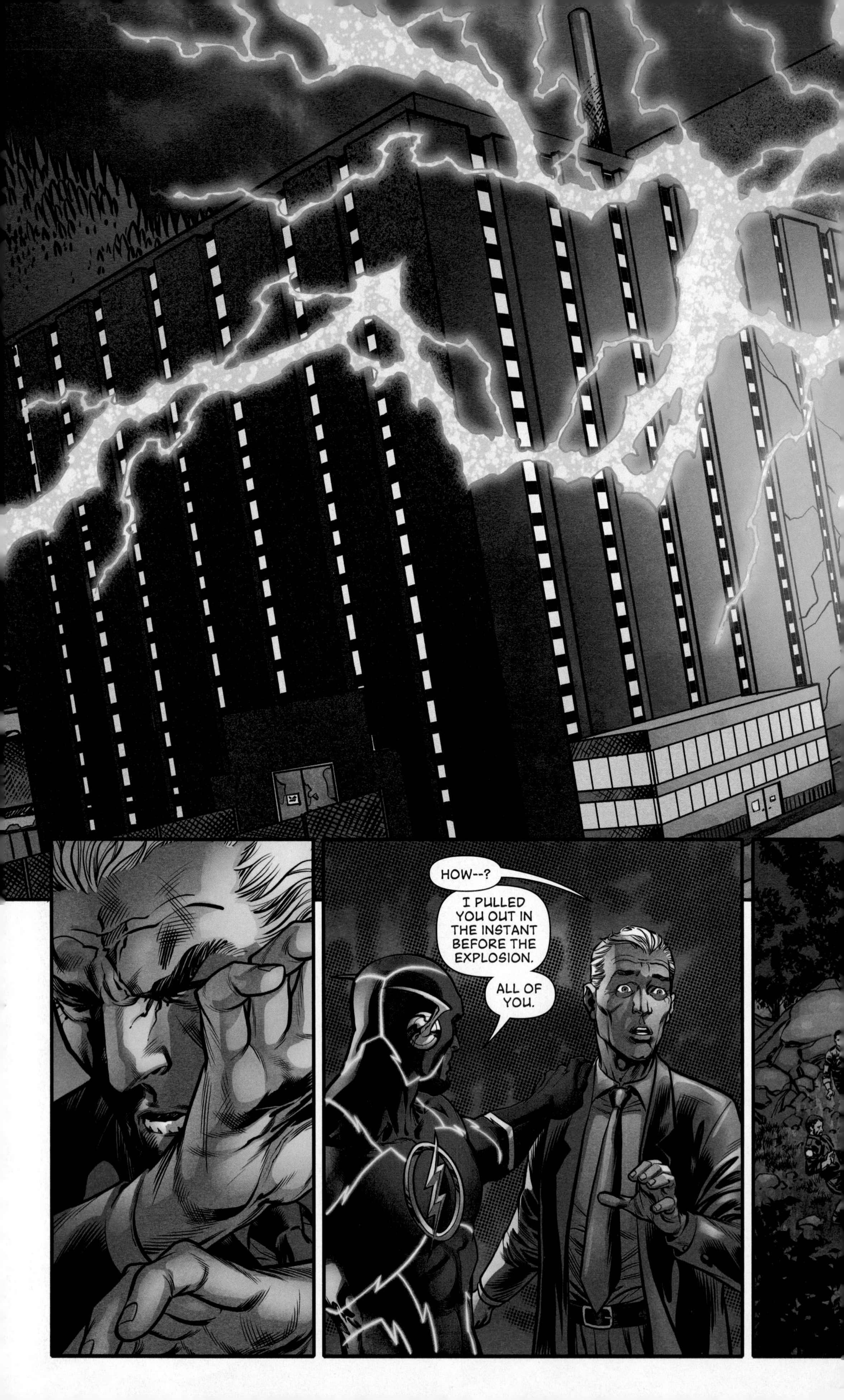
HOW--?
I PULLED YOU OUT IN THE INSTANT BEFORE THE EXPLOSION.
ALL OF YOU.

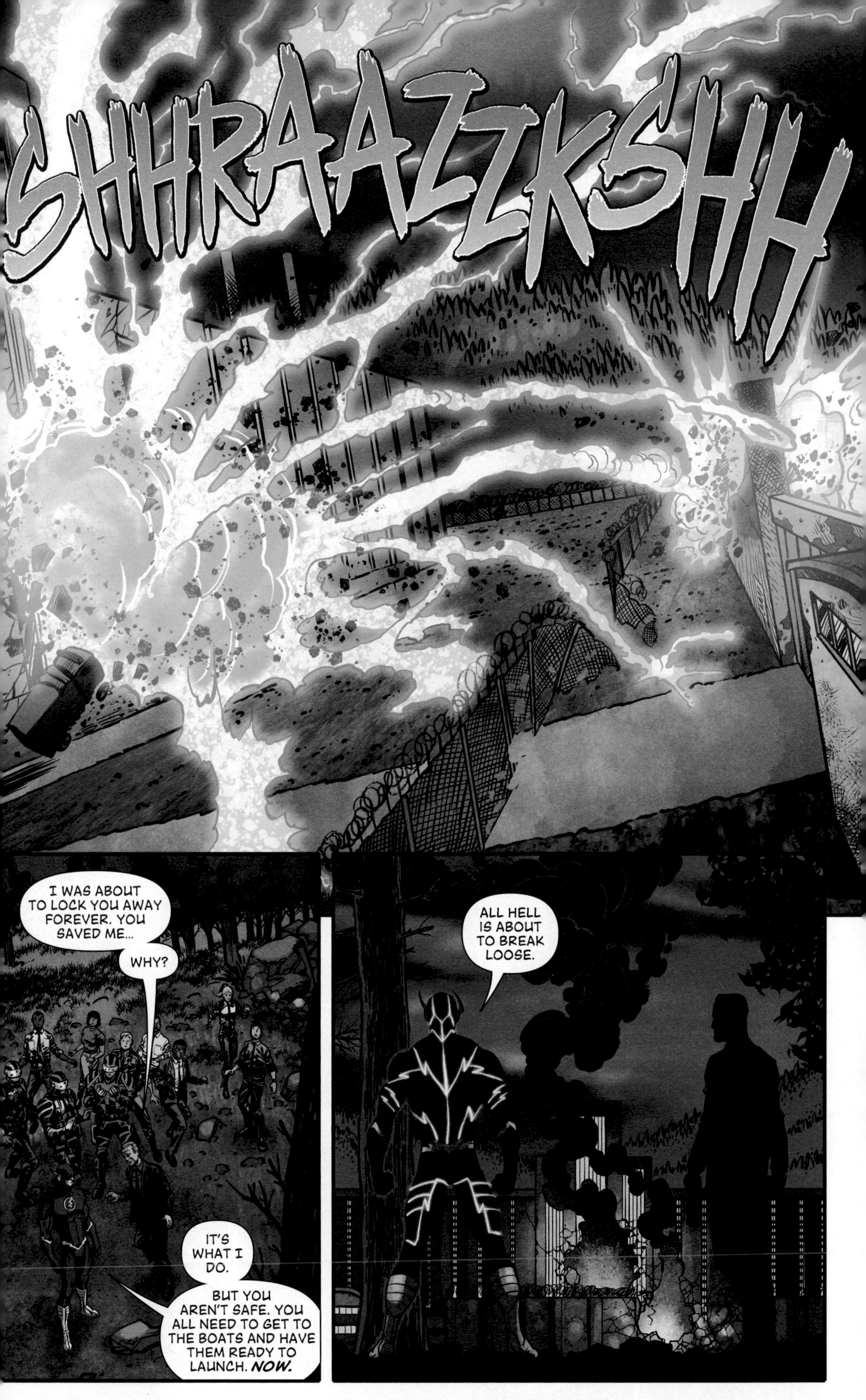
SHHRAAZZKSHH
I WAS ABOUT TO LOCK YOU AWAY FOREVER. YOU SAVED ME...
WHY?
IT'S WHAT I DO.
BUT YOU AREN'T SAFE. YOU ALL NEED TO GET TO THE BOATS AND HAVE THEM READY TO LAUNCH. NOW.
ALL HELL IS ABOUT TO BREAK LOOSE.

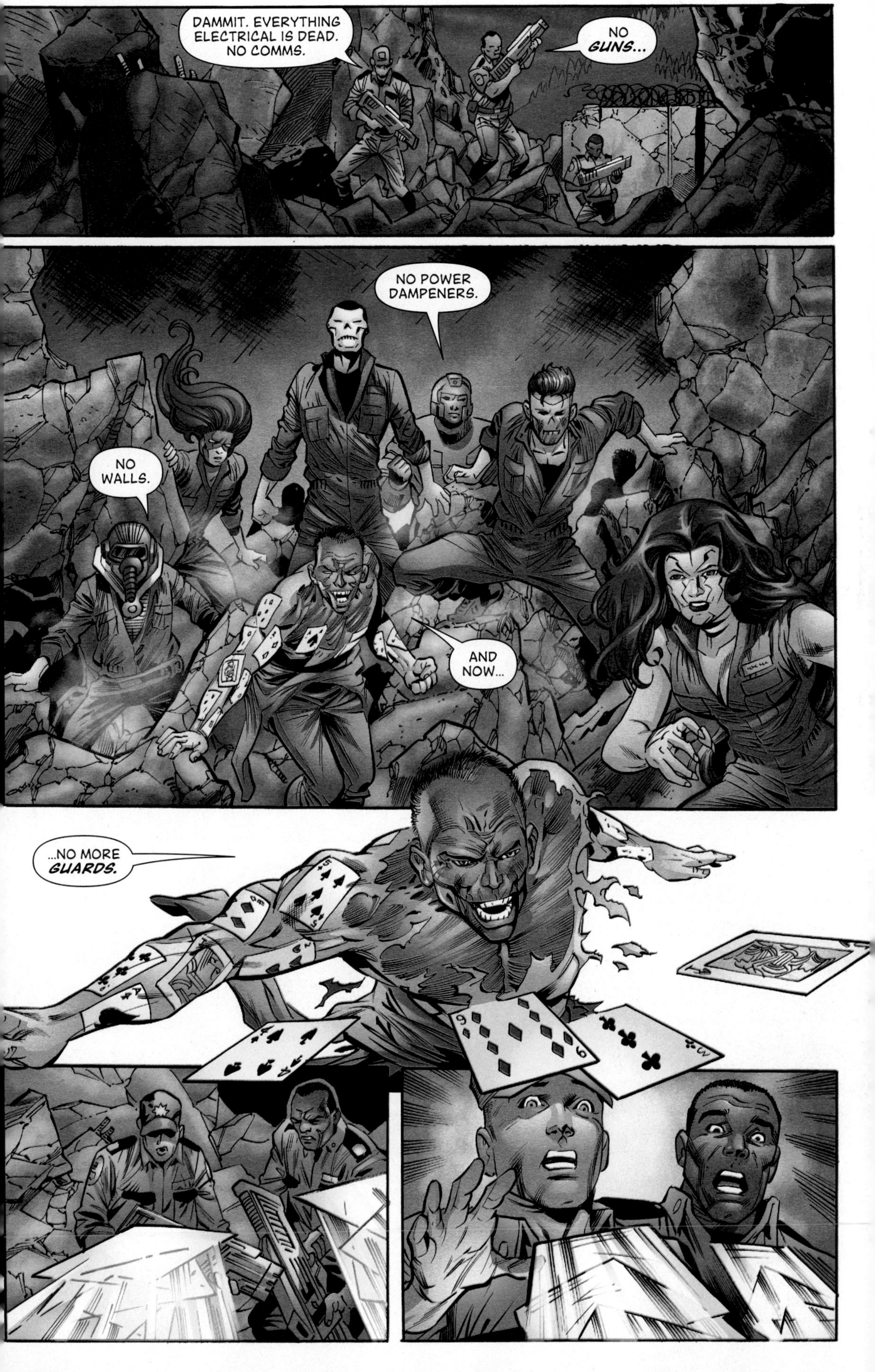
DAMMIT. EVERYTHING ELECTRICAL IS DEAD. NO COMMS.
NO GUNS...
NO POWER DAMPENERS.
NO WALLS.
AND NOW...
...NO MORE GUARDS.

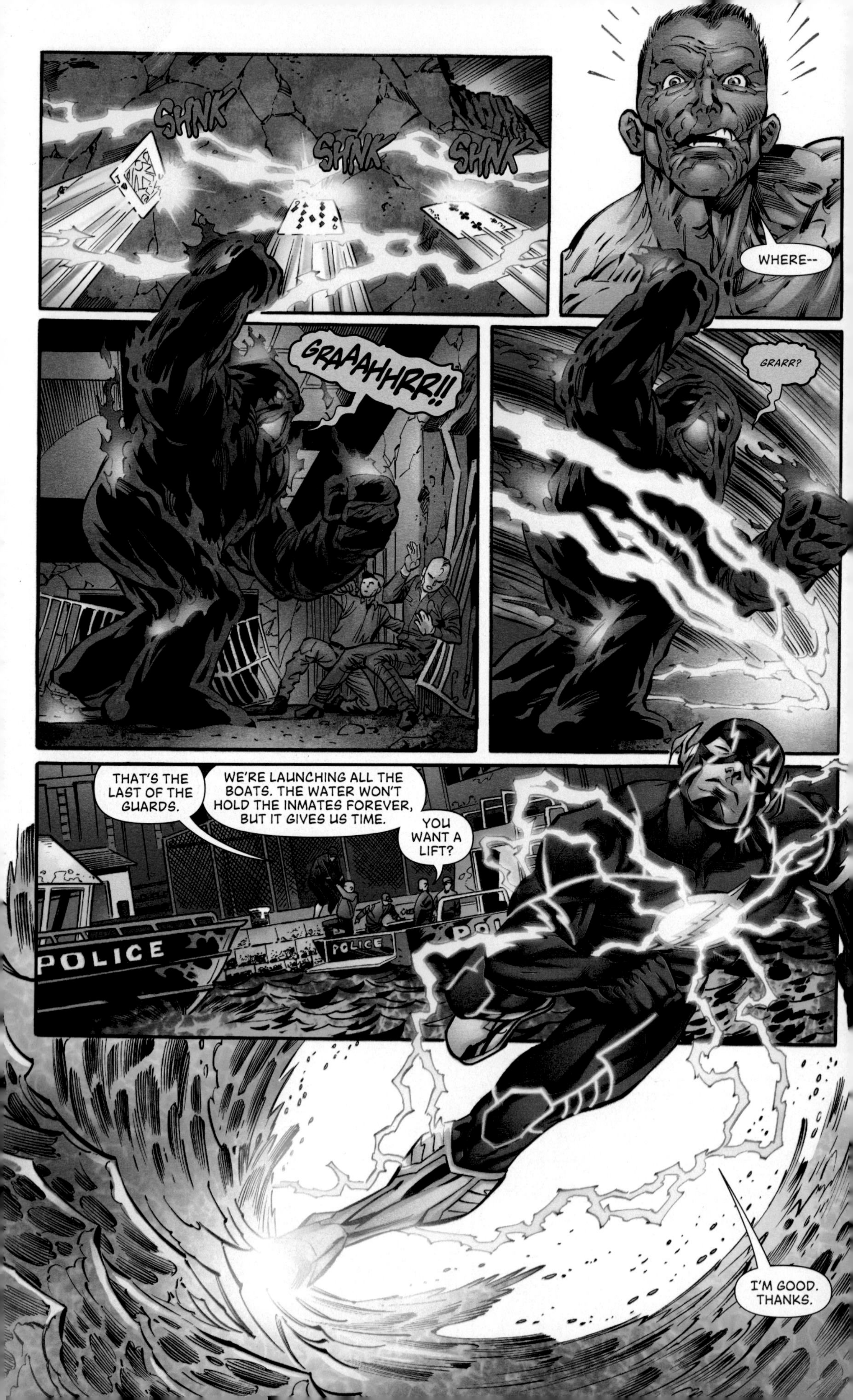
SHNK
SHNK
SHNK
WHERE--
GRAAAHHRR!!
GRARR?
THAT'S THE LAST OF THE GUARDS.
WE'RE LAUNCHING ALL THE BOATS. THE WATER WON'T HOLD THE INMATES FOREVER, BUT IT GIVES US TIME.
YOU WANT A LIFT?
POLICE
POLICE
I'M GOOD. THANKS.

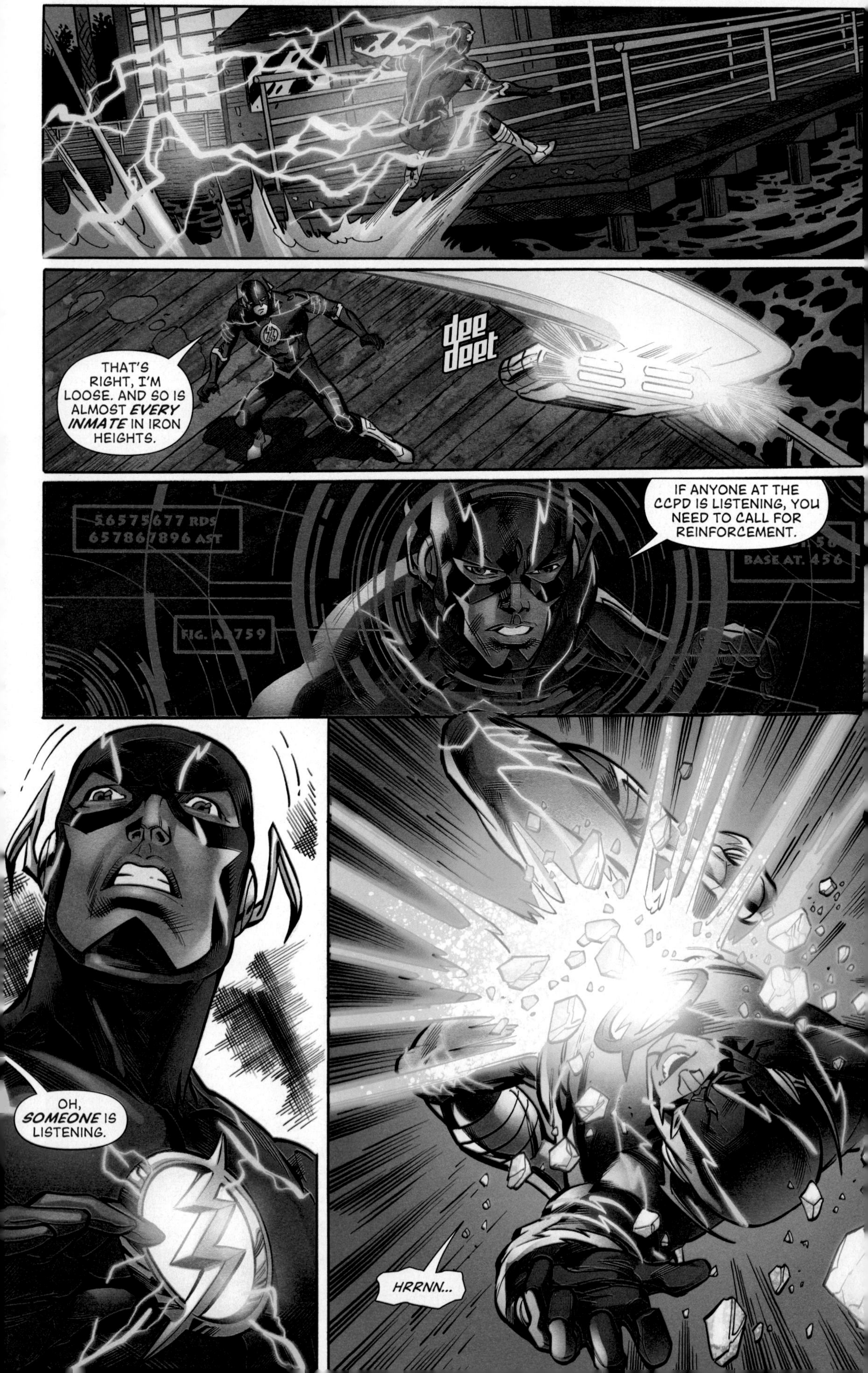
THAT'S RIGHT, I'M LOOSE. AND SO IS ALMOST EVERY INMATE IN IRON HEIGHTS.
dee deet
IF ANYONE AT THE CCPD IS LISTENING, YOU NEED TO CALL FOR REINFORCEMENT.
OH, SOMEONE IS LISTENING.
HRRNN...

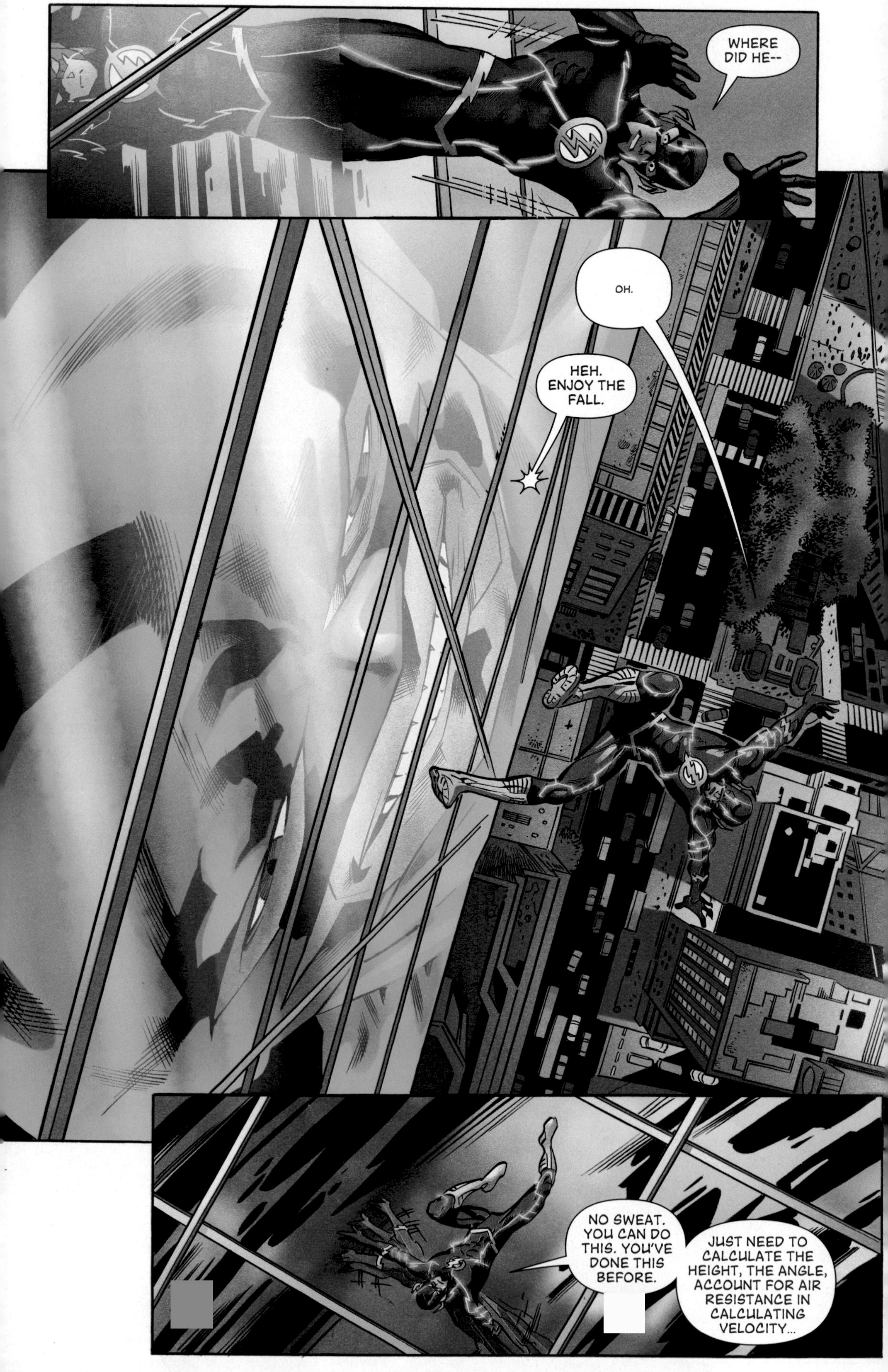
WHERE DID HE--
OH.
HEH. ENJOY THE FALL.
NO SWEAT. YOU CAN DO THIS. YOU'VE DONE THIS BEFORE.
JUST NEED TO CALCULATE THE HEIGHT, THE ANGLE, ACCOUNT FOR AIR RESISTANCE IN CALCULATING VELOCITY...

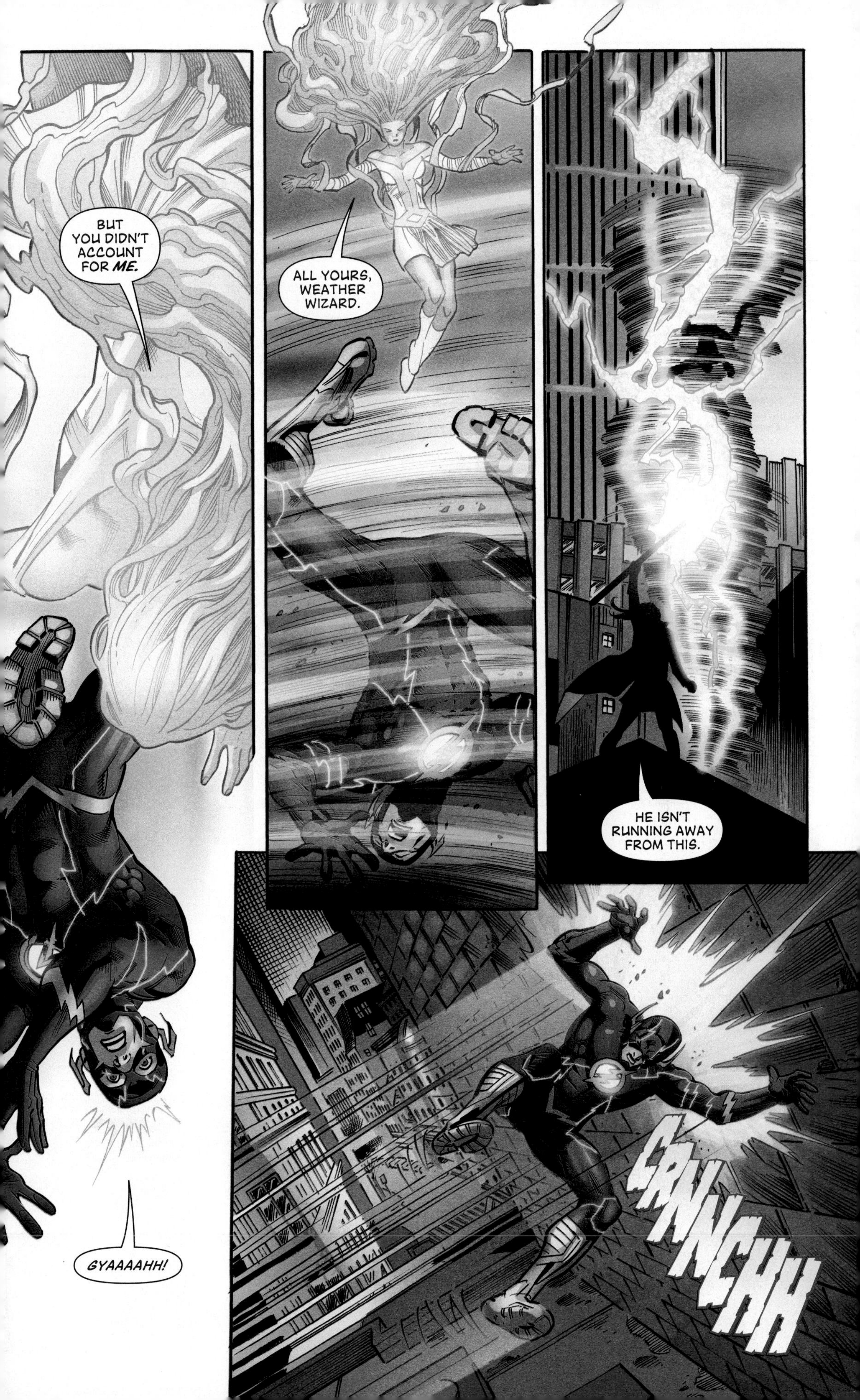
BUT YOU DIDN'T ACCOUNT FOR **ME.**
ALL YOURS, WEATHER WIZARD.
HE ISN'T RUNNING AWAY FROM THIS.
GYAAAAHH!
CRNNCHH

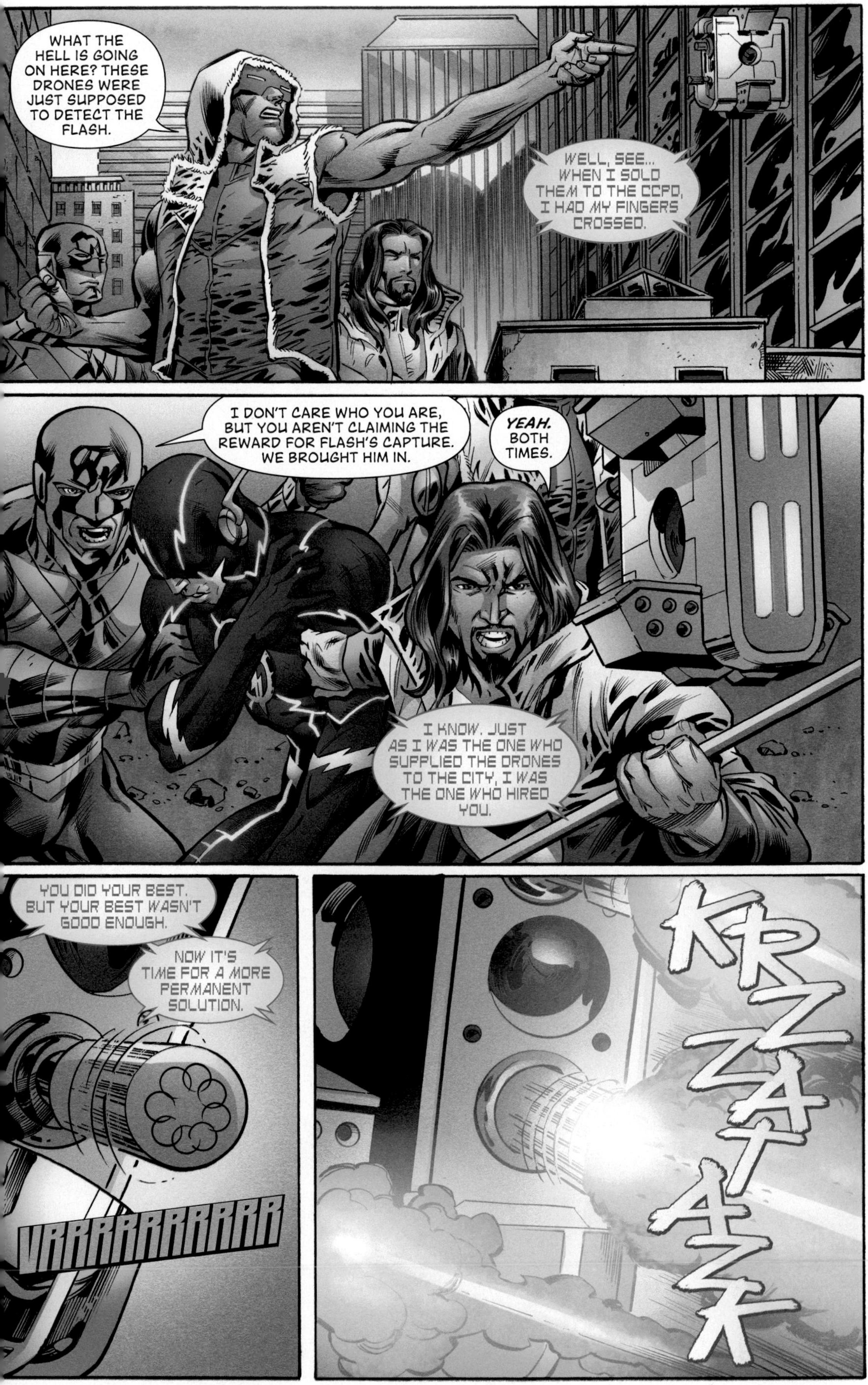
WHAT THE HELL IS GOING ON HERE? THESE DRONES WERE JUST SUPPOSED TO DETECT THE FLASH.
WELL, SEE... WHEN I SOLD THEM TO THE CCPD, I HAD MY FINGERS CROSSED.
I DON'T CARE WHO YOU ARE, BUT YOU AREN'T CLAIMING THE REWARD FOR FLASH'S CAPTURE. WE BROUGHT HIM IN.
YEAH. BOTH TIMES.
I KNOW. JUST AS I WAS THE ONE WHO SUPPLIED THE DRONES TO THE CITY, I WAS THE ONE WHO HIRED YOU.
YOU DID YOUR BEST. BUT YOUR BEST WASN'T GOOD ENOUGH.
NOW IT'S TIME FOR A MORE PERMANENT SOLUTION.
VRRRRRRRRRR
KRZZATAZK

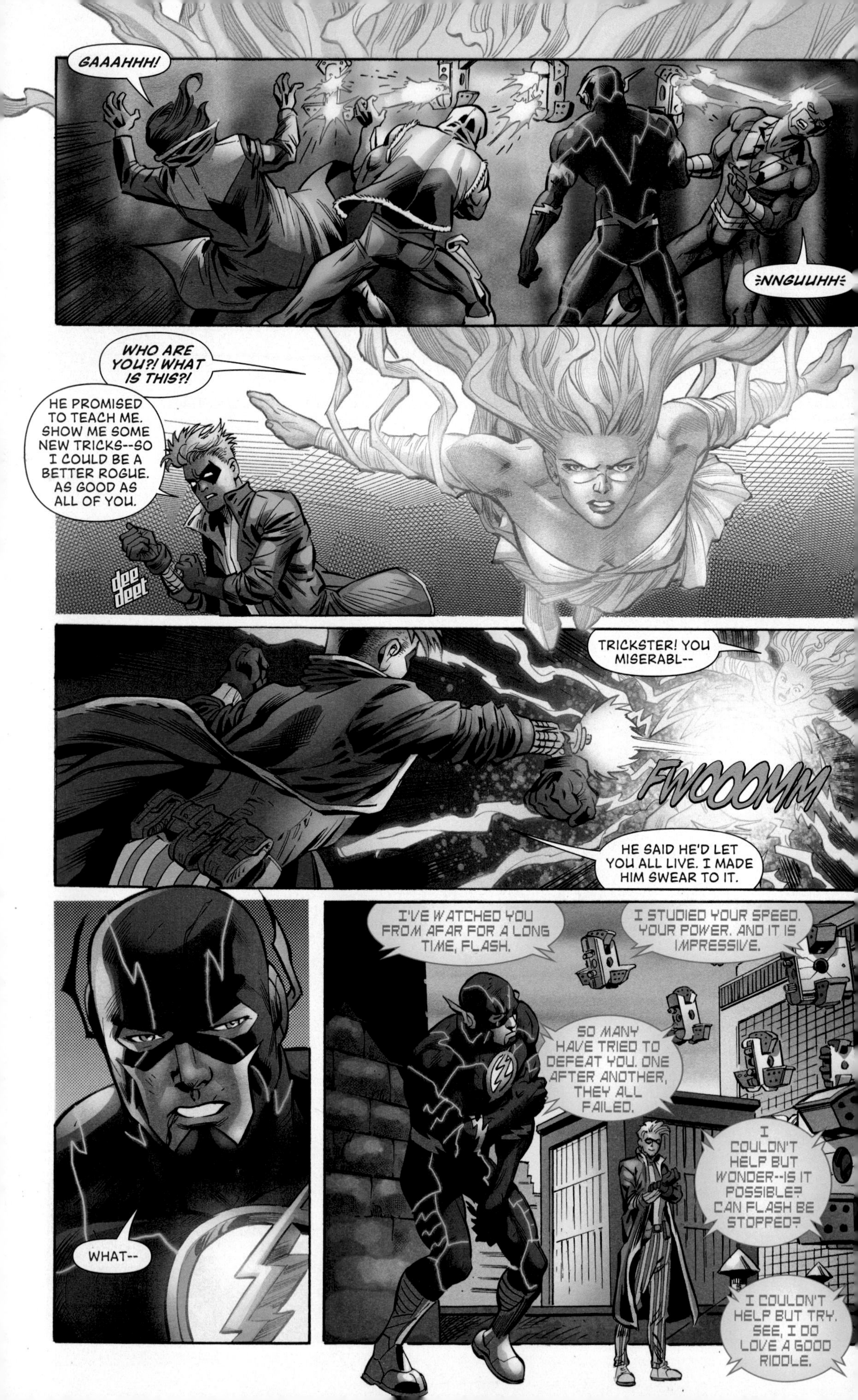
GAAAHHH!
NNGUUHH
WHO ARE YOU?! WHAT IS THIS?!
HE PROMISED TO TEACH ME. SHOW ME SOME NEW TRICKS--SO I COULD BE A BETTER ROGUE. AS GOOD AS ALL OF YOU.
dee deet
TRICKSTER! YOU MISERABL--
FWOOOMM
HE SAID HE'D LET YOU ALL LIVE. I MADE HIM SWEAR TO IT.
WHAT--
I'VE WATCHED YOU FROM AFAR FOR A LONG TIME, FLASH.
I STUDIED YOUR SPEED. YOUR POWER. AND IT IS IMPRESSIVE.
SO MANY HAVE TRIED TO DEFEAT YOU. ONE AFTER ANOTHER, THEY ALL FAILED.
I COULDN'T HELP BUT WONDER--IS IT POSSIBLE? CAN FLASH BE STOPPED?
I COULDN'T HELP BUT TRY. SEE, I DO LOVE A GOOD RIDDLE.

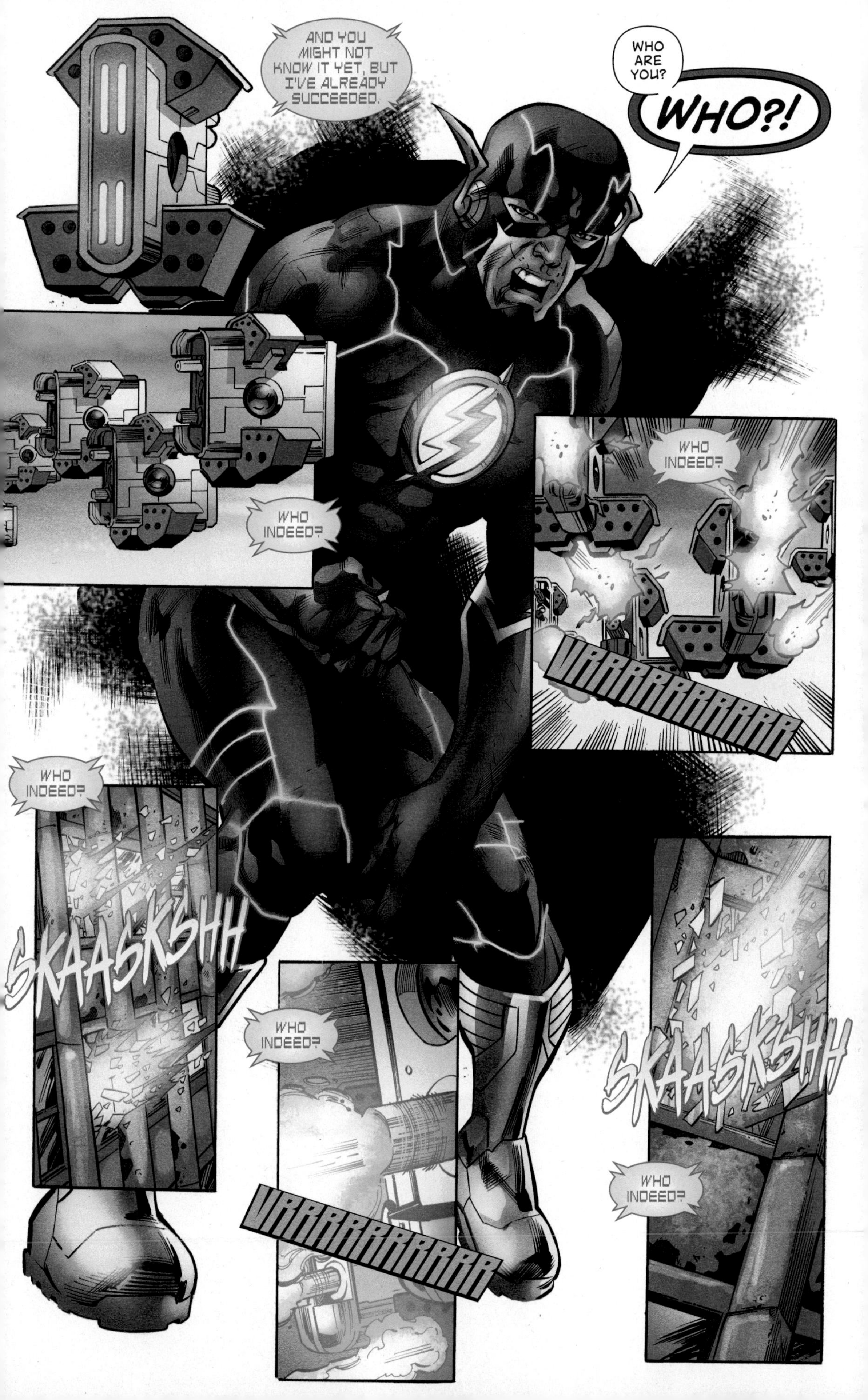
AND YOU MIGHT NOT KNOW IT YET, BUT I'VE ALREADY SUCCEEDED.
WHO ARE YOU?
WHO?!
WHO INDEED?
WHO INDEED?
VRRRRRRRRRRRR
WHO INDEED?
SKAASKSHH
WHO INDEED?
VRRRRRRRRRRR
SKAASKSHH
WHO INDEED?

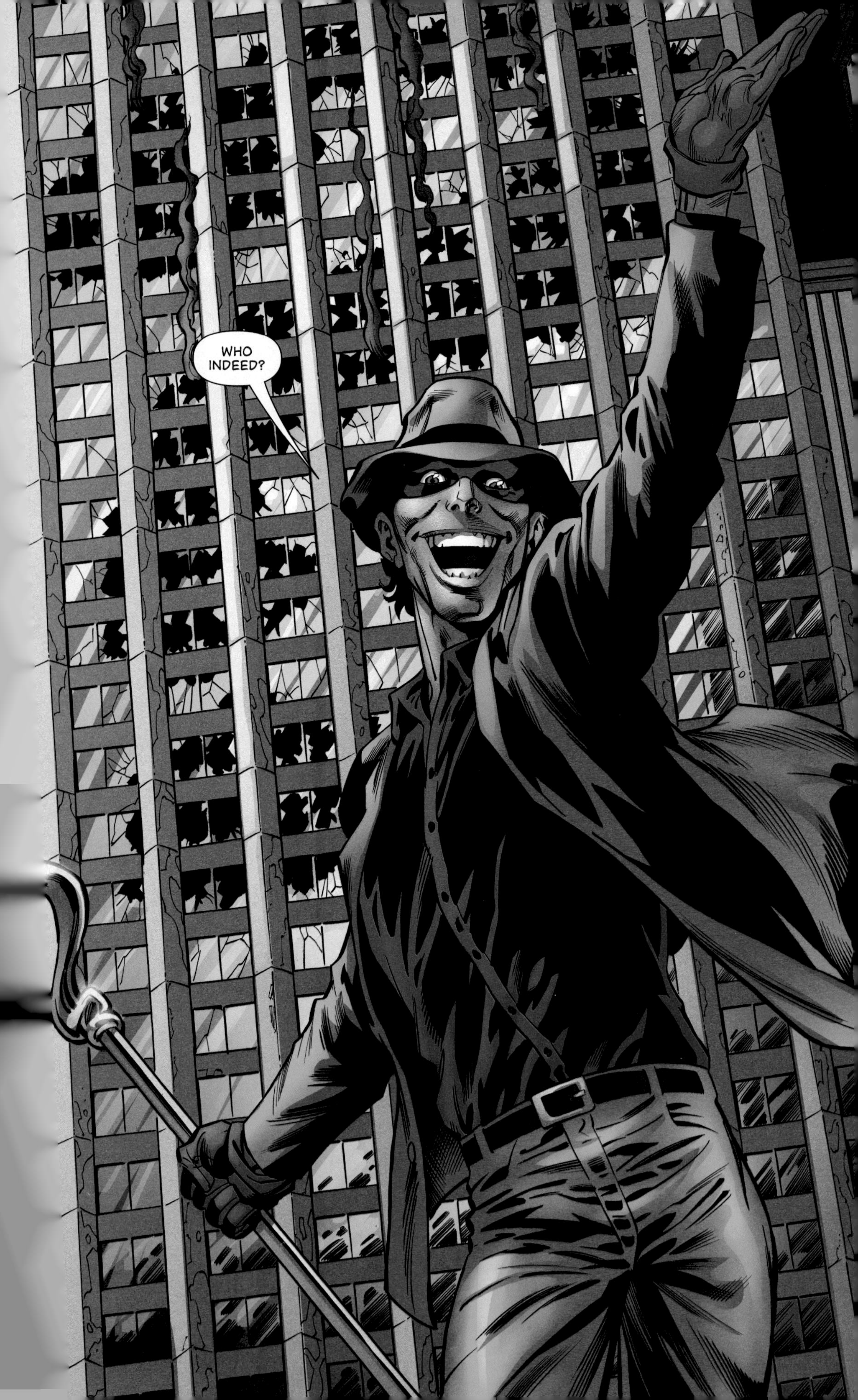
WHO INDEED?

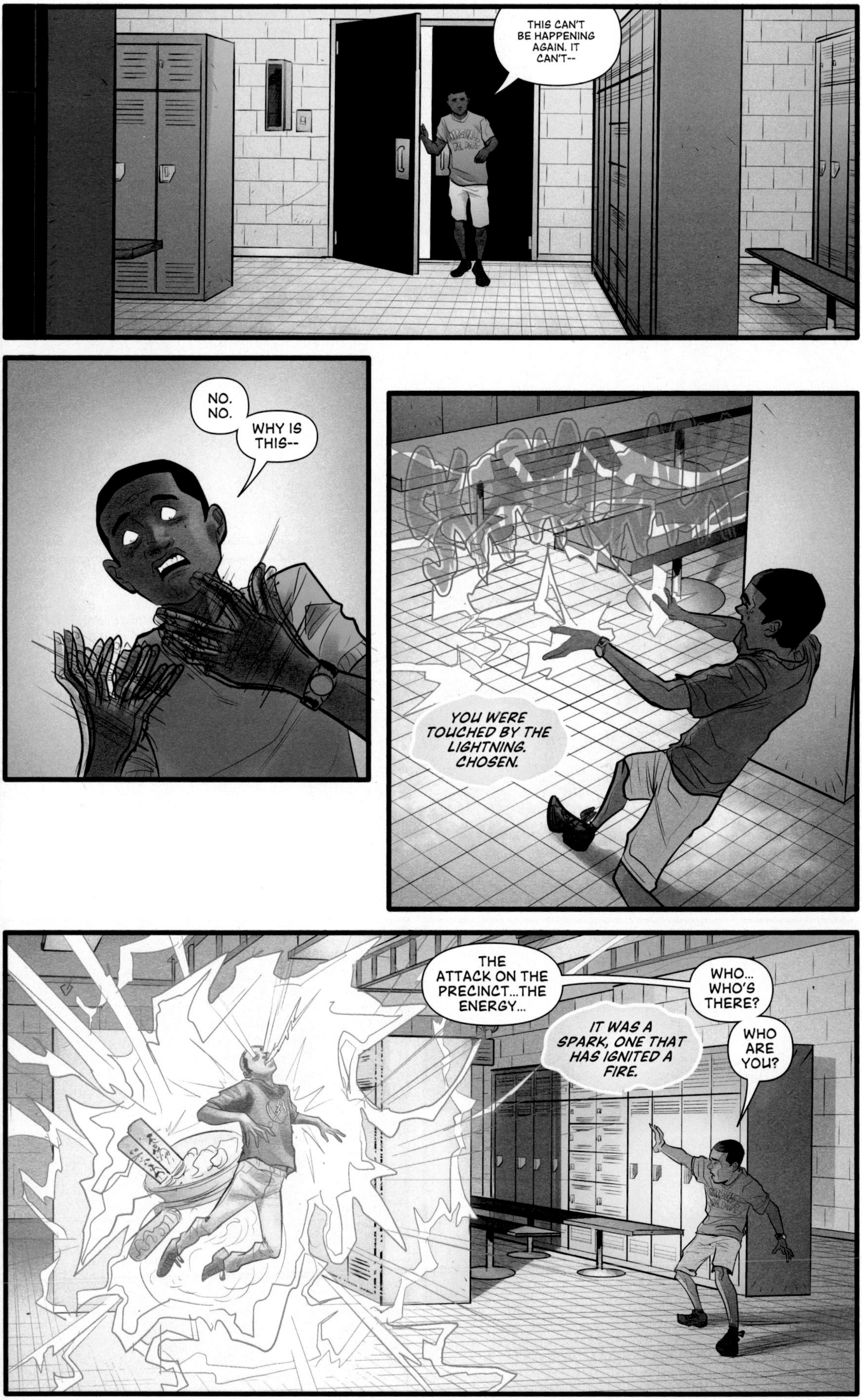
THIS CAN'T BE HAPPENING AGAIN. IT CAN'T--
NO. NO.
WHY IS THIS--
YOU WERE TOUCHED BY THE LIGHTNING. CHOSEN.
THE ATTACK ON THE PRECINCT...THE ENERGY...
WHO... WHO'S THERE?
IT WAS A SPARK, ONE THAT HAS IGNITED A FIRE.
WHO ARE YOU?

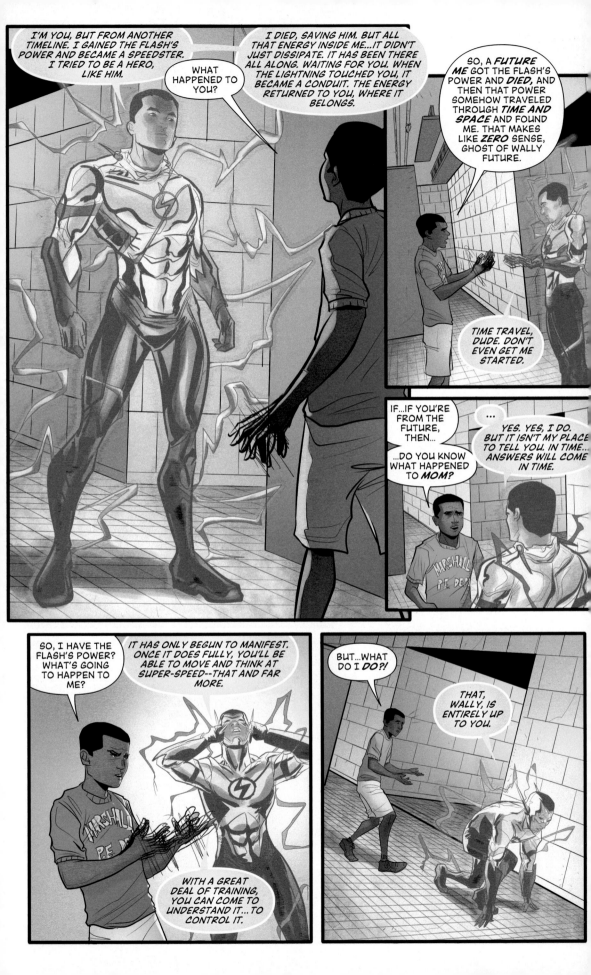

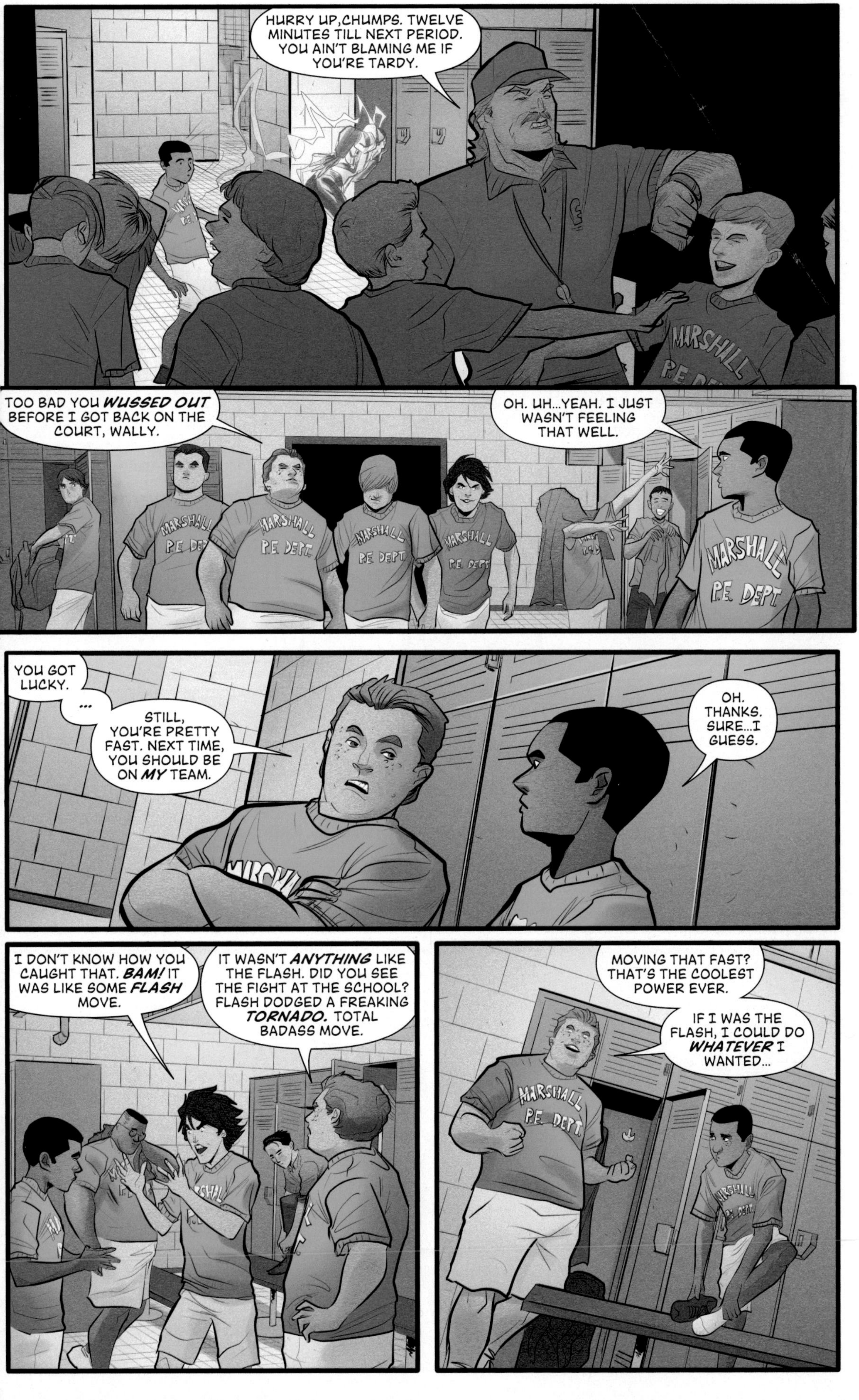
HURRY UP, CHUMPS. TWELVE MINUTES TILL NEXT PERIOD. YOU AIN'T BLAMING ME IF YOU'RE TARDY.
TOO BAD YOU WUSSED OUT BEFORE I GOT BACK ON THE COURT, WALLY.
OH. UH...YEAH. I JUST WASN'T FEELING THAT WELL.
YOU GOT LUCKY.
...
STILL, YOU'RE PRETTY FAST. NEXT TIME, YOU SHOULD BE ON MY TEAM.
OH. THANKS. SURE...I GUESS.
I DON'T KNOW HOW YOU CAUGHT THAT. BAM! IT WAS LIKE SOME FLASH MOVE.
IT WASN'T ANYTHING LIKE THE FLASH. DID YOU SEE THE FIGHT AT THE SCHOOL? FLASH DODGED A FREAKING TORNADO. TOTAL BADASS MOVE.
MOVING THAT FAST? THAT'S THE COOLEST POWER EVER.
IF I WAS THE FLASH, I COULD DO WHATEVER I WANTED...

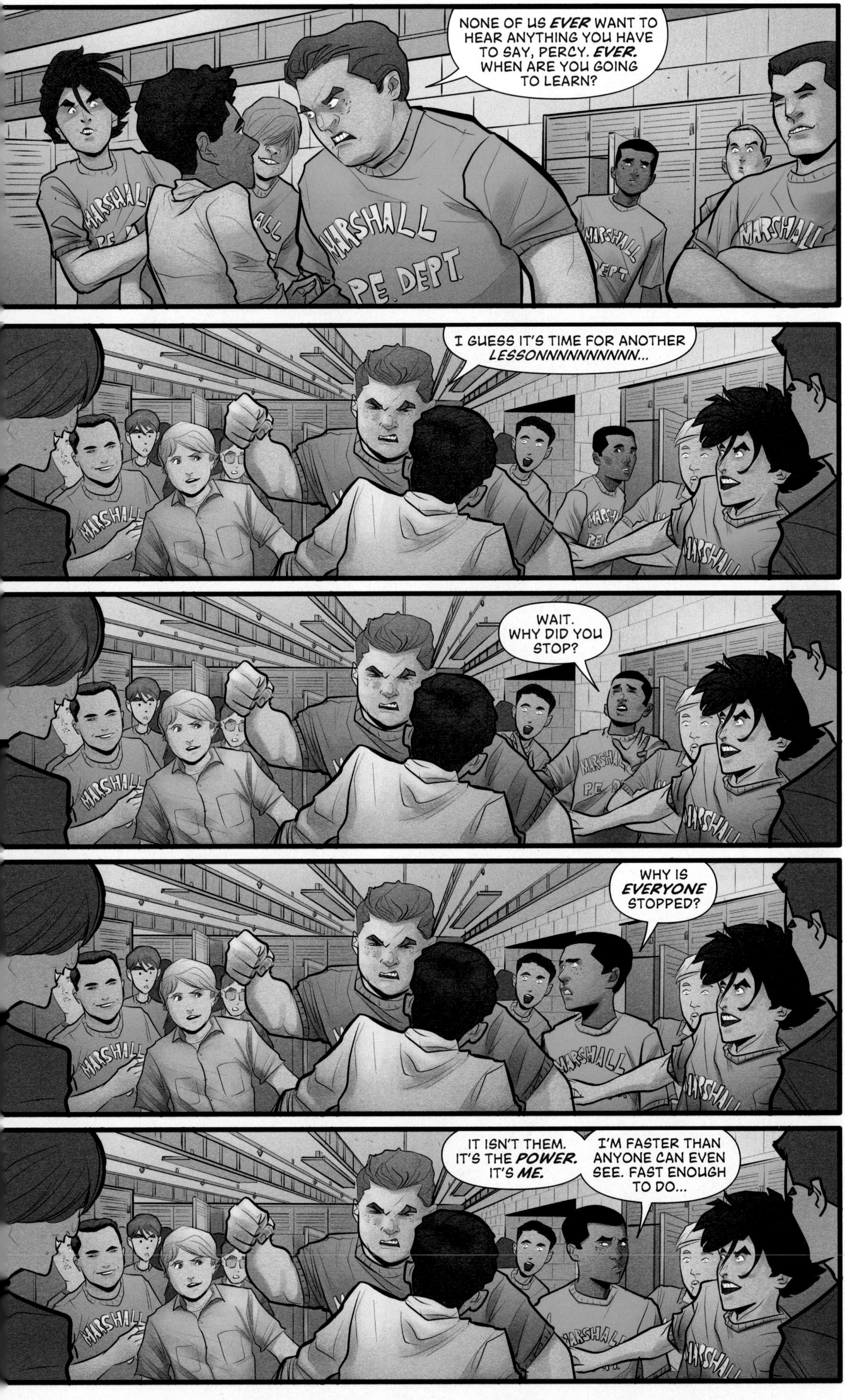
NONE OF US *EVER* WANT TO HEAR ANYTHING YOU HAVE TO SAY, PERCY. *EVER.* WHEN ARE YOU GOING TO LEARN?
MARSHALL
MARSHALL P.E. DEPT.
MARSHALL
MARSHALL
I GUESS IT'S TIME FOR ANOTHER *LESSONNNNNNNNNN...*
MARSHALL
MARSHALL
WAIT. WHY DID YOU STOP?
MARSHALL
MARSHALL
WHY IS *EVERYONE* STOPPED?
MARSHALL
MARSHALL
IT ISN'T THEM. IT'S THE *POWER.* IT'S *ME.*
I'M FASTER THAN ANYONE CAN EVEN SEE. FAST ENOUGH TO DO...
MARSHALL
MARSHALL

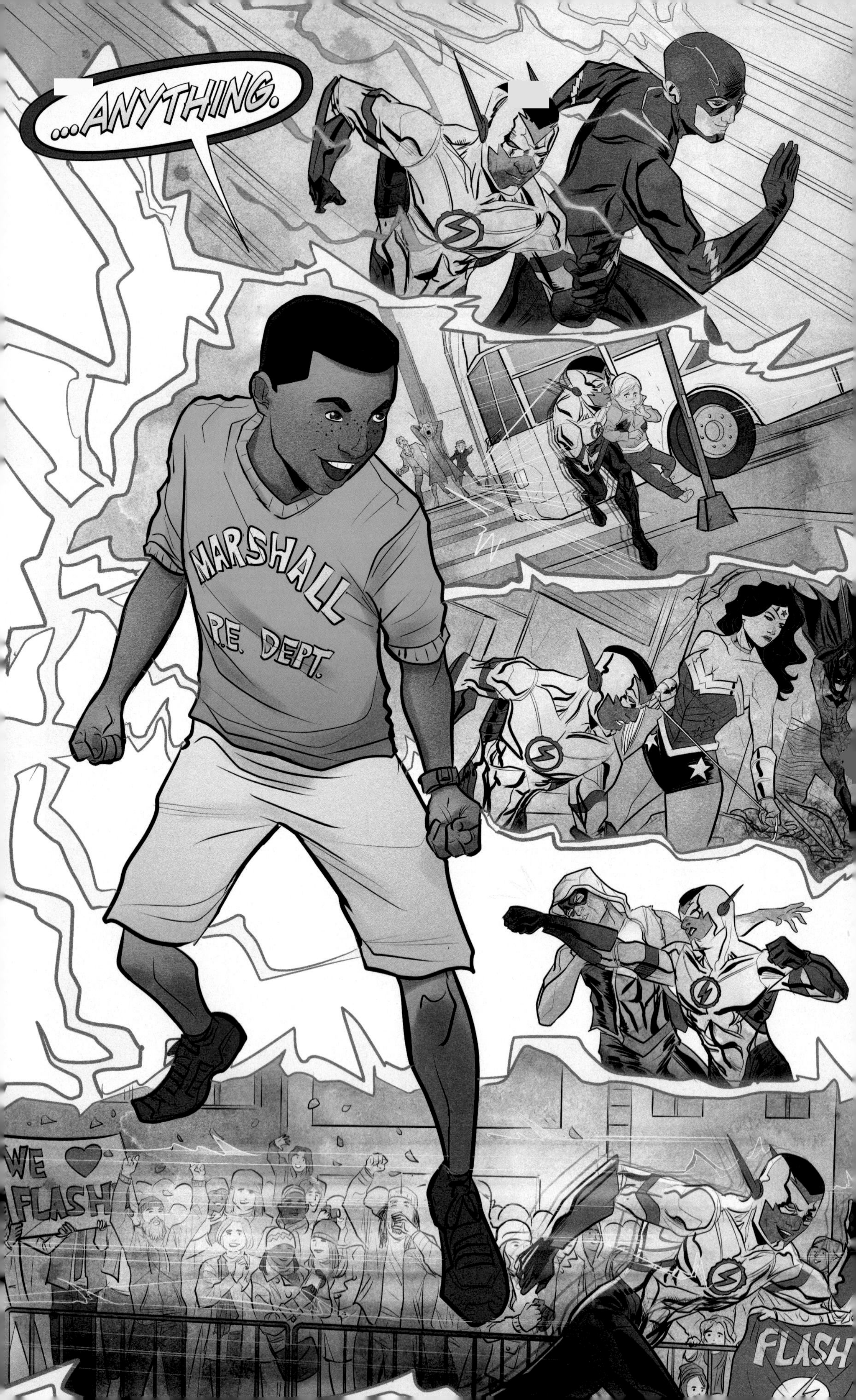
...ANYTHING.
MARSHALL
P.E. DEPT.
WE ♥ FLASH
FLASH

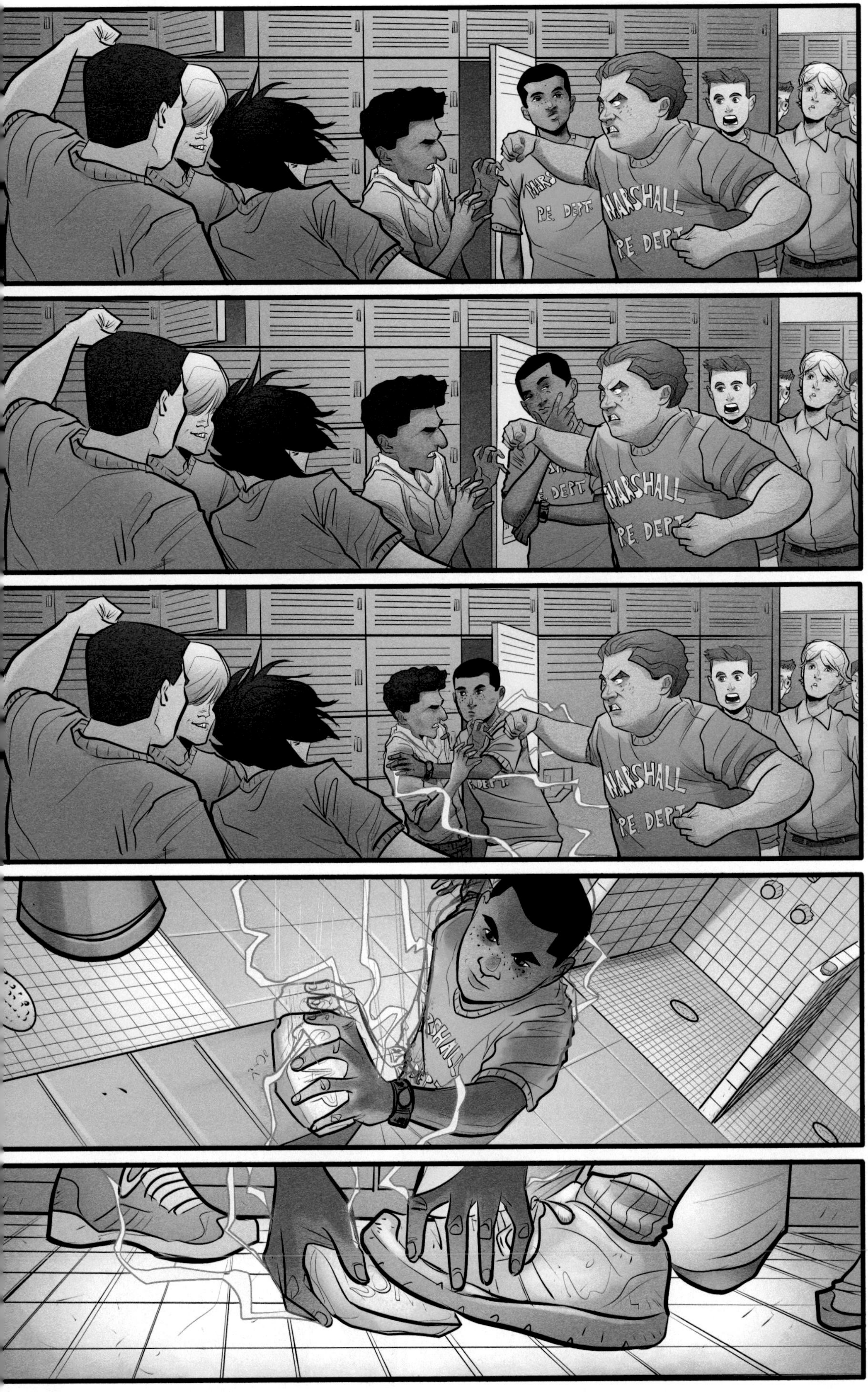
MARSHALL
P.E. DEPT

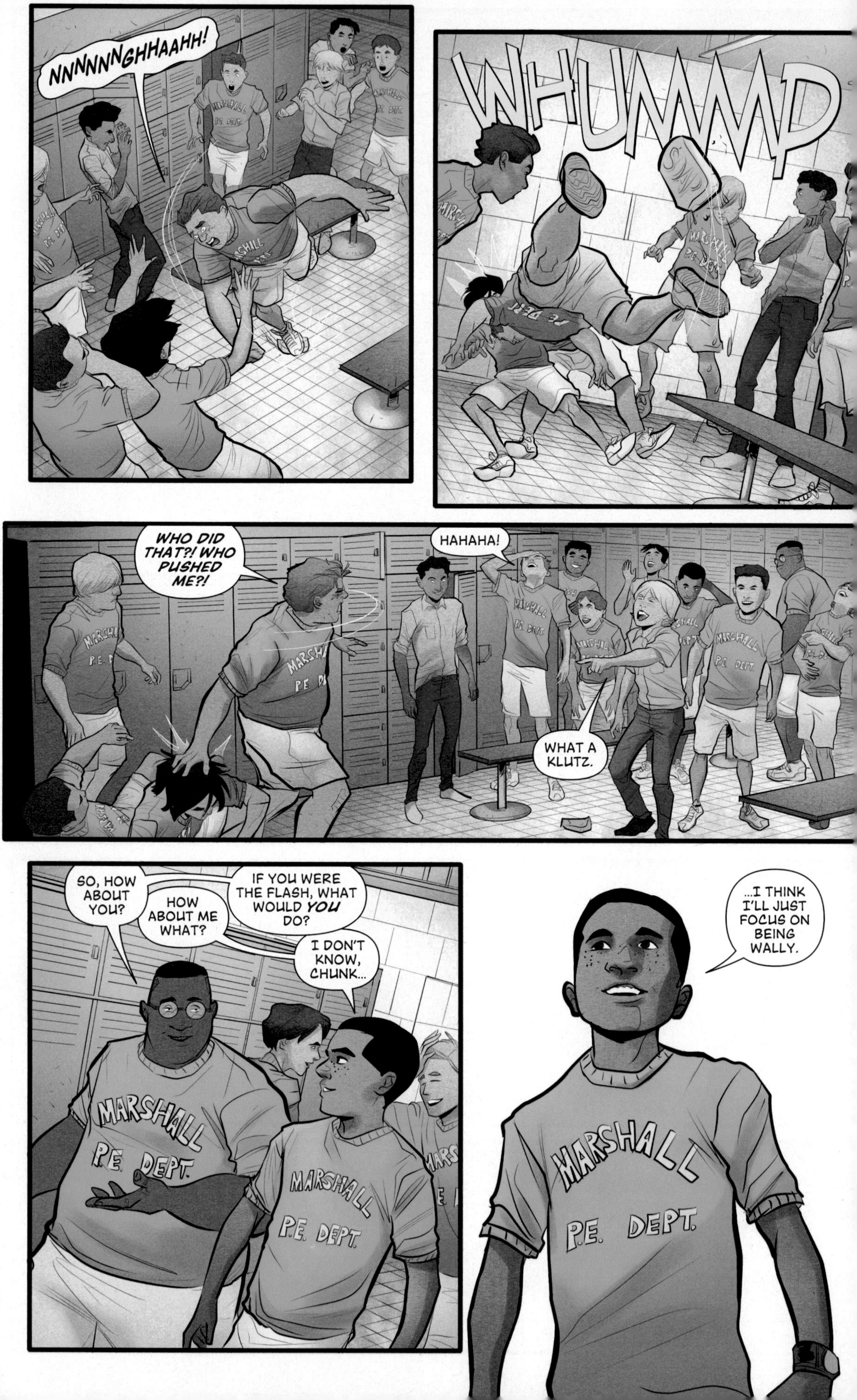
NNNNNNGHHAAHH!
WHUMMP
WHO DID THAT?! WHO PUSHED ME?!
HAHAHA!
WHAT A KLUTZ.
SO, HOW ABOUT YOU?
HOW ABOUT ME WHAT?
IF YOU WERE THE FLASH, WHAT WOULD *YOU* DO?
I DON'T KNOW, CHUNK...
...I THINK I'LL JUST FOCUS ON BEING WALLY.

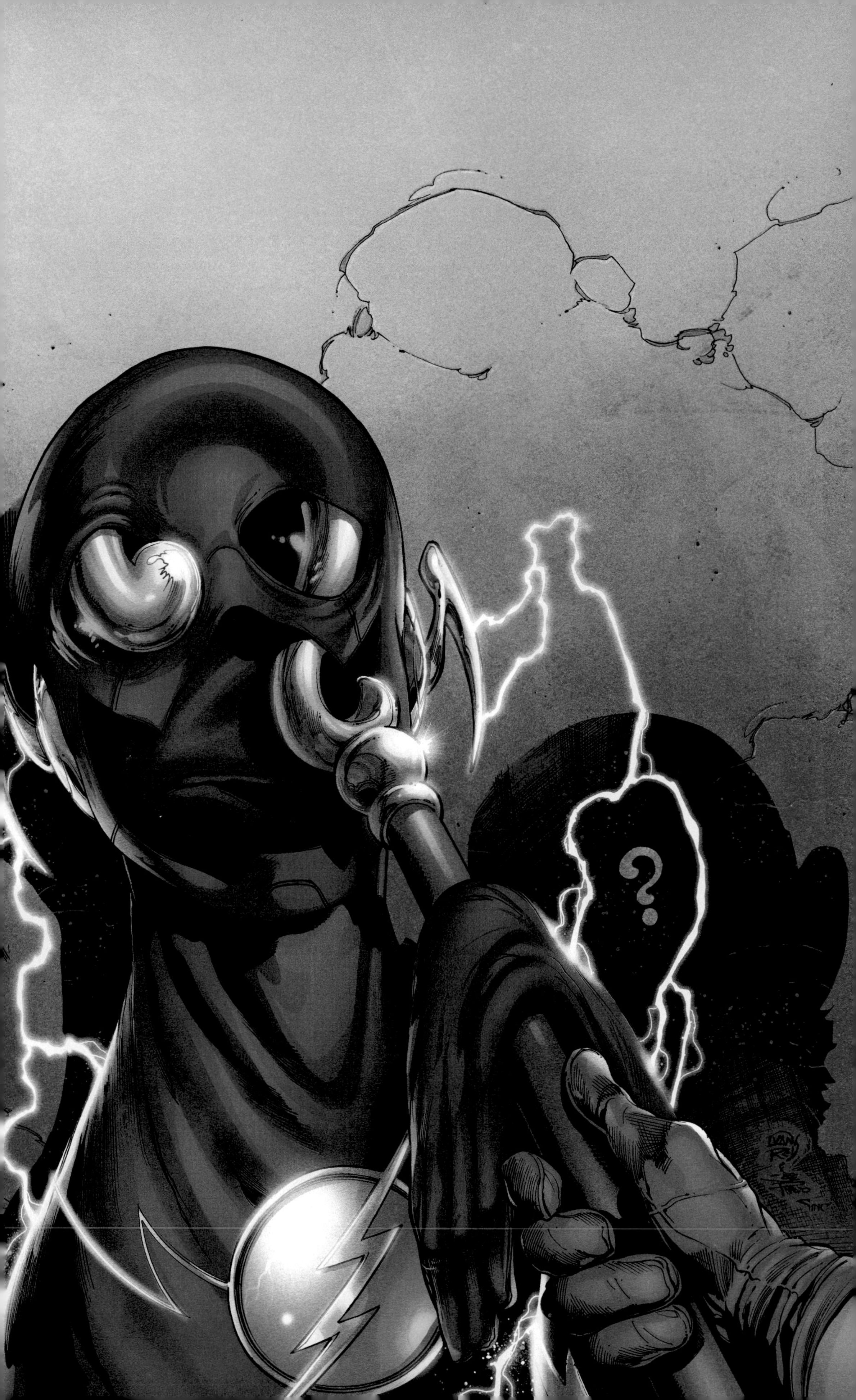

UNDER THE GUN

VAN JENSEN writer **GUS VAZQUEZ JOE EISMA** artists **GUY MAJOR** colorist **PAT BROSSEAU** letterer **IVAN REIS JOE PRADO ALEX SINCLAIR** cover

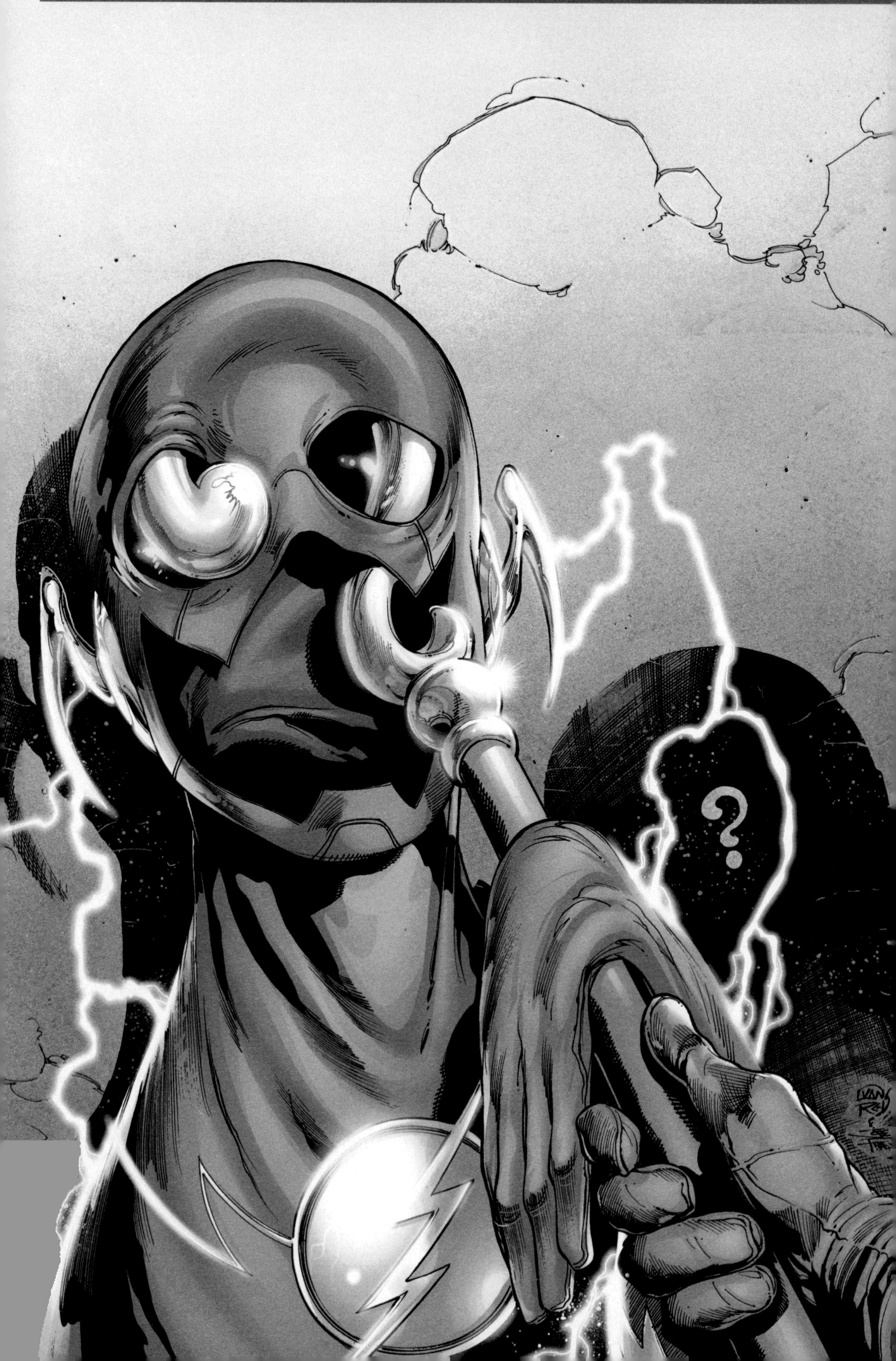
?

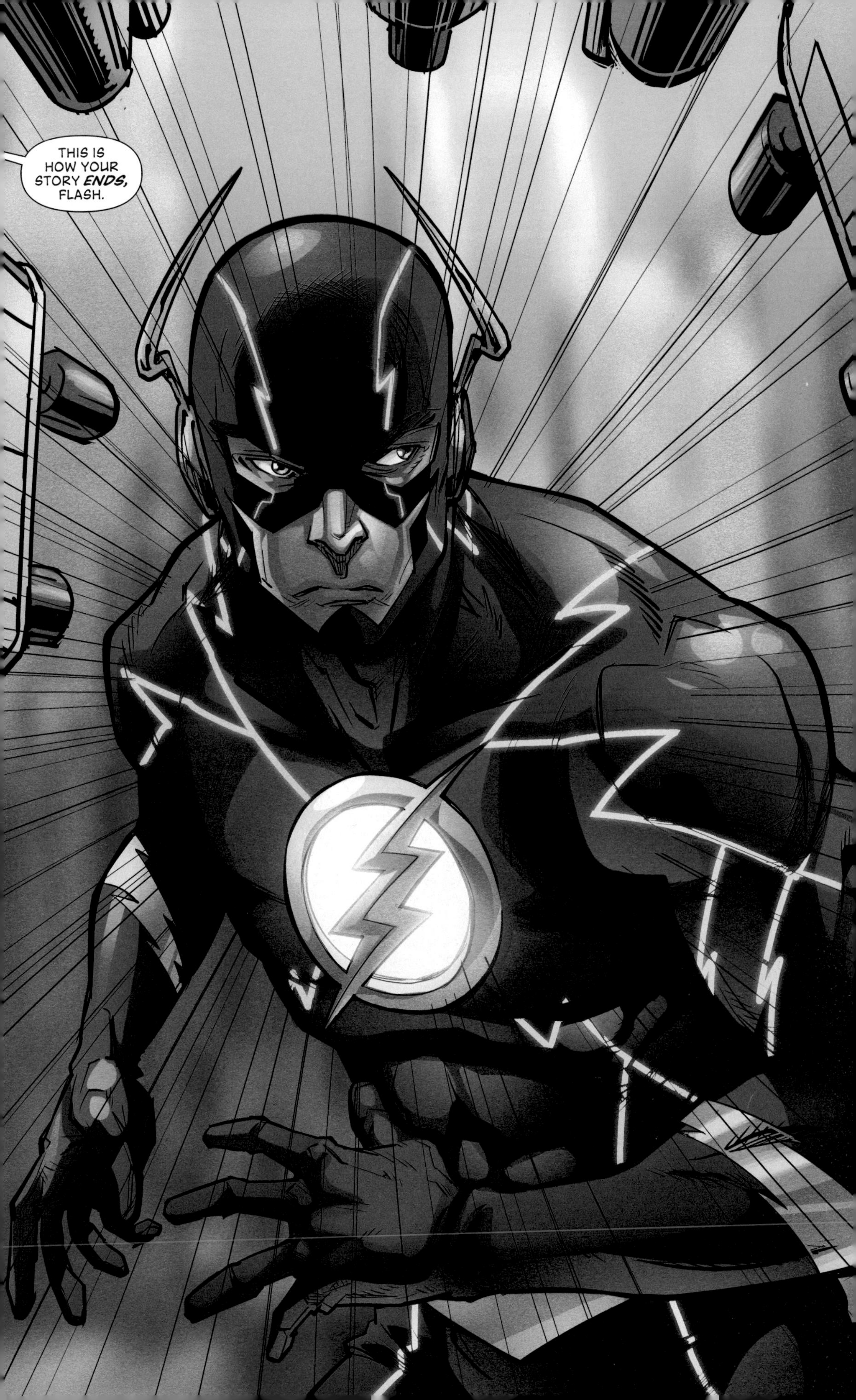
THIS IS HOW YOUR STORY *ENDS,* FLASH.

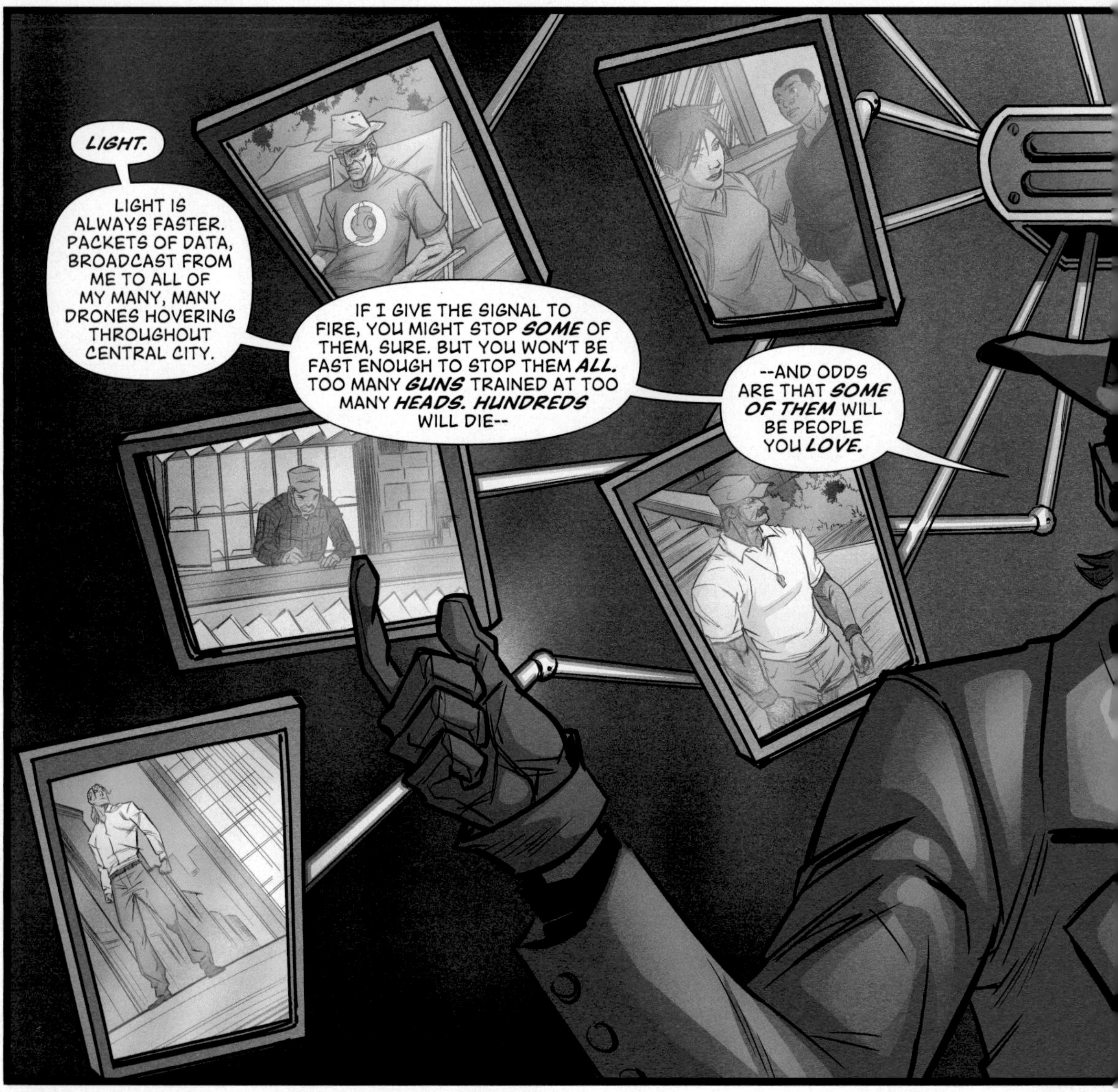
LIGHT.
LIGHT IS ALWAYS FASTER. PACKETS OF DATA, BROADCAST FROM ME TO ALL OF MY MANY, MANY DRONES HOVERING THROUGHOUT CENTRAL CITY.
IF I GIVE THE SIGNAL TO FIRE, YOU MIGHT STOP SOME OF THEM, SURE. BUT YOU WON'T BE FAST ENOUGH TO STOP THEM ALL. TOO MANY GUNS TRAINED AT TOO MANY HEADS. HUNDREDS WILL DIE--
--AND ODDS ARE THAT SOME OF THEM WILL BE PEOPLE YOU LOVE.

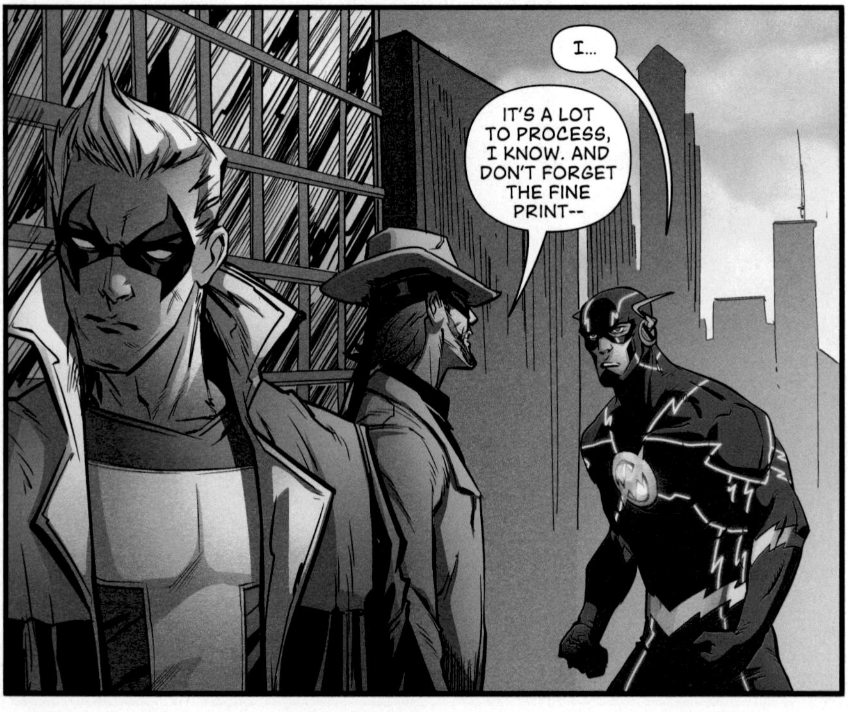
I...
IT'S A LOT TO PROCESS, I KNOW. AND DON'T FORGET THE FINE PRINT--

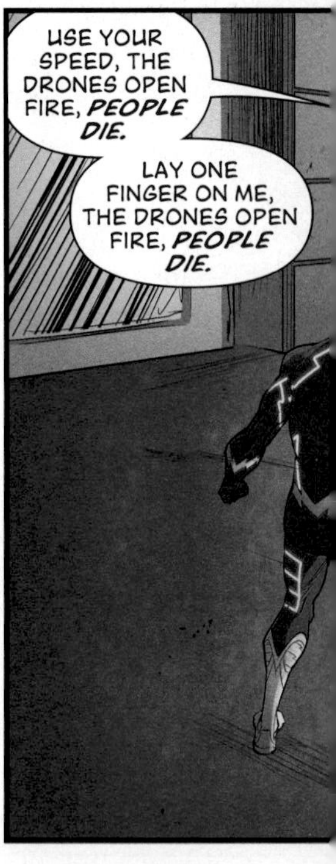
USE YOUR SPEED, THE DRONES OPEN FIRE, PEOPLE DIE.
LAY ONE FINGER ON ME, THE DRONES OPEN FIRE, PEOPLE DIE.

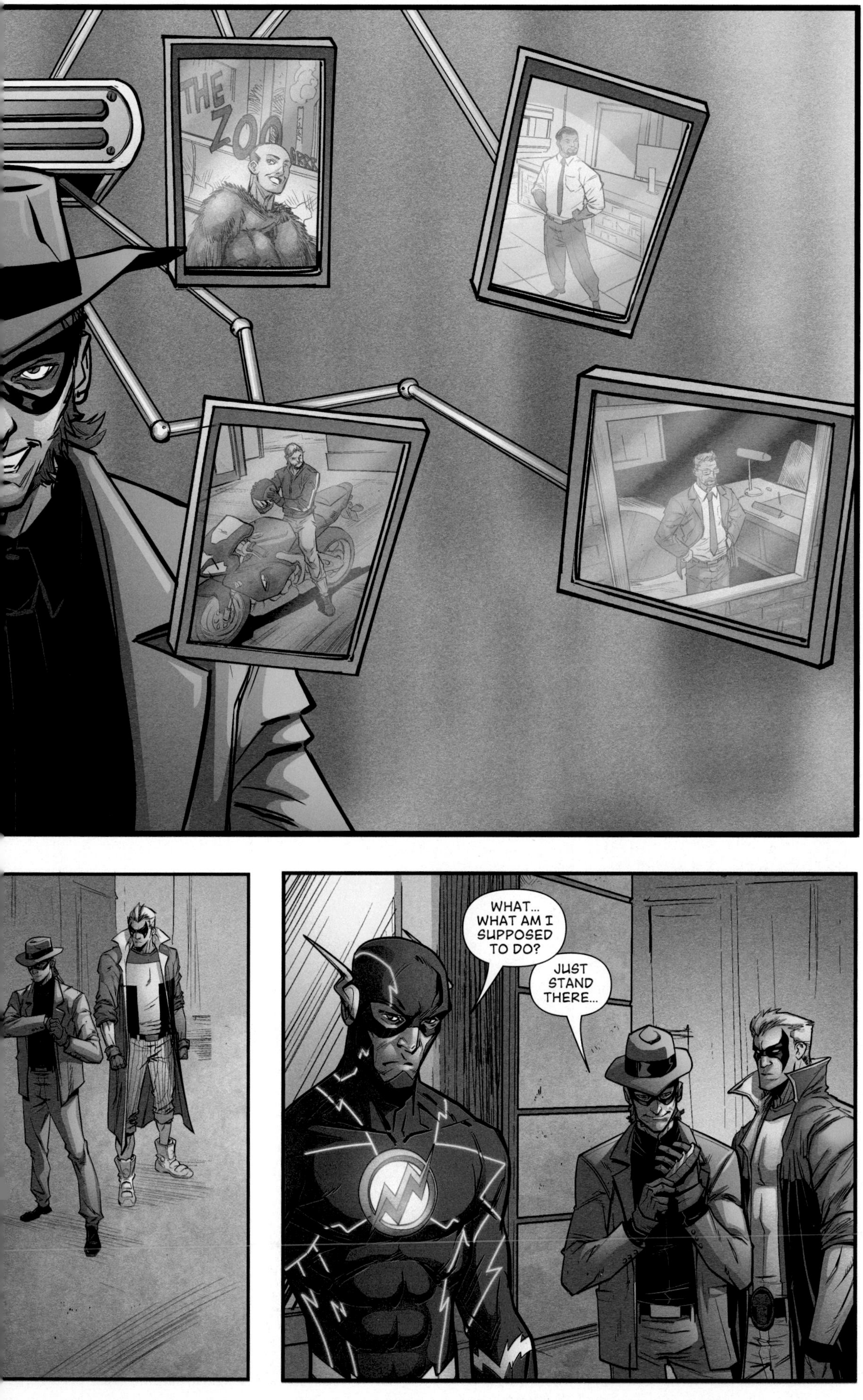
THE ZOO
WHAT... WHAT AM I SUPPOSED TO DO?
JUST STAND THERE...

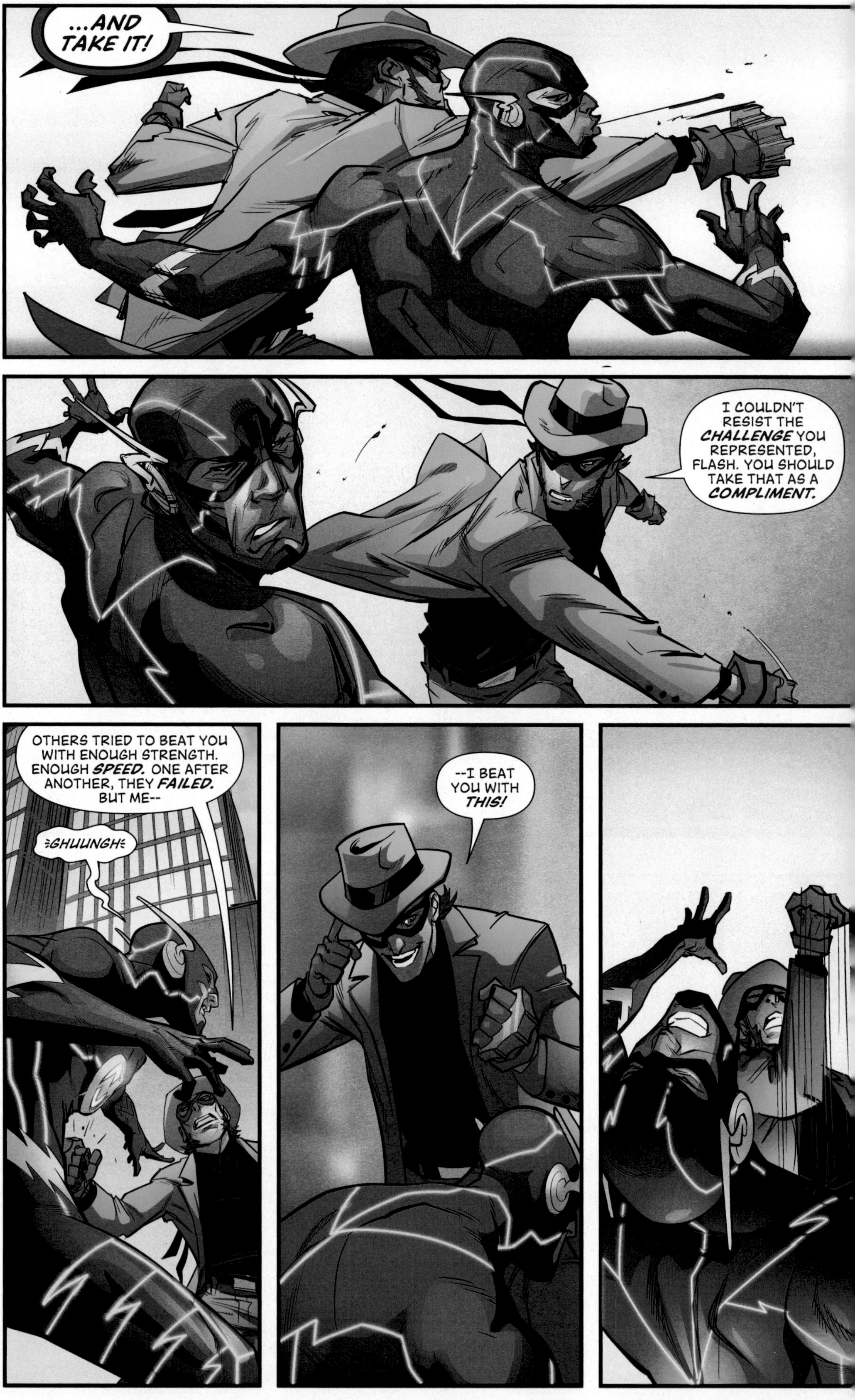
...AND TAKE IT!
I COULDN'T RESIST THE CHALLENGE YOU REPRESENTED, FLASH. YOU SHOULD TAKE THAT AS A COMPLIMENT.
OTHERS TRIED TO BEAT YOU WITH ENOUGH STRENGTH. ENOUGH SPEED. ONE AFTER ANOTHER, THEY FAILED. BUT ME--
GHUUNGH
--I BEAT YOU WITH THIS!

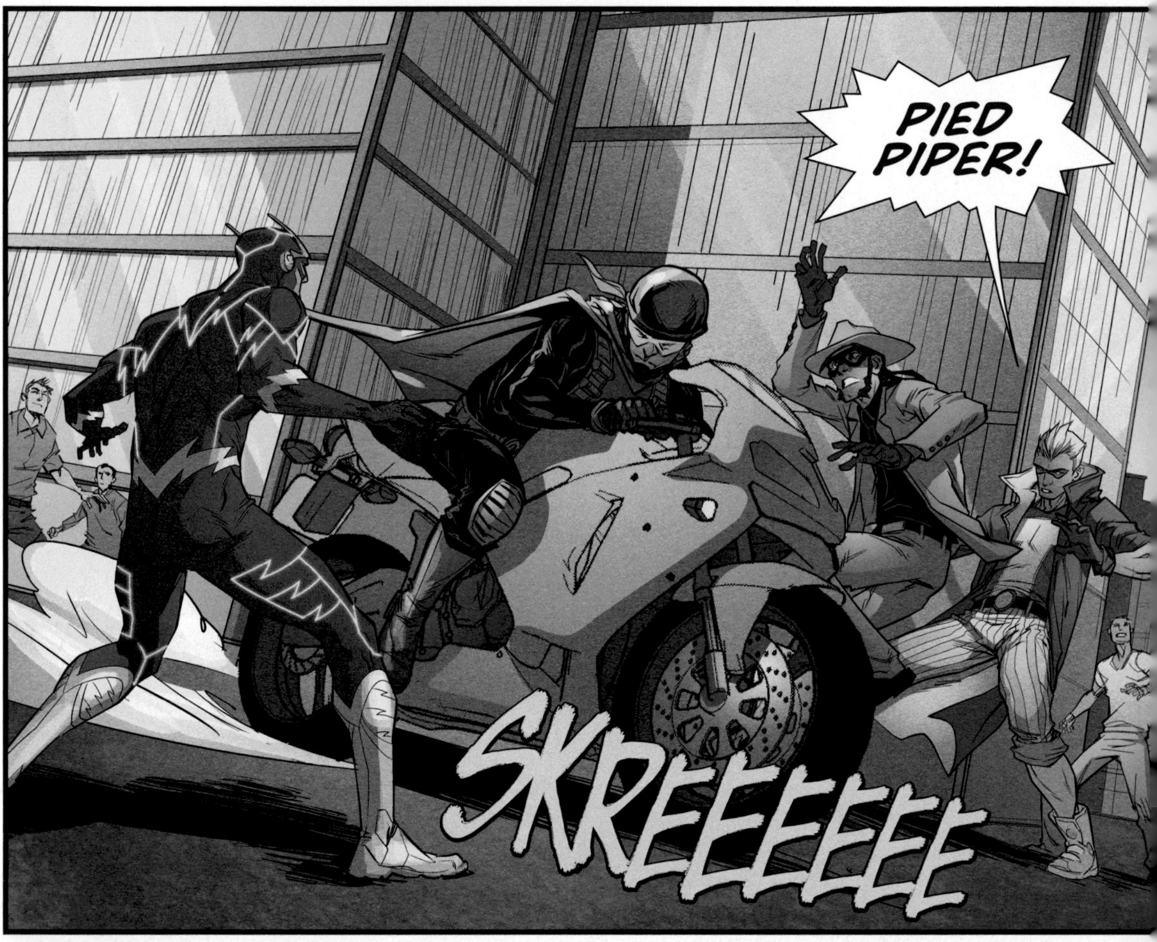
PIED PIPER!
SKREEEEEEE

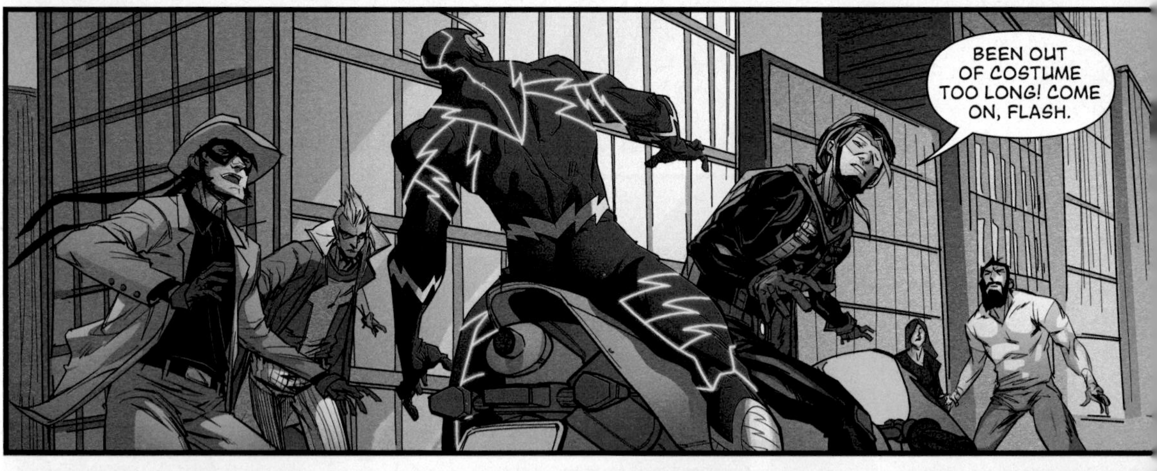
BEEN OUT OF COSTUME TOO LONG! COME ON, FLASH.

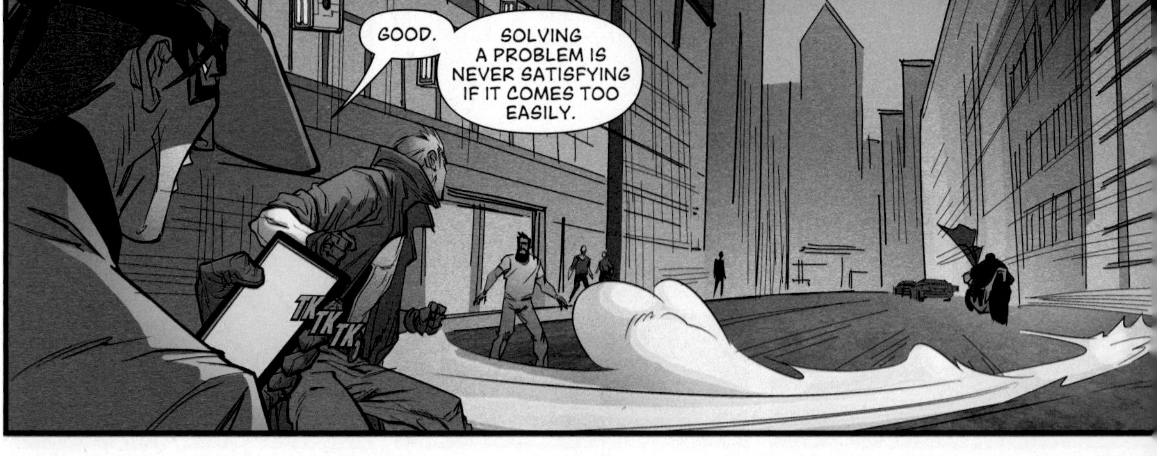
GOOD.
SOLVING A PROBLEM IS NEVER SATISFYING IF IT COMES TOO EASILY.
TK TK TK

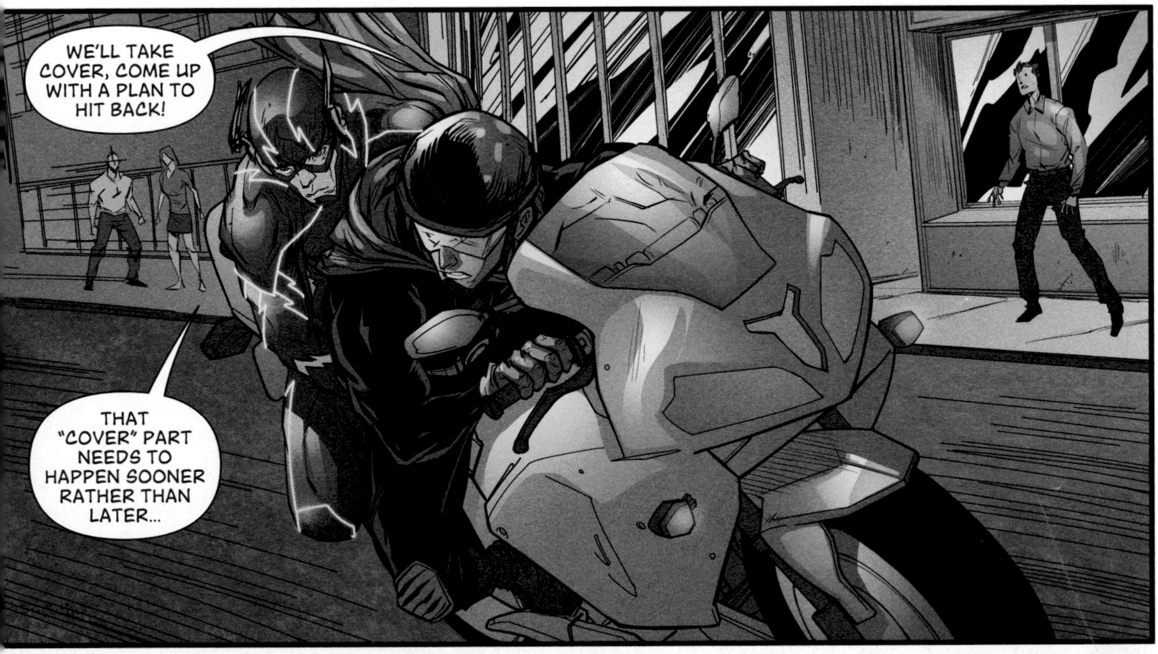
WE'LL TAKE COVER, COME UP WITH A PLAN TO HIT BACK!
THAT "COVER" PART NEEDS TO HAPPEN SOONER RATHER THAN LATER...

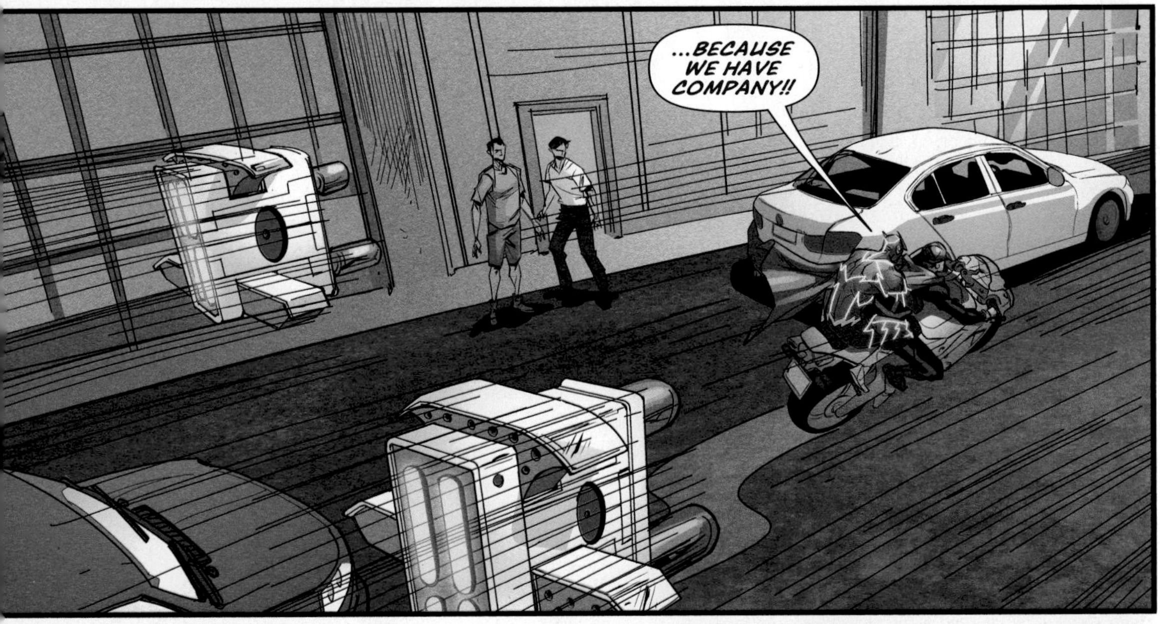
...BECAUSE WE HAVE COMPANY!!

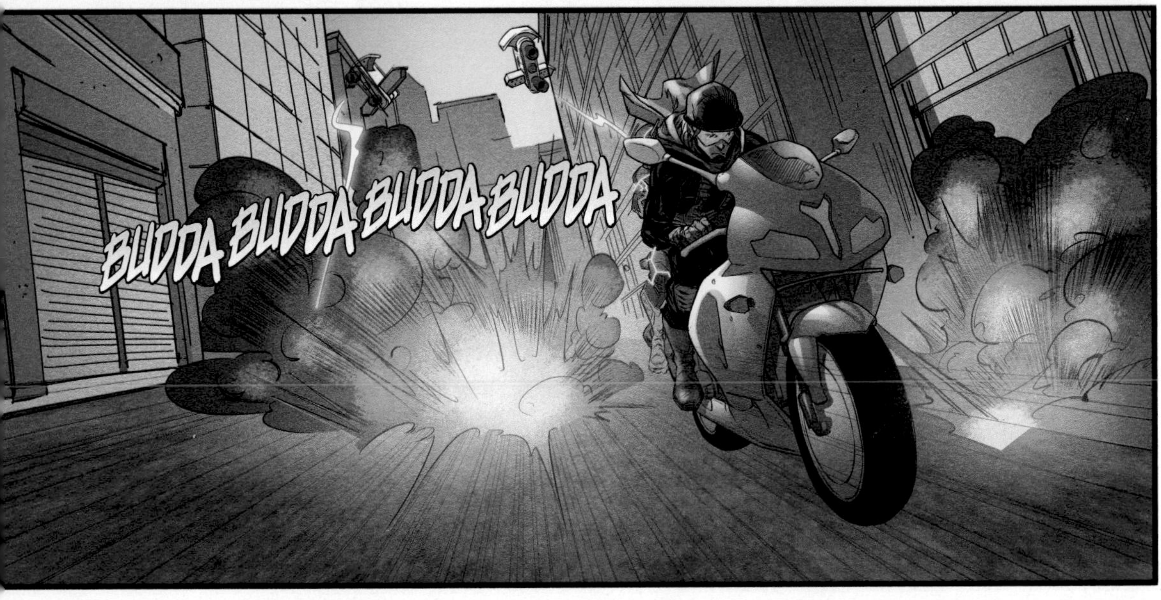
BUDDA BUDDA BUDDA BUDDA

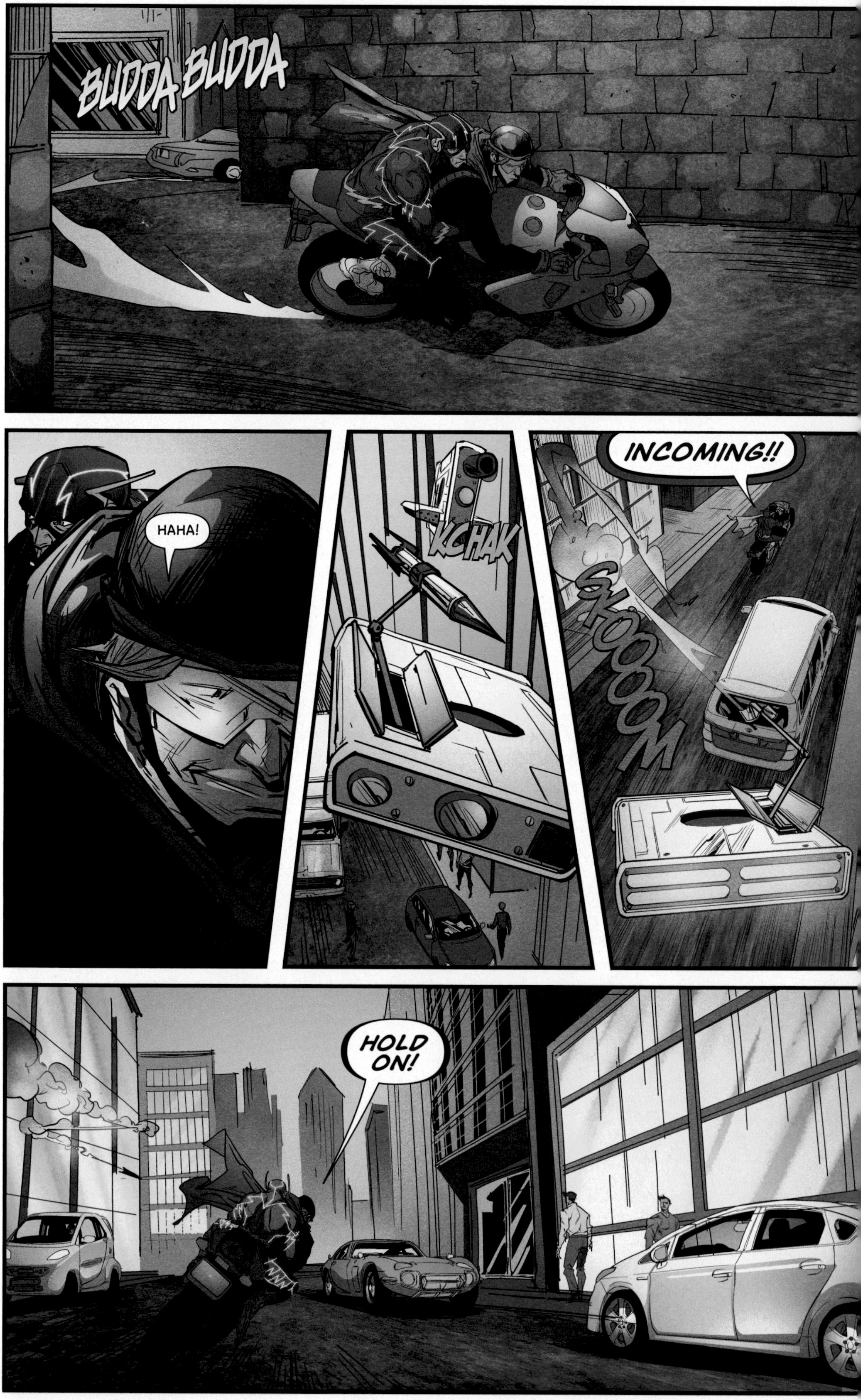
BUDDA BUDDA
HAHA!
KCHAK
INCOMING!!
SKOOOOM
HOLD ON!

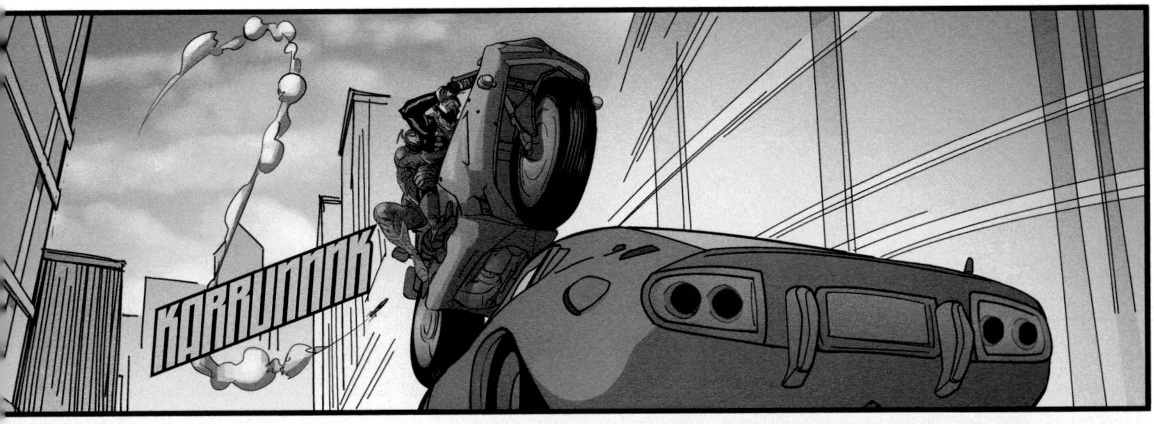
KRRUNNNK

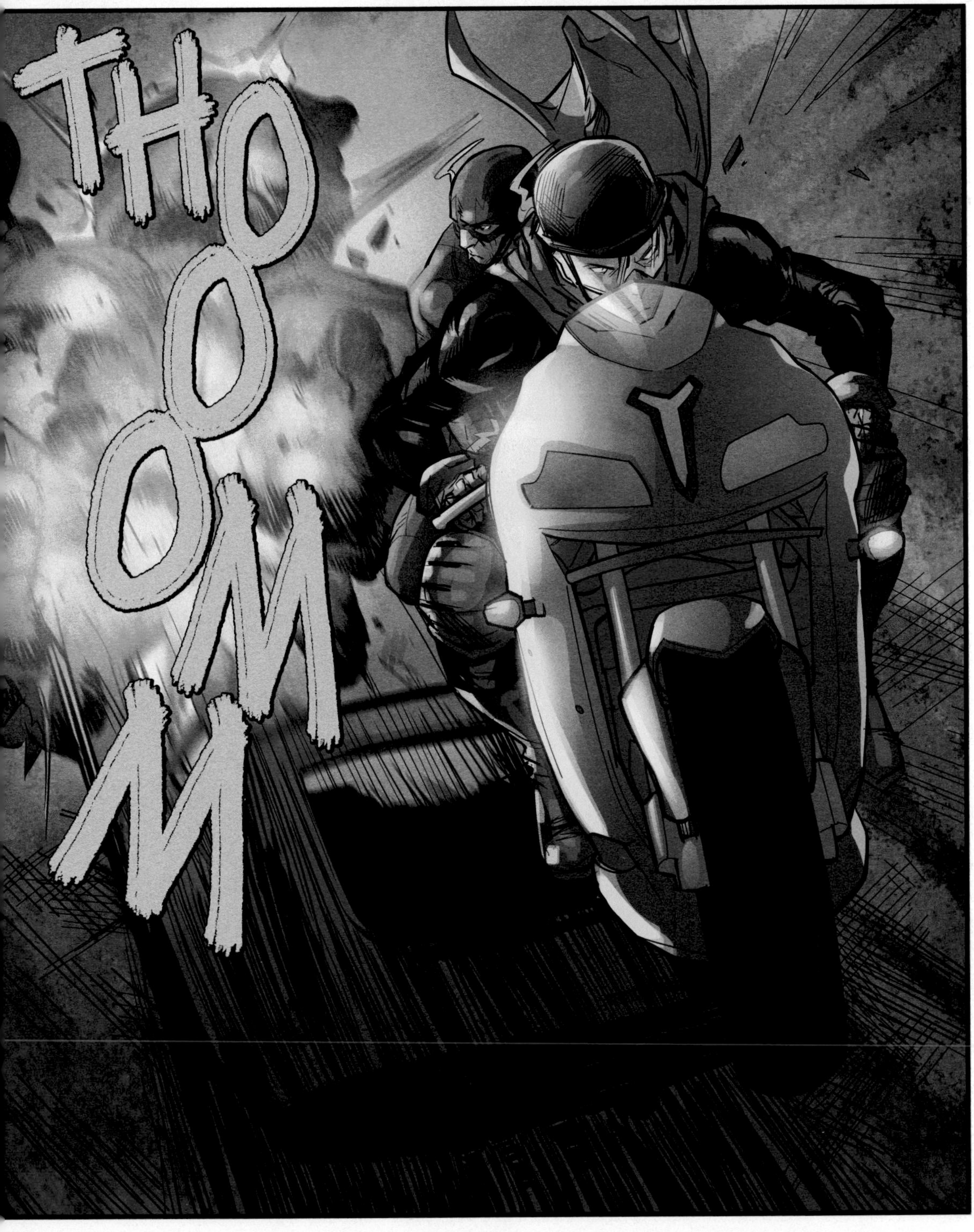
THOOOOMM

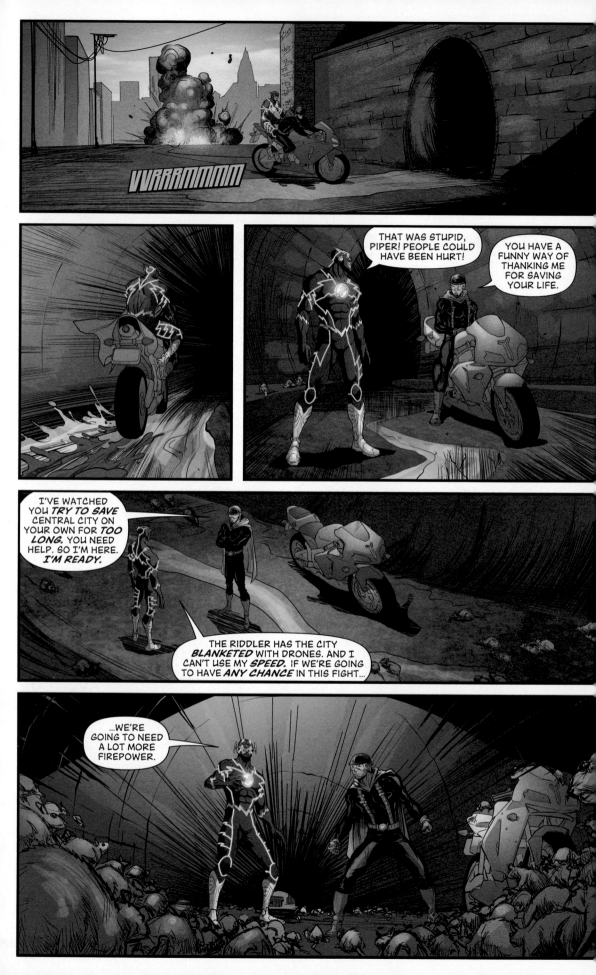

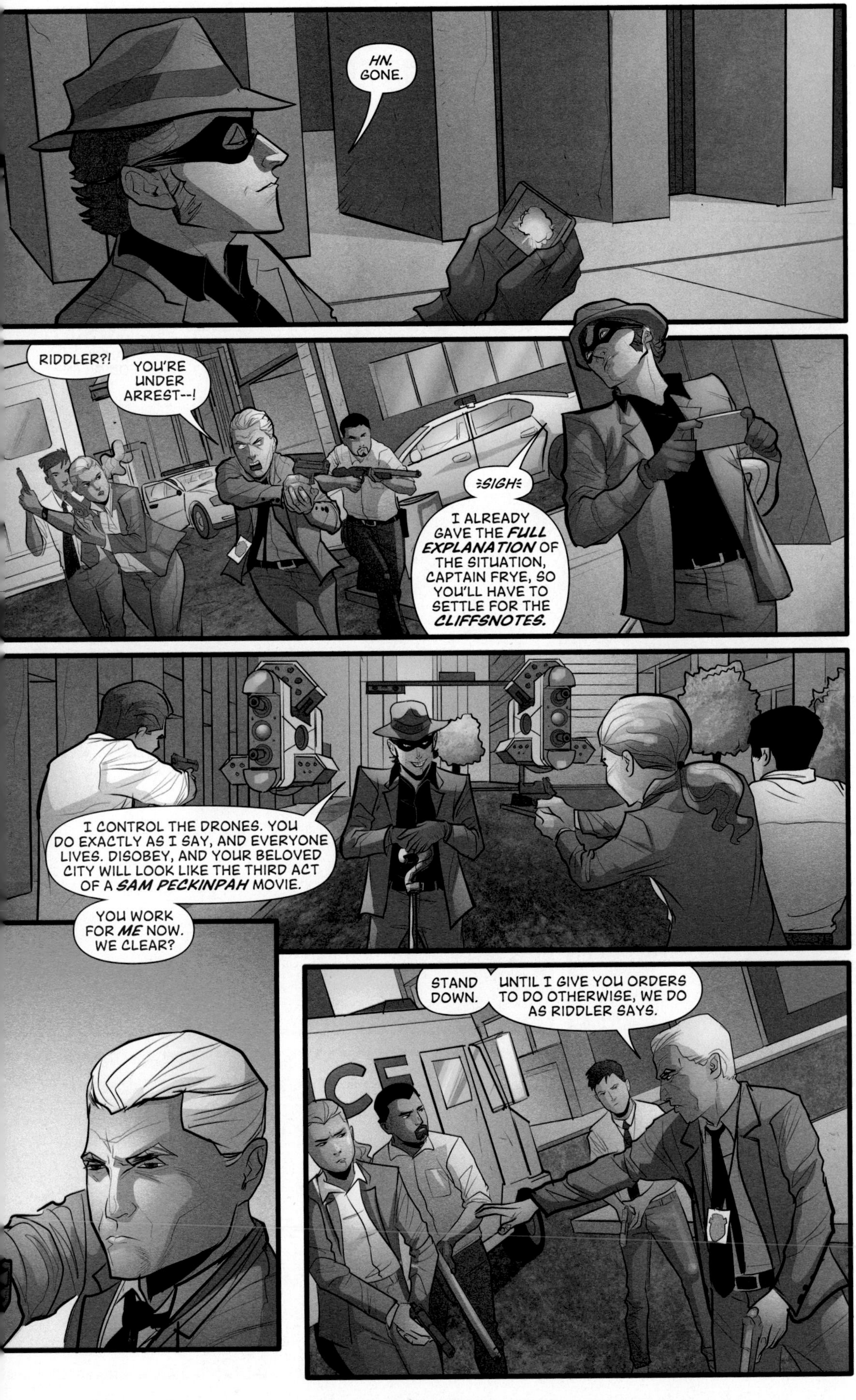
HN. GONE.
RIDDLER?!
YOU'RE UNDER ARREST--!
≈SIGH≈
I ALREADY GAVE THE FULL EXPLANATION OF THE SITUATION, CAPTAIN FRYE, SO YOU'LL HAVE TO SETTLE FOR THE CLIFFSNOTES.
I CONTROL THE DRONES. YOU DO EXACTLY AS I SAY, AND EVERYONE LIVES. DISOBEY, AND YOUR BELOVED CITY WILL LOOK LIKE THE THIRD ACT OF A SAM PECKINPAH MOVIE.
YOU WORK FOR ME NOW. WE CLEAR?
STAND DOWN.
UNTIL I GIVE YOU ORDERS TO DO OTHERWISE, WE DO AS RIDDLER SAYS.

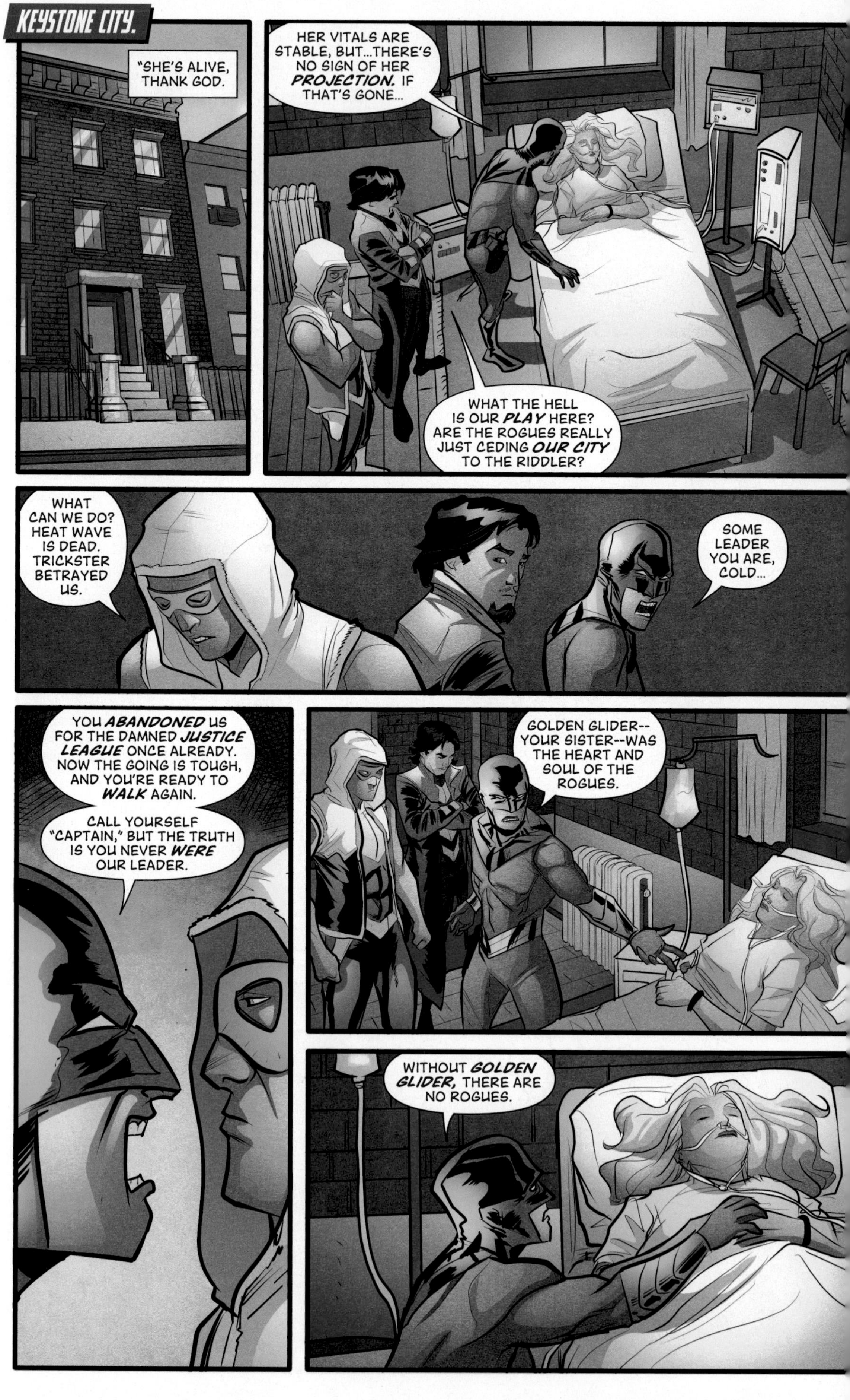
KEYSTONE CITY.
"SHE'S ALIVE, THANK GOD.
HER VITALS ARE STABLE, BUT...THERE'S NO SIGN OF HER PROJECTION. IF THAT'S GONE...
WHAT THE HELL IS OUR PLAY HERE? ARE THE ROGUES REALLY JUST CEDING OUR CITY TO THE RIDDLER?
WHAT CAN WE DO? HEAT WAVE IS DEAD. TRICKSTER BETRAYED US.
SOME LEADER YOU ARE, COLD...
YOU ABANDONED US FOR THE DAMNED JUSTICE LEAGUE ONCE ALREADY. NOW THE GOING IS TOUGH, AND YOU'RE READY TO WALK AGAIN.
CALL YOURSELF "CAPTAIN," BUT THE TRUTH IS YOU NEVER WERE OUR LEADER.
GOLDEN GLIDER--YOUR SISTER--WAS THE HEART AND SOUL OF THE ROGUES.
WITHOUT GOLDEN GLIDER, THERE ARE NO ROGUES.

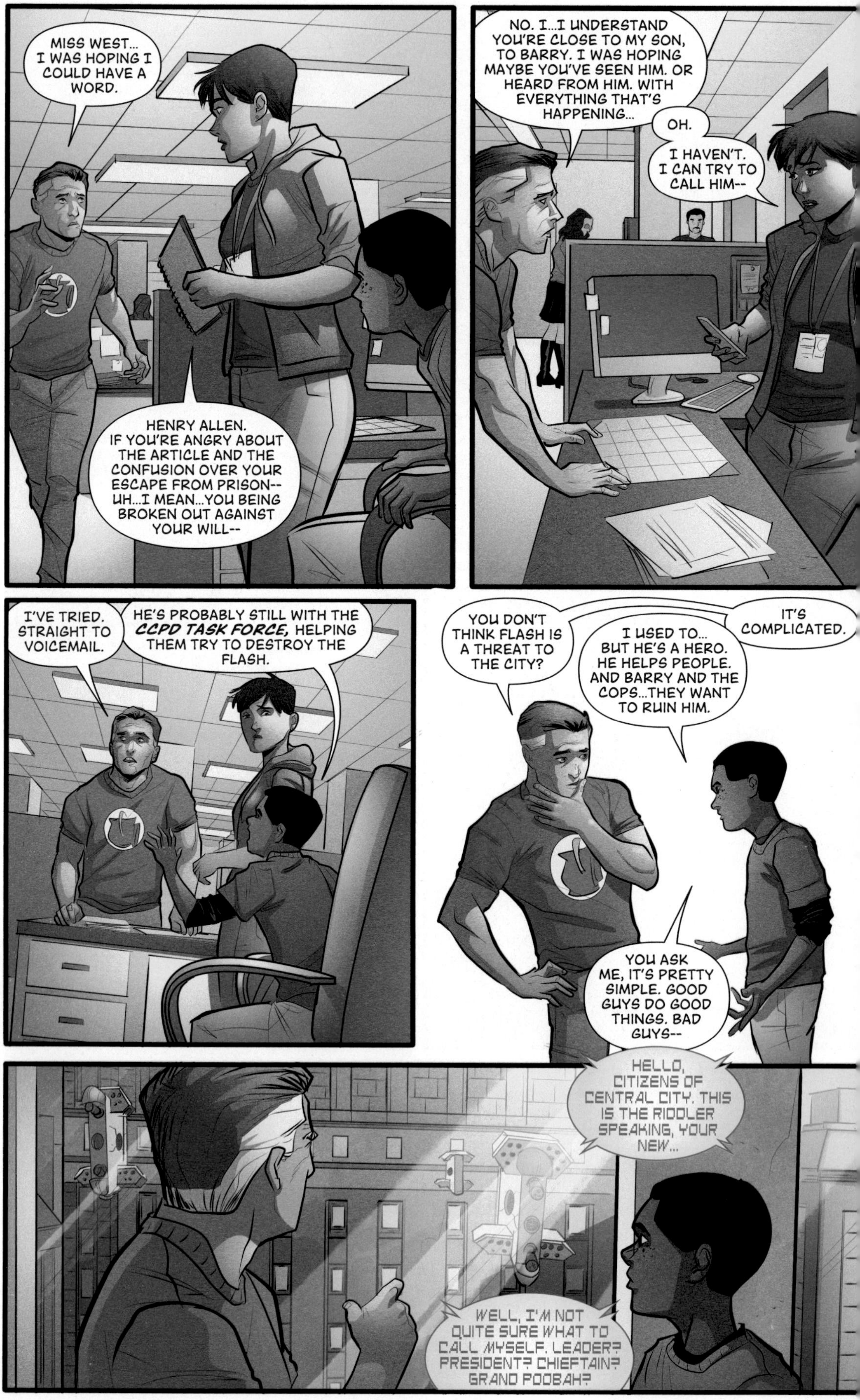
MISS WEST... I WAS HOPING I COULD HAVE A WORD.
HENRY ALLEN. IF YOU'RE ANGRY ABOUT THE ARTICLE AND THE CONFUSION OVER YOUR ESCAPE FROM PRISON-- UH...I MEAN...YOU BEING BROKEN OUT AGAINST YOUR WILL--
NO. I...I UNDERSTAND YOU'RE CLOSE TO MY SON, TO BARRY. I WAS HOPING MAYBE YOU'VE SEEN HIM. OR HEARD FROM HIM. WITH EVERYTHING THAT'S HAPPENING...
OH.
I HAVEN'T. I CAN TRY TO CALL HIM--
I'VE TRIED. STRAIGHT TO VOICEMAIL.
HE'S PROBABLY STILL WITH THE *CCPD TASK FORCE,* HELPING THEM TRY TO DESTROY THE FLASH.
YOU DON'T THINK FLASH IS A THREAT TO THE CITY?
IT'S COMPLICATED.
I USED TO... BUT HE'S A HERO. HE HELPS PEOPLE. AND BARRY AND THE COPS...THEY WANT TO RUIN HIM.
YOU ASK ME, IT'S PRETTY SIMPLE. GOOD GUYS DO GOOD THINGS. BAD GUYS--
HELLO, CITIZENS OF CENTRAL CITY. THIS IS THE RIDDLER SPEAKING, YOUR NEW...
WELL, I'M NOT QUITE SURE WHAT TO CALL MYSELF. LEADER? PRESIDENT? CHIEFTAIN? GRAND POOBAH?

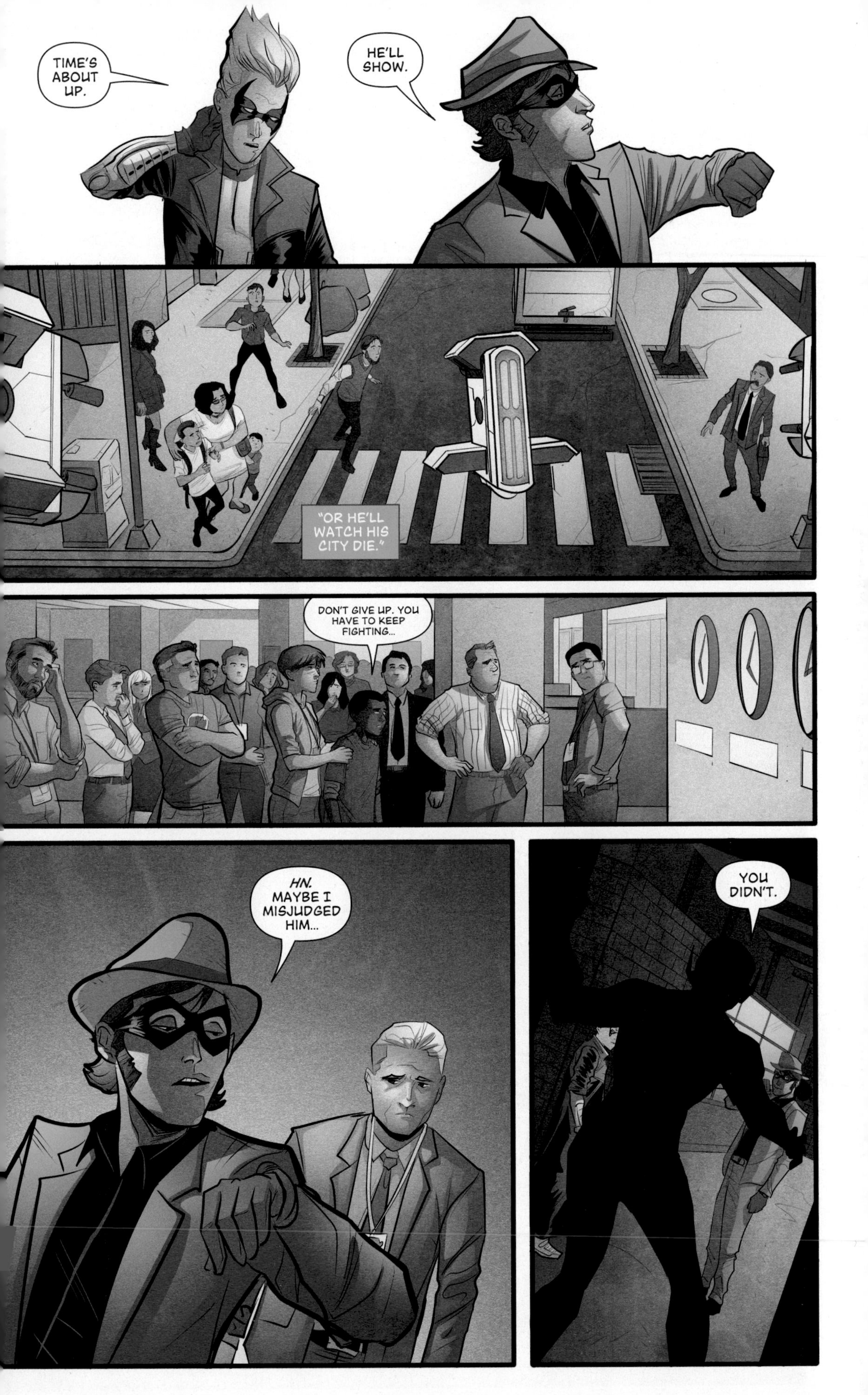

TIME'S ABOUT UP.
HE'LL SHOW.
"OR HE'LL WATCH HIS CITY DIE."
DON'T GIVE UP. YOU HAVE TO KEEP FIGHTING...
HN. MAYBE I MISJUDGED HIM...
YOU DIDN'T.

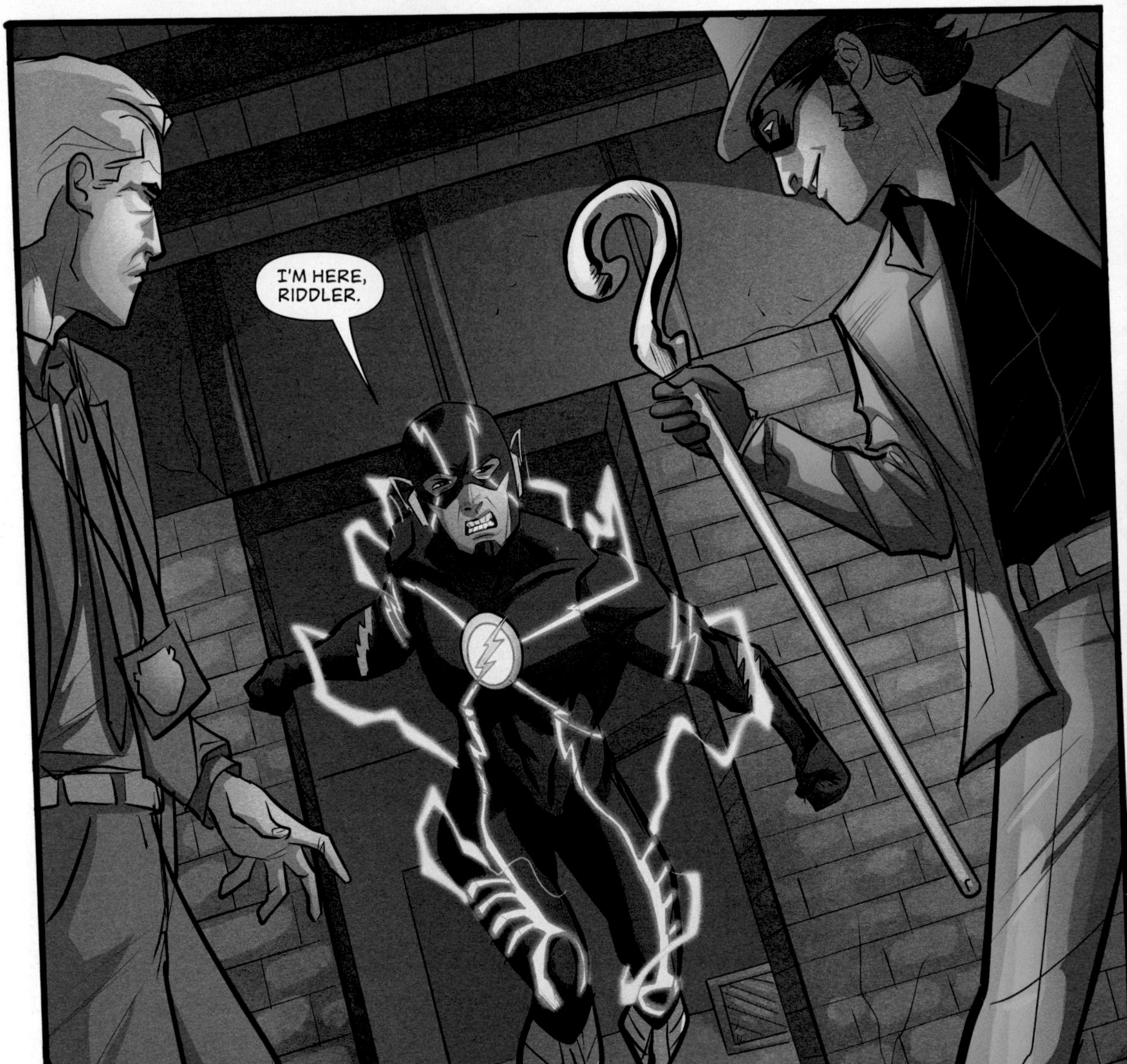
I'M HERE, RIDDLER.

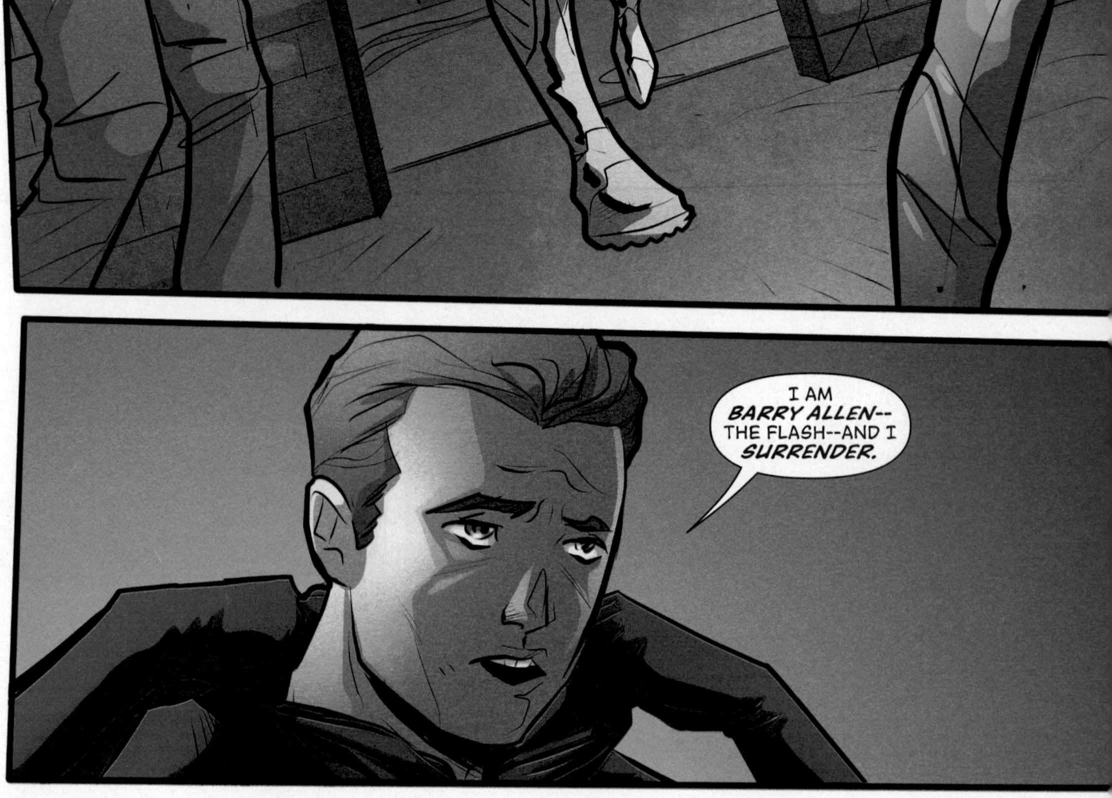
I AM *BARRY ALLEN*-- THE FLASH--AND I *SURRENDER.*

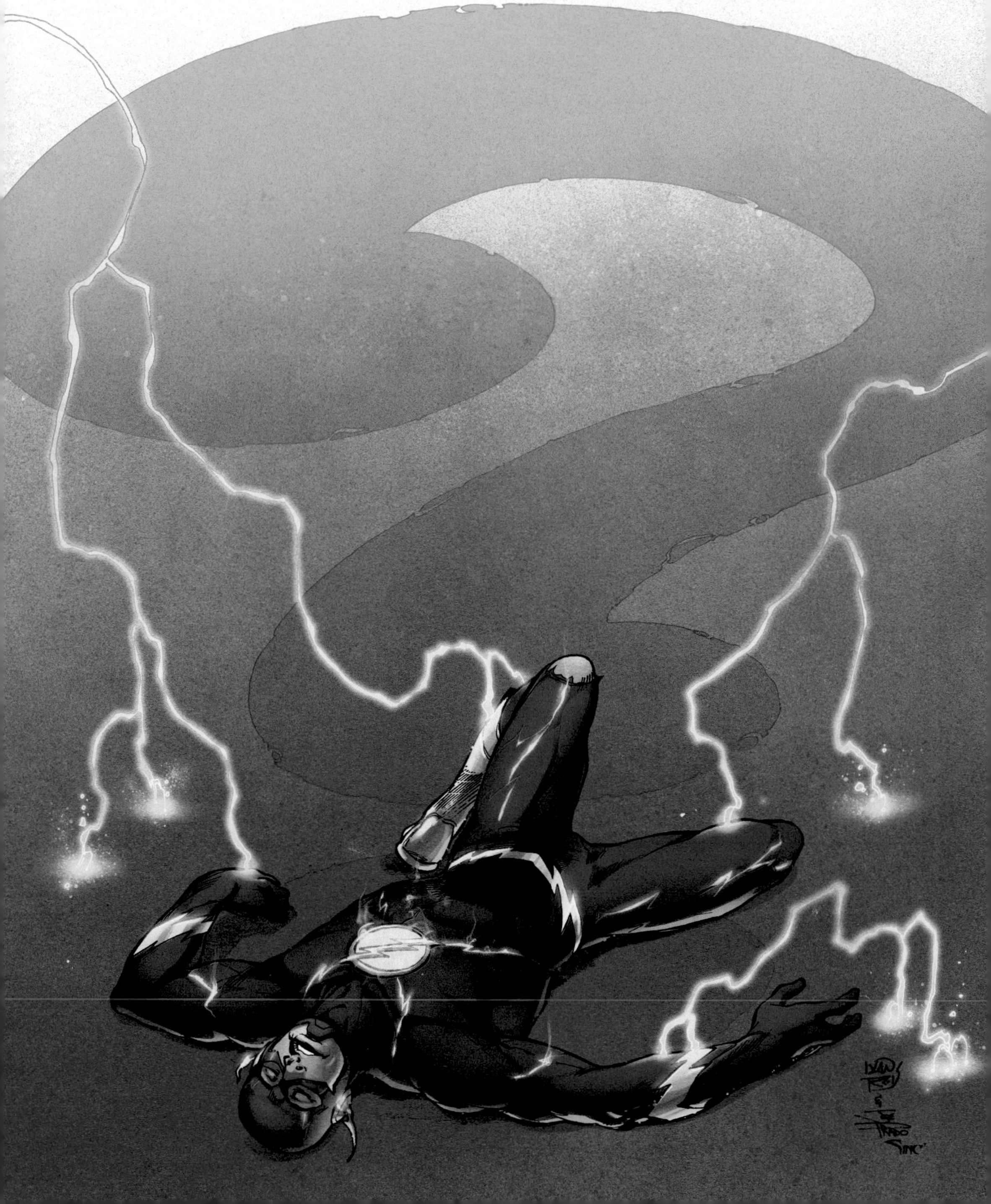

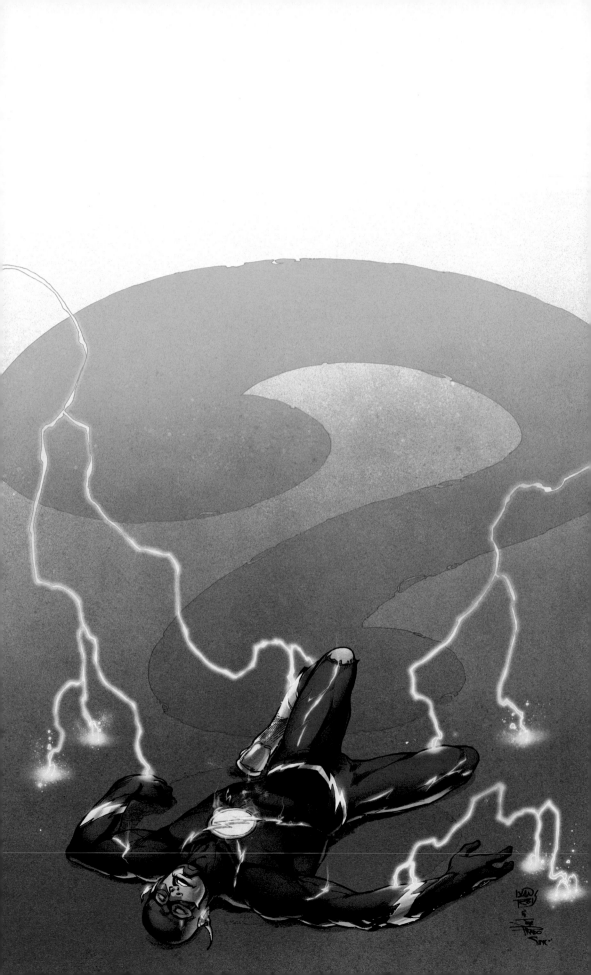

FULL STOP

VAN JENSEN writer **JESÚS MERINO** artist **GUY MAJOR** colorist **PAT BROSSEAU** letterer **IVAN REIS JOE PRADO ALEX SINCLAIR** cover

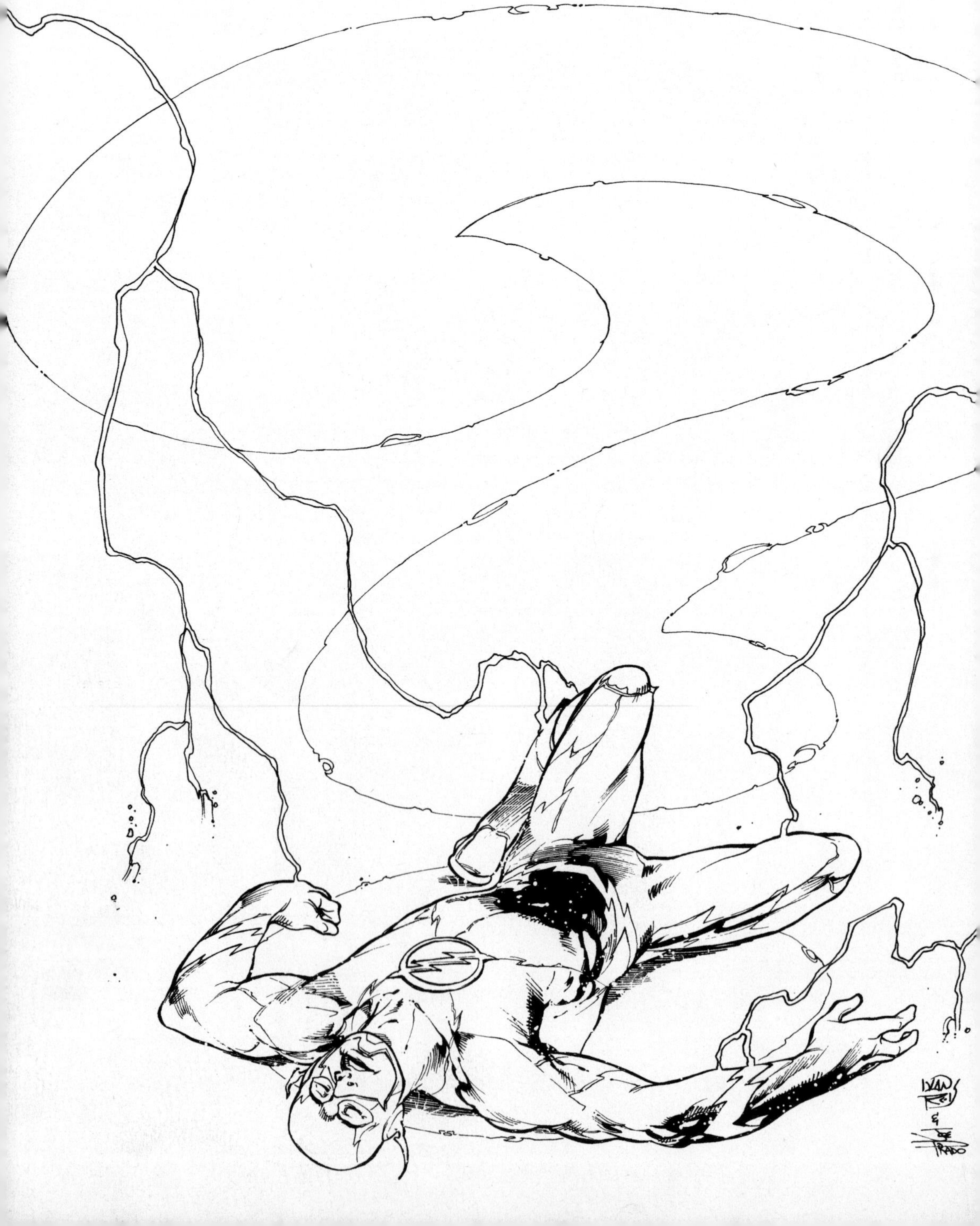

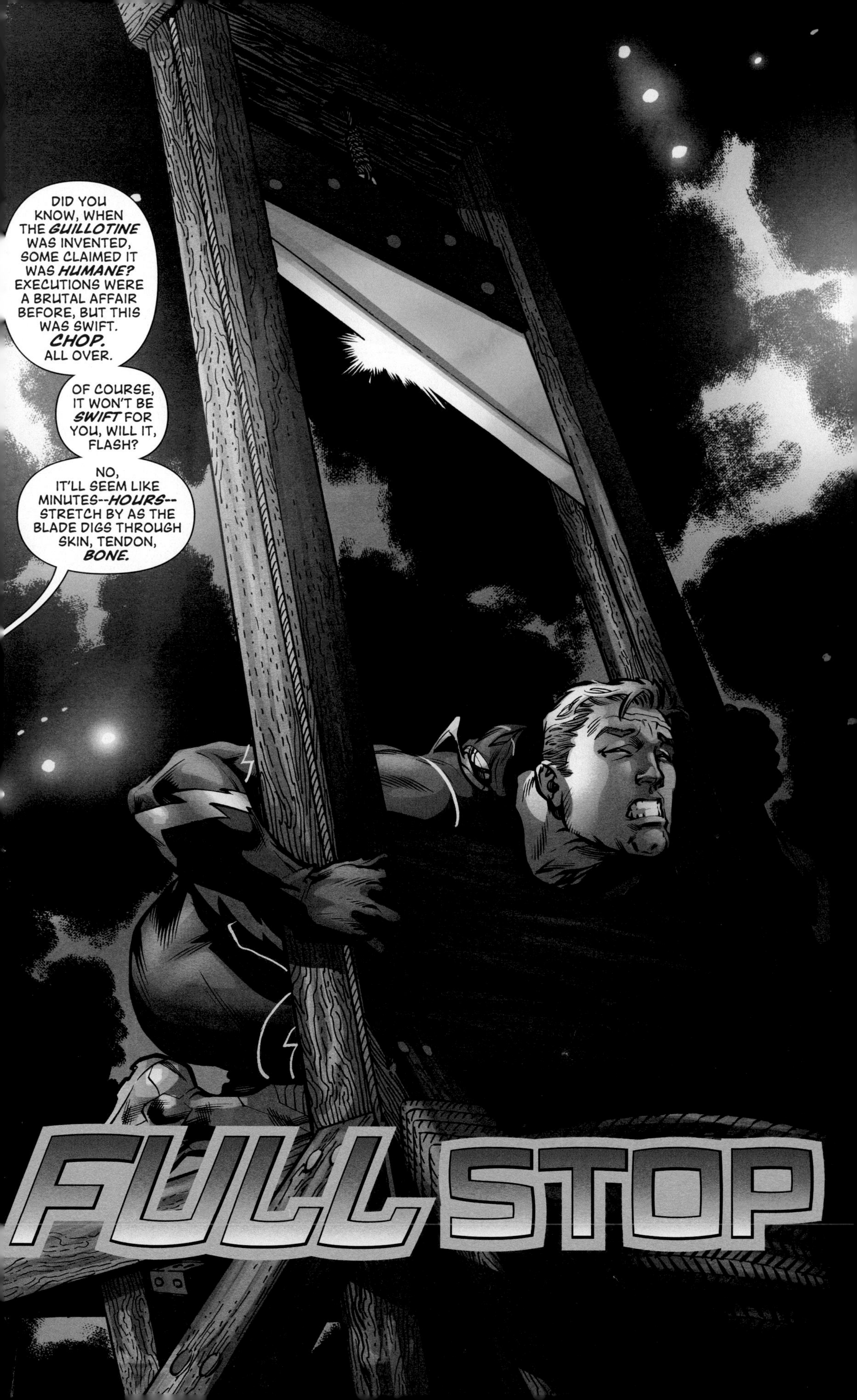
DID YOU KNOW, WHEN THE GUILLOTINE WAS INVENTED, SOME CLAIMED IT WAS HUMANE? EXECUTIONS WERE A BRUTAL AFFAIR BEFORE, BUT THIS WAS SWIFT. CHOP. ALL OVER.
OF COURSE, IT WON'T BE SWIFT FOR YOU, WILL IT, FLASH?
NO, IT'LL SEEM LIKE MINUTES--HOURS-- STRETCH BY AS THE BLADE DIGS THROUGH SKIN, TENDON, BONE.
FULL STOP

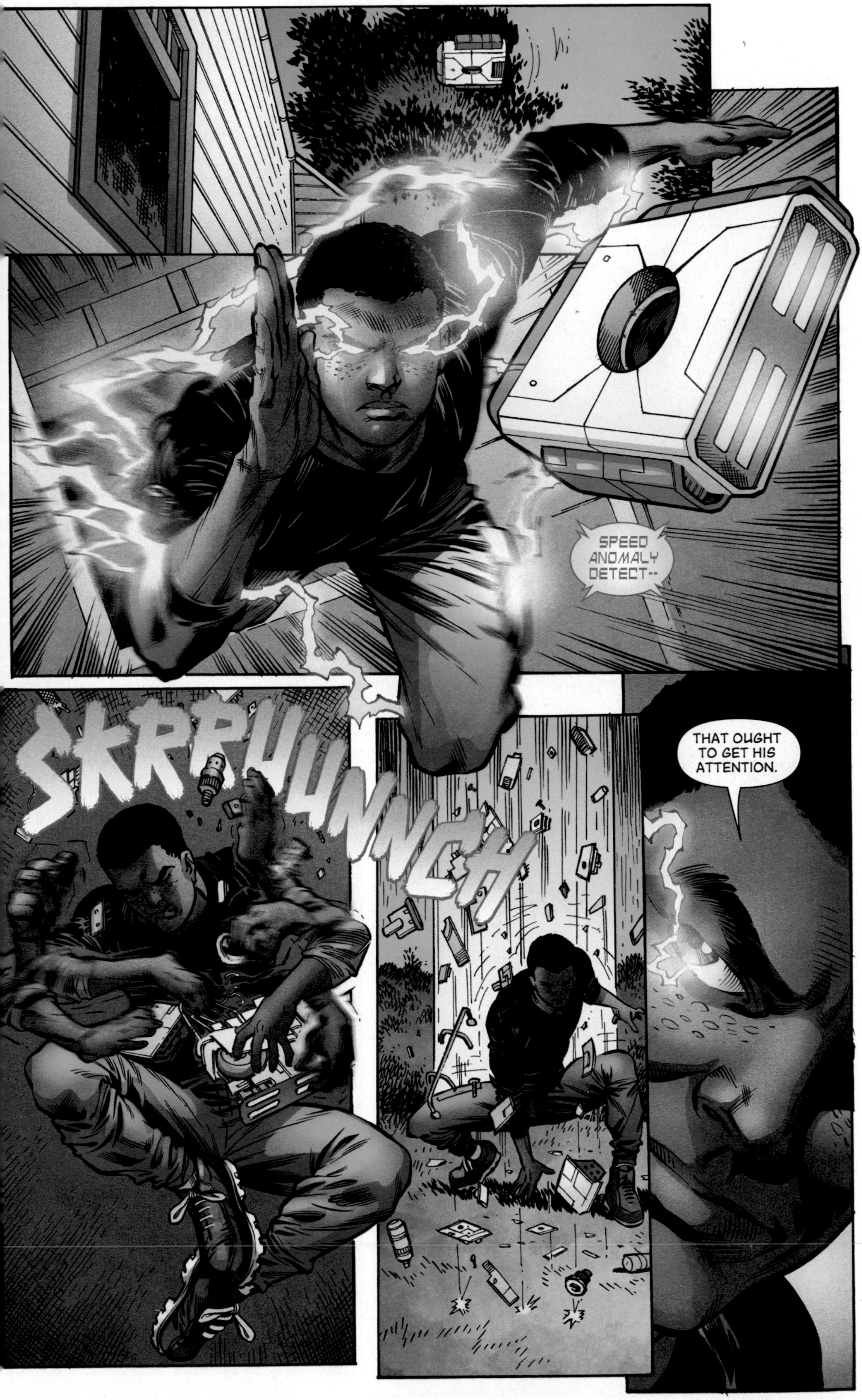
SPEED
ANOMALY
DETECT--
SKRRUUNNCH
THAT OUGHT
TO GET HIS
ATTENTION.

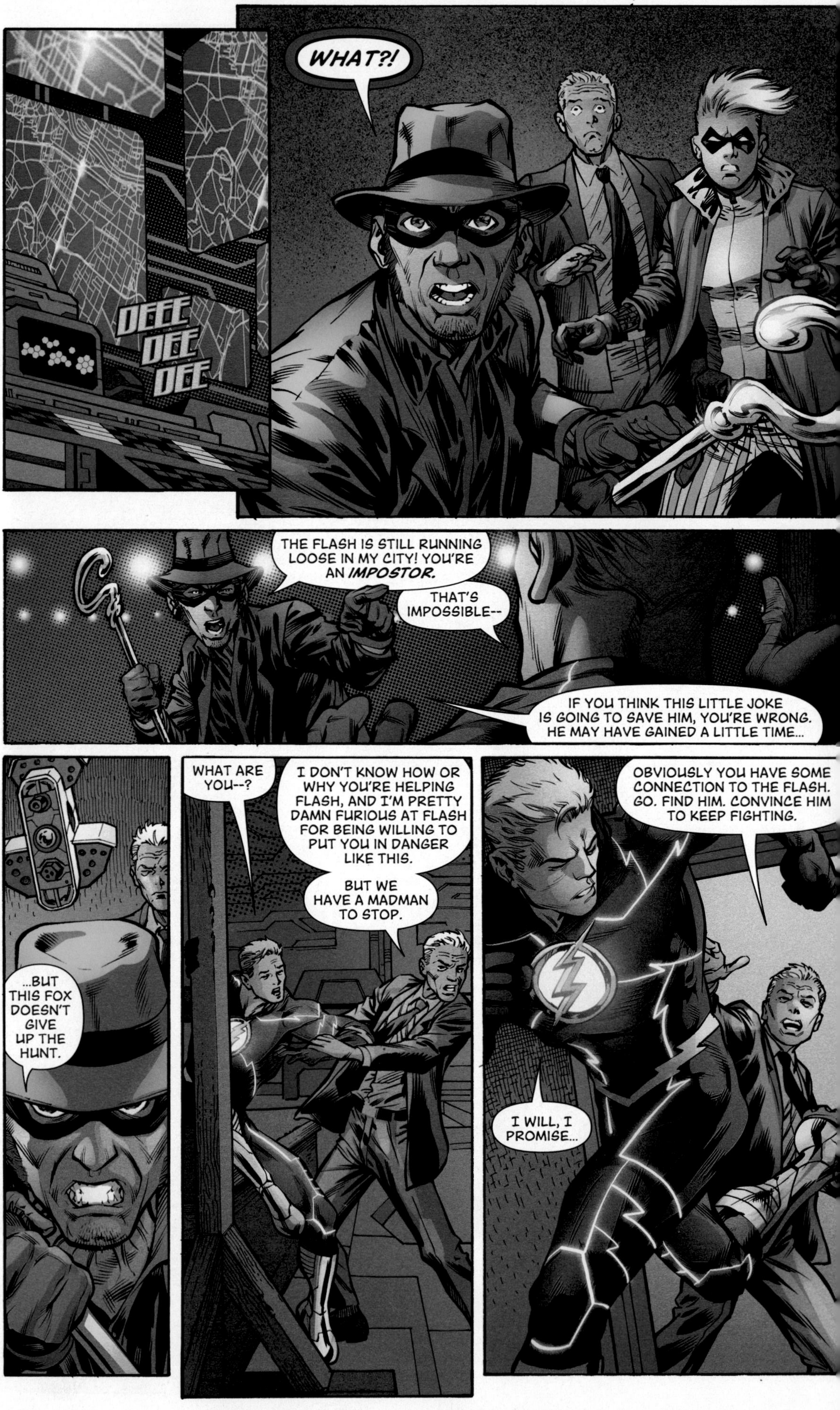

DEEE
DEE
DEE
WHAT?!
THE FLASH IS STILL RUNNING LOOSE IN MY CITY! YOU'RE AN *IMPOSTOR.*
THAT'S IMPOSSIBLE--
IF YOU THINK THIS LITTLE JOKE IS GOING TO SAVE HIM, YOU'RE WRONG. HE MAY HAVE GAINED A LITTLE TIME...
...BUT THIS FOX DOESN'T GIVE UP THE HUNT.
WHAT ARE YOU--?
I DON'T KNOW HOW OR WHY YOU'RE HELPING FLASH, AND I'M PRETTY DAMN FURIOUS AT FLASH FOR BEING WILLING TO PUT YOU IN DANGER LIKE THIS.
BUT WE HAVE A MADMAN TO STOP.
OBVIOUSLY YOU HAVE SOME CONNECTION TO THE FLASH. GO. FIND HIM. CONVINCE HIM TO KEEP FIGHTING.
I WILL, I PROMISE...

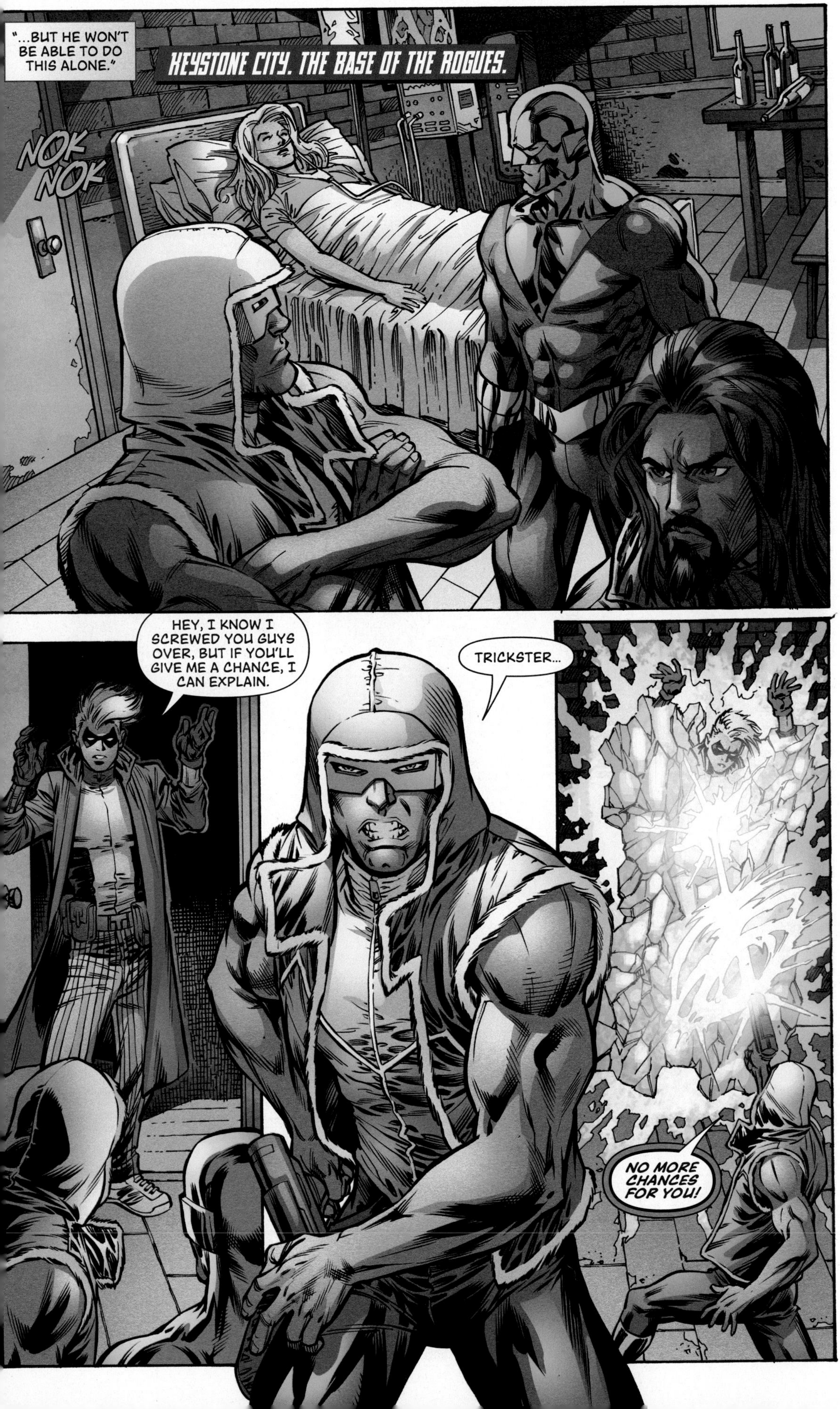
"...BUT HE WON'T BE ABLE TO DO THIS ALONE."
KEYSTONE CITY. THE BASE OF THE ROGUES.
NOK NOK
HEY, I KNOW I SCREWED YOU GUYS OVER, BUT IF YOU'LL GIVE ME A CHANCE, I CAN EXPLAIN.
TRICKSTER...
NO MORE CHANCES FOR YOU!

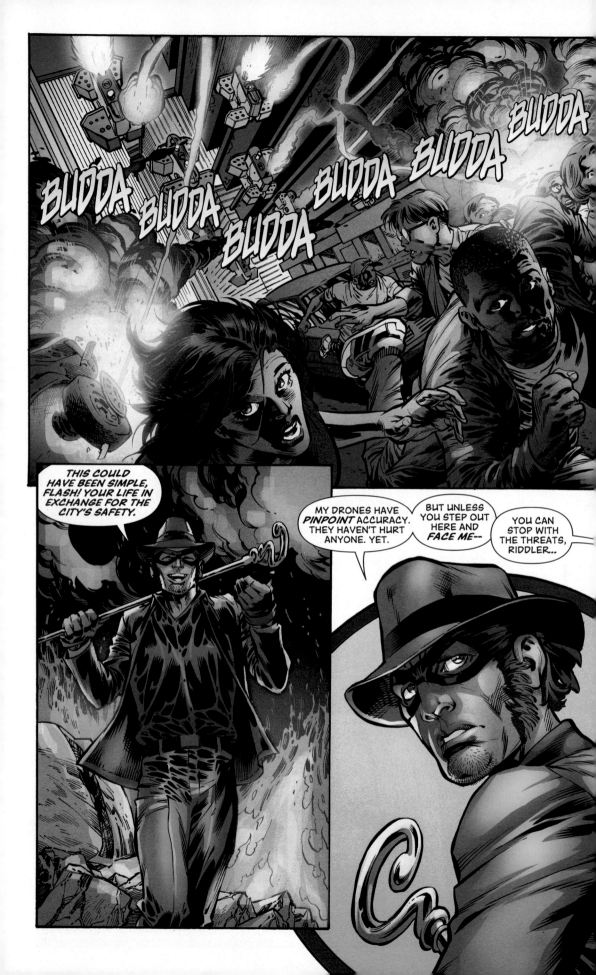

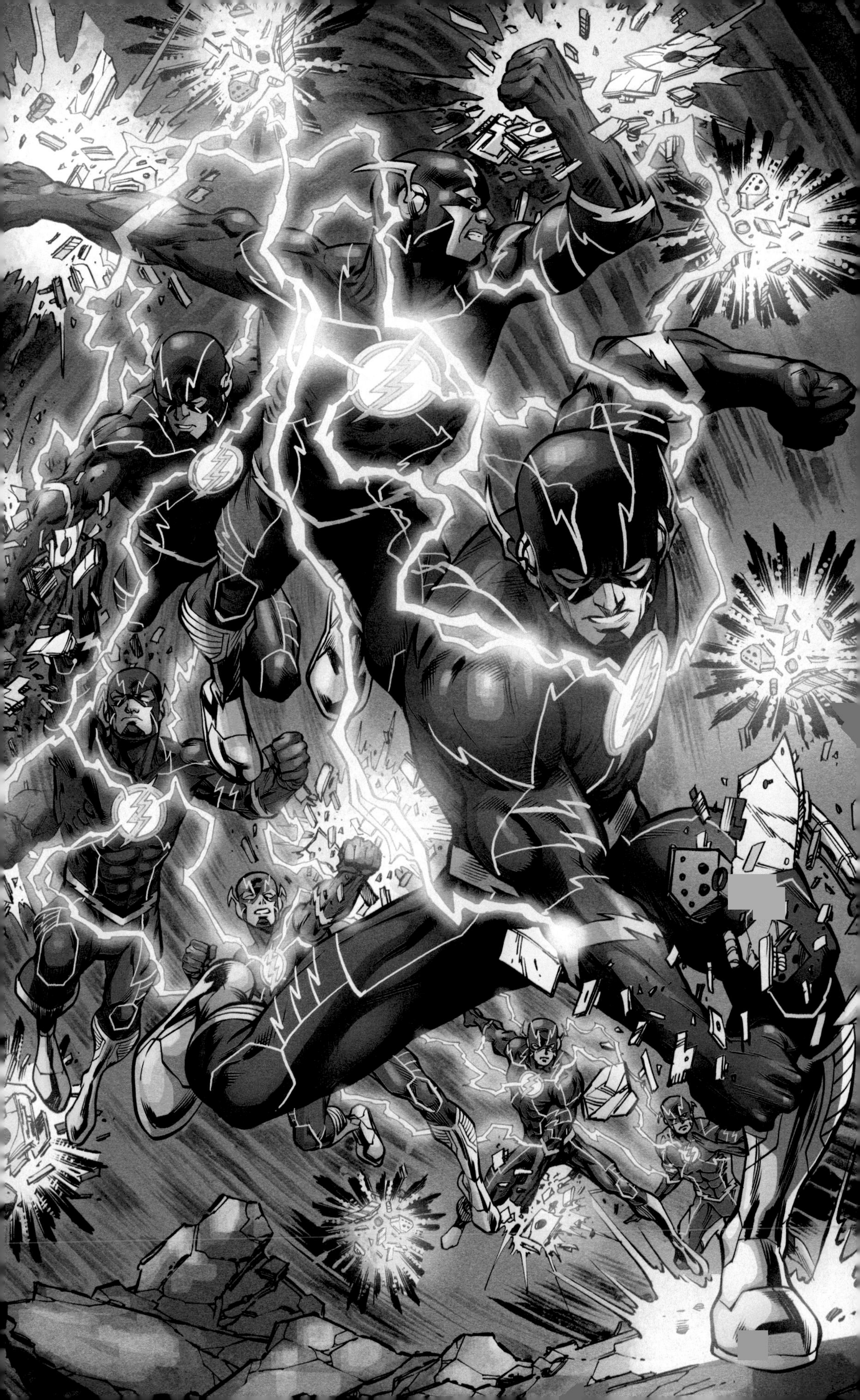

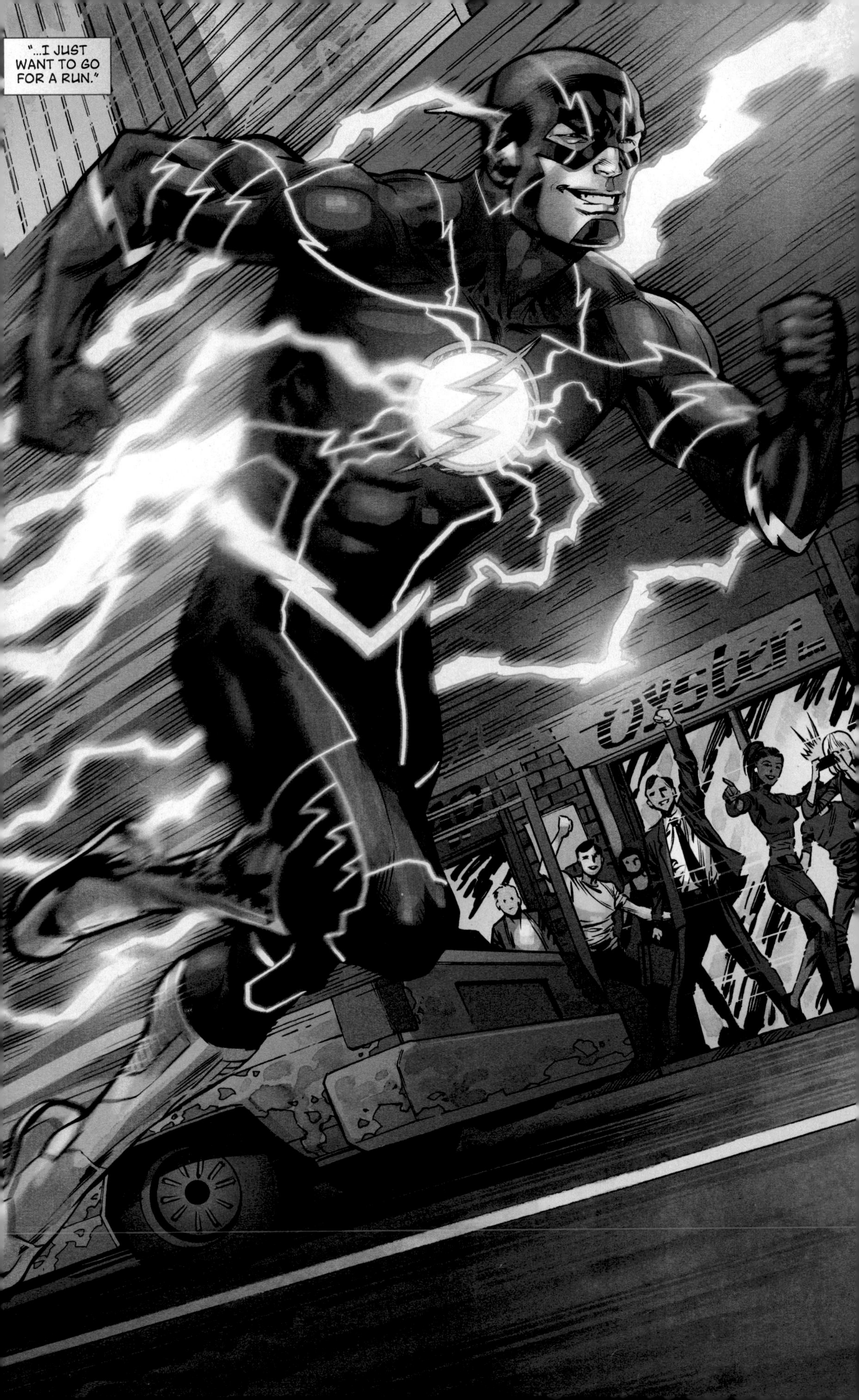
"...I JUST WANT TO GO FOR A RUN."
Oyster

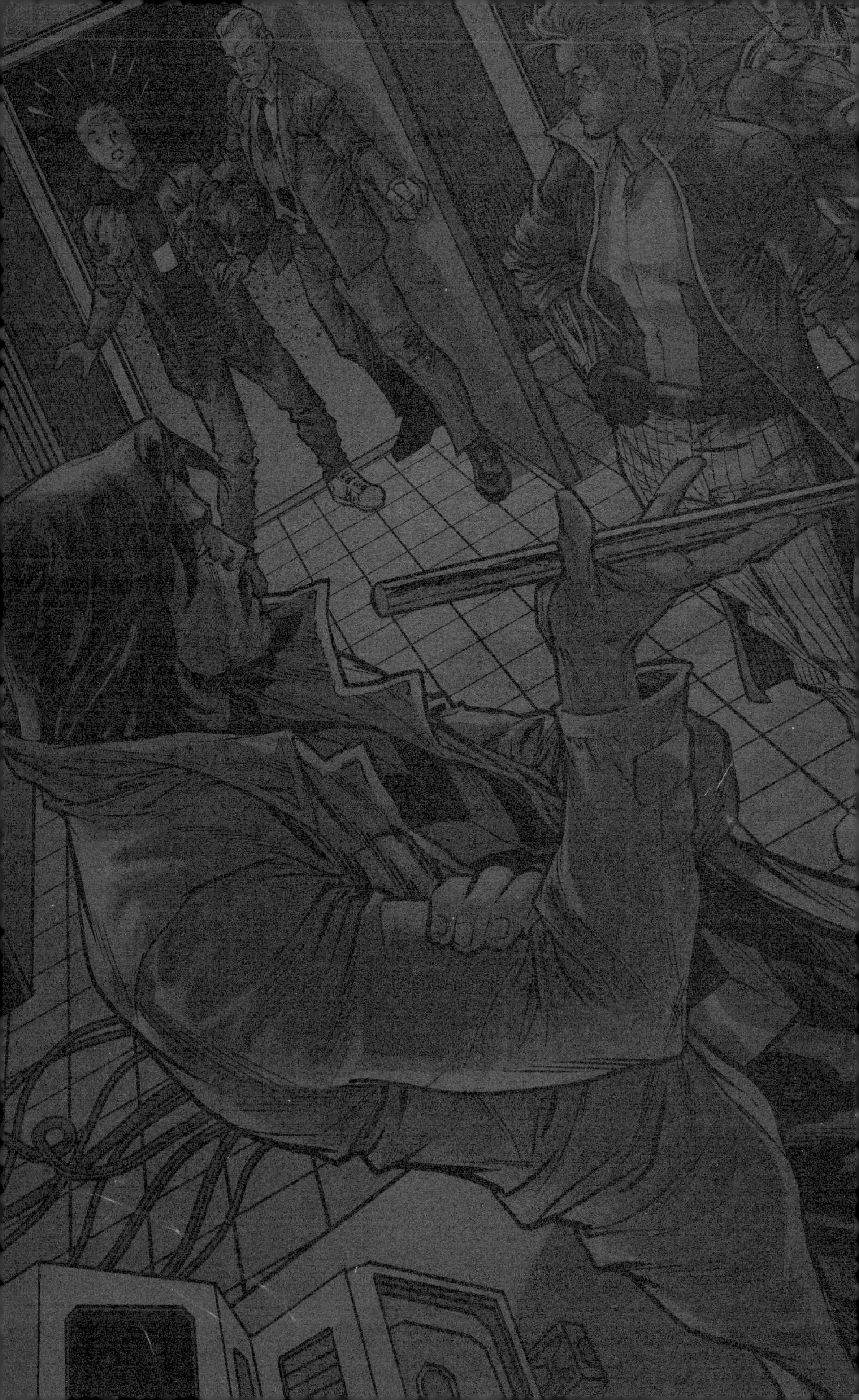

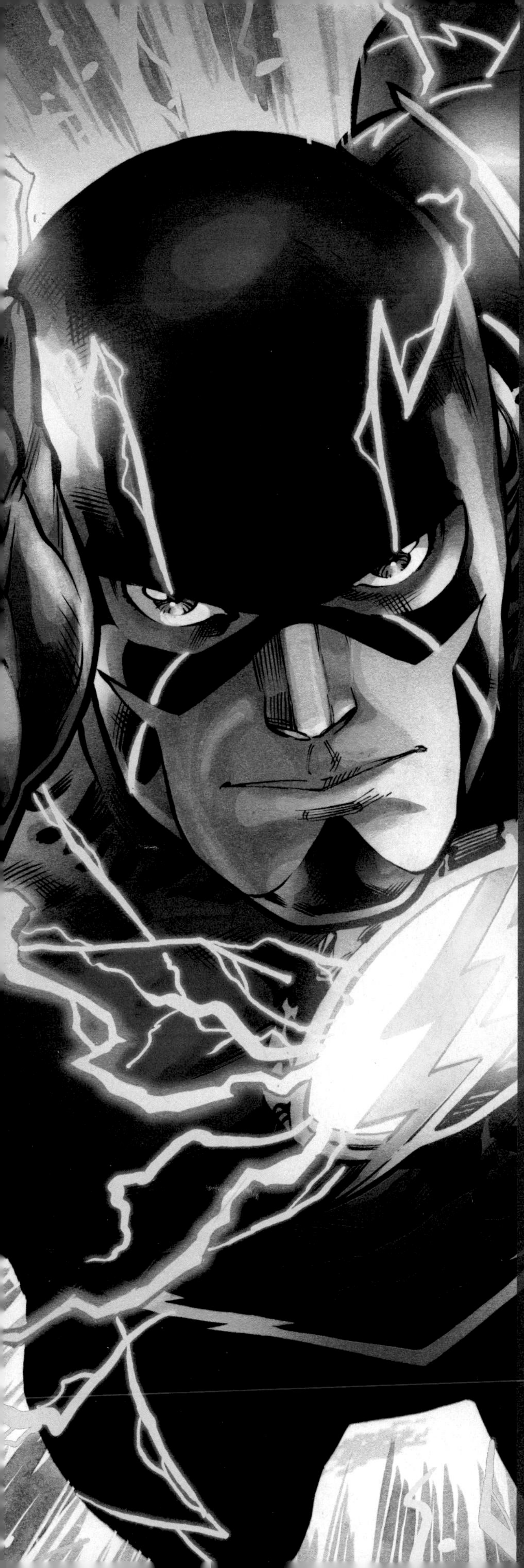

VARIANT COVER GALLERY

THE FLASH #48
COLORING BOOK VARIANT
BY DEREC DONOVAN

THE FLASH #49
NEAL ADAMS VARIANT
BY NEAL ADAMS
& FRANK MILLER

THE FLASH #50
BATMAN V SUPERMAN VARIANT
BY DUNCAN FEGREDO

THE FLASH #51
JOHN ROMITA JR. VARIANT
BY JOHN ROMITA JR.
DANNY MIKI
ALEX SINCLAIR

THE FLASH #52
THE NEW 52 VARIANT
BY JESÚS MERINO GUY MAJOR

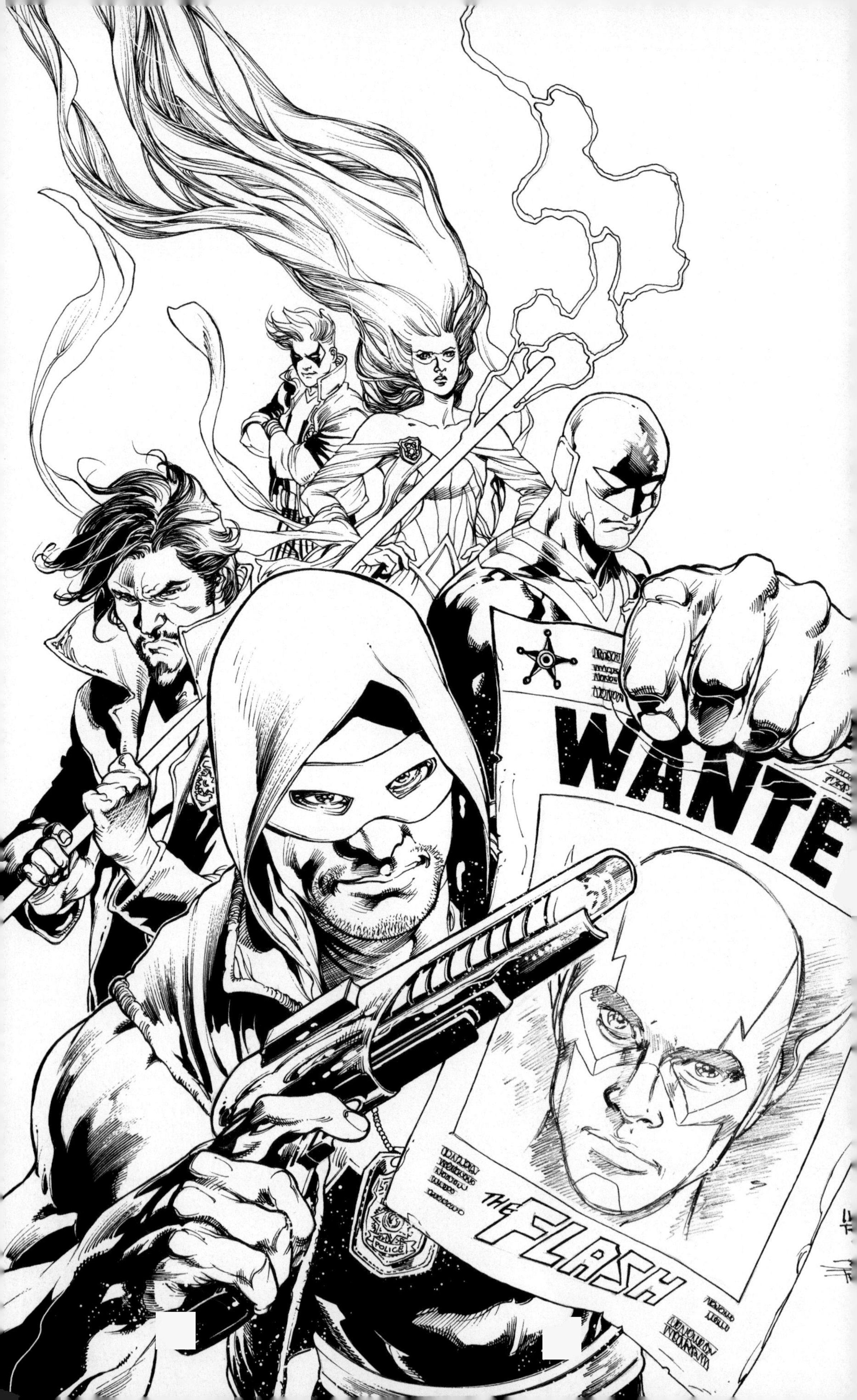
WANTE
THE FLASH
POLICE

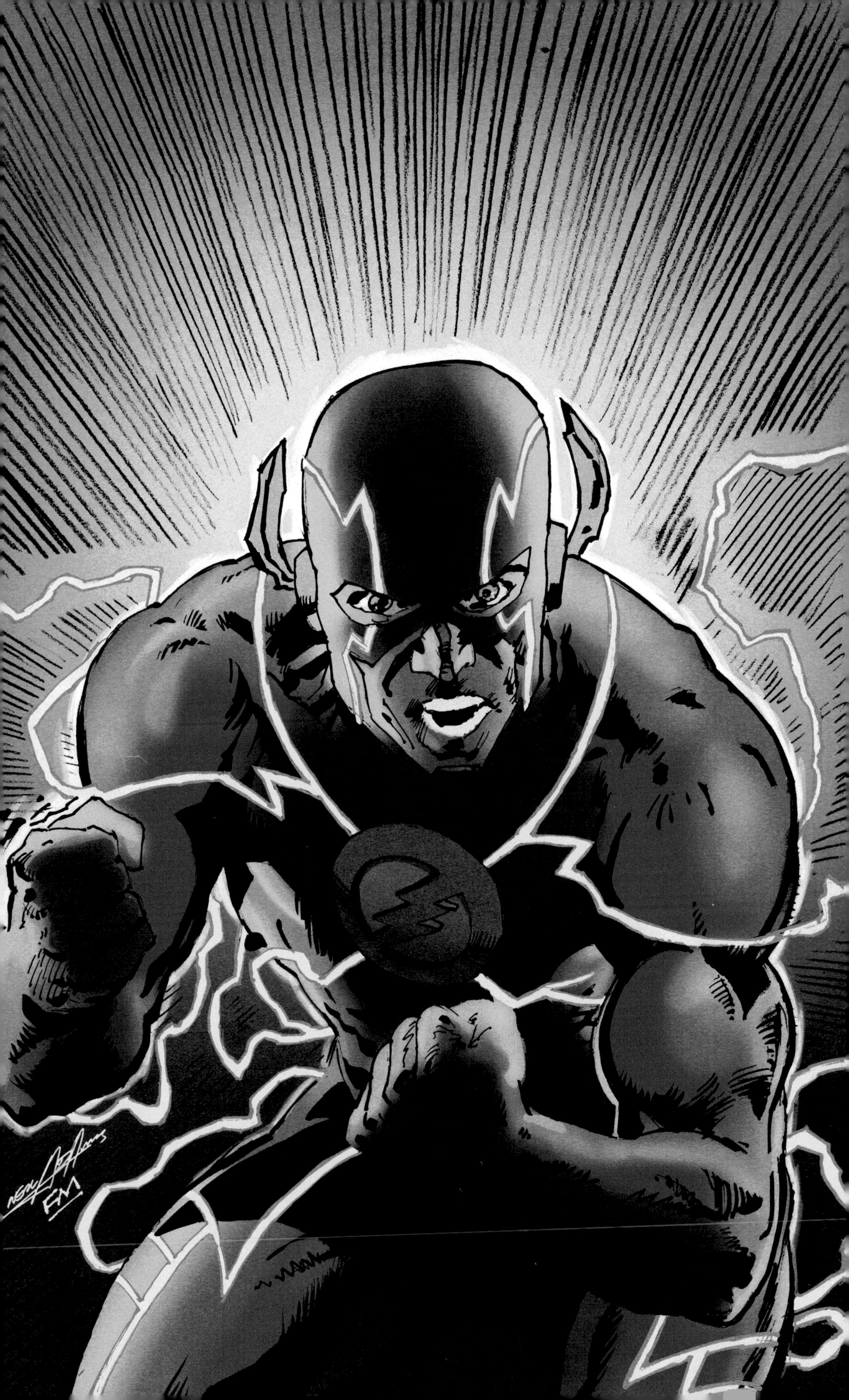

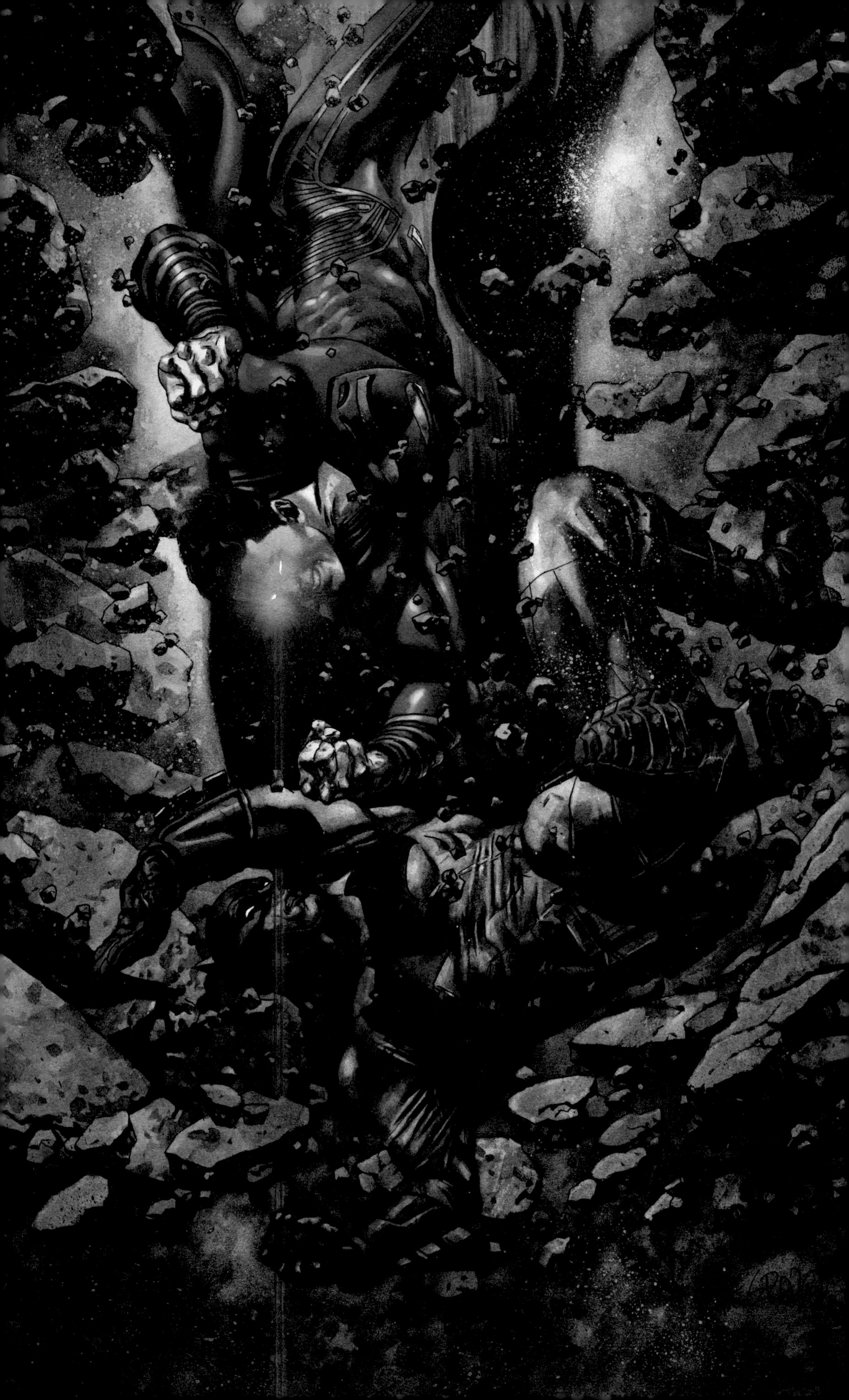

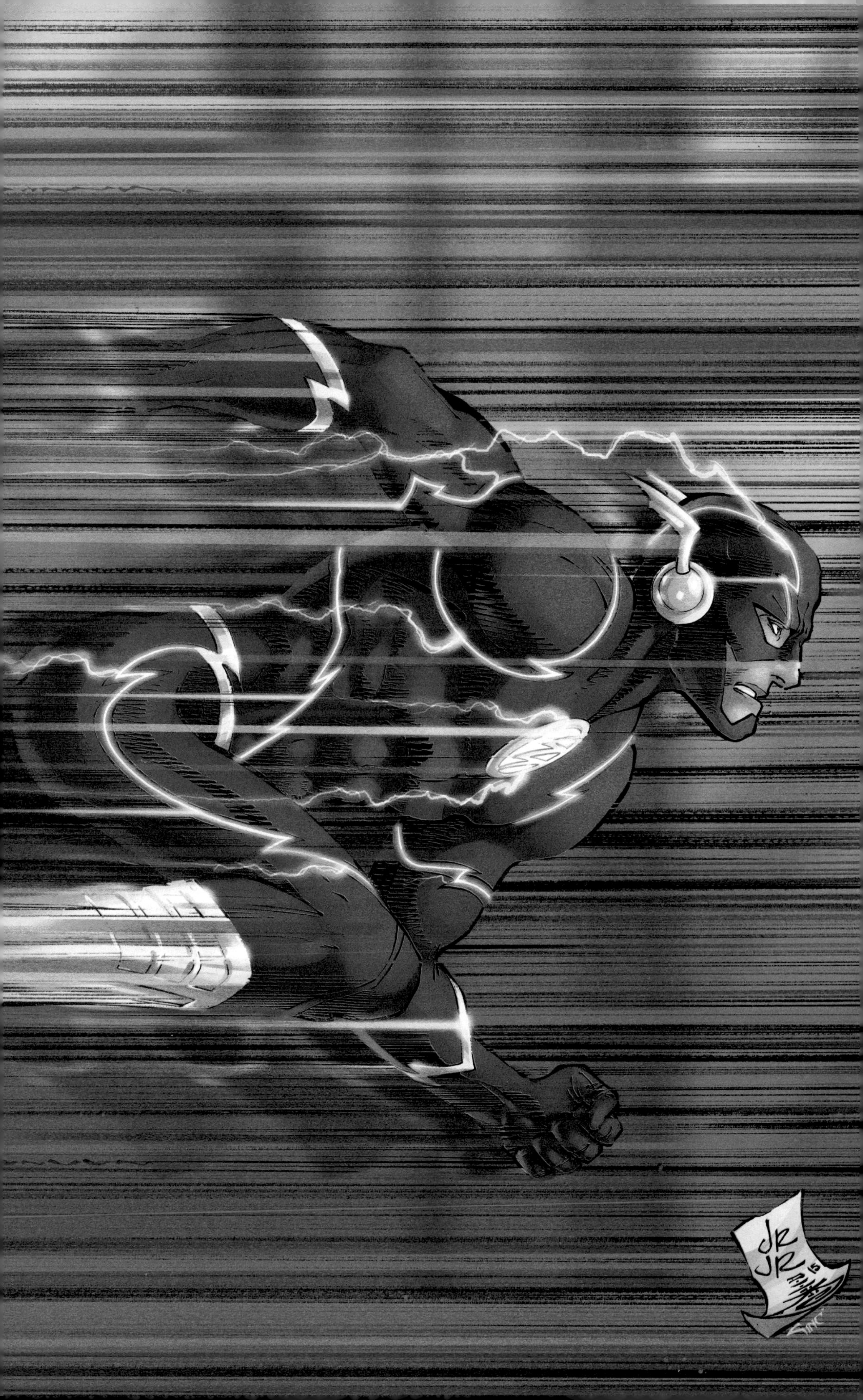

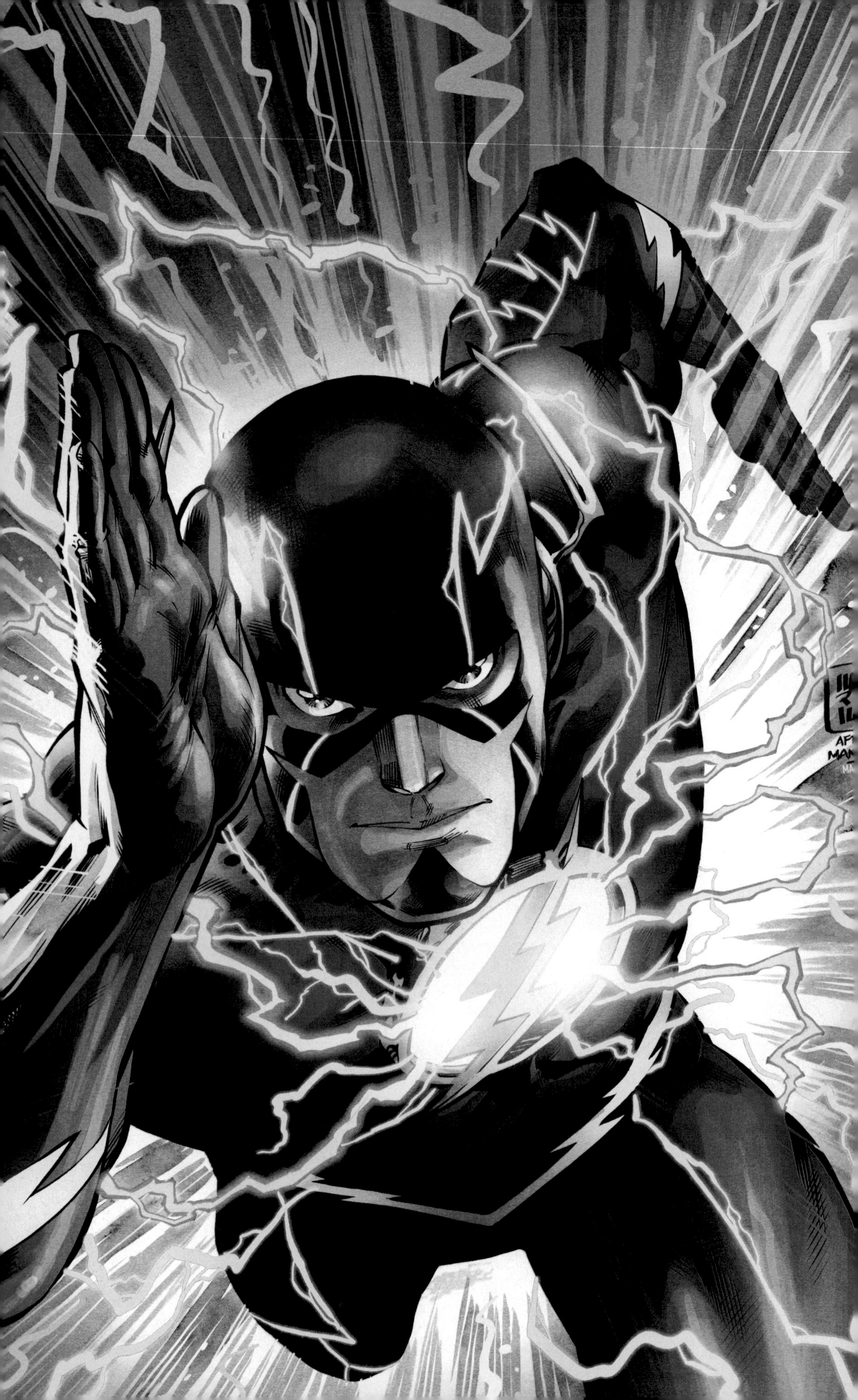

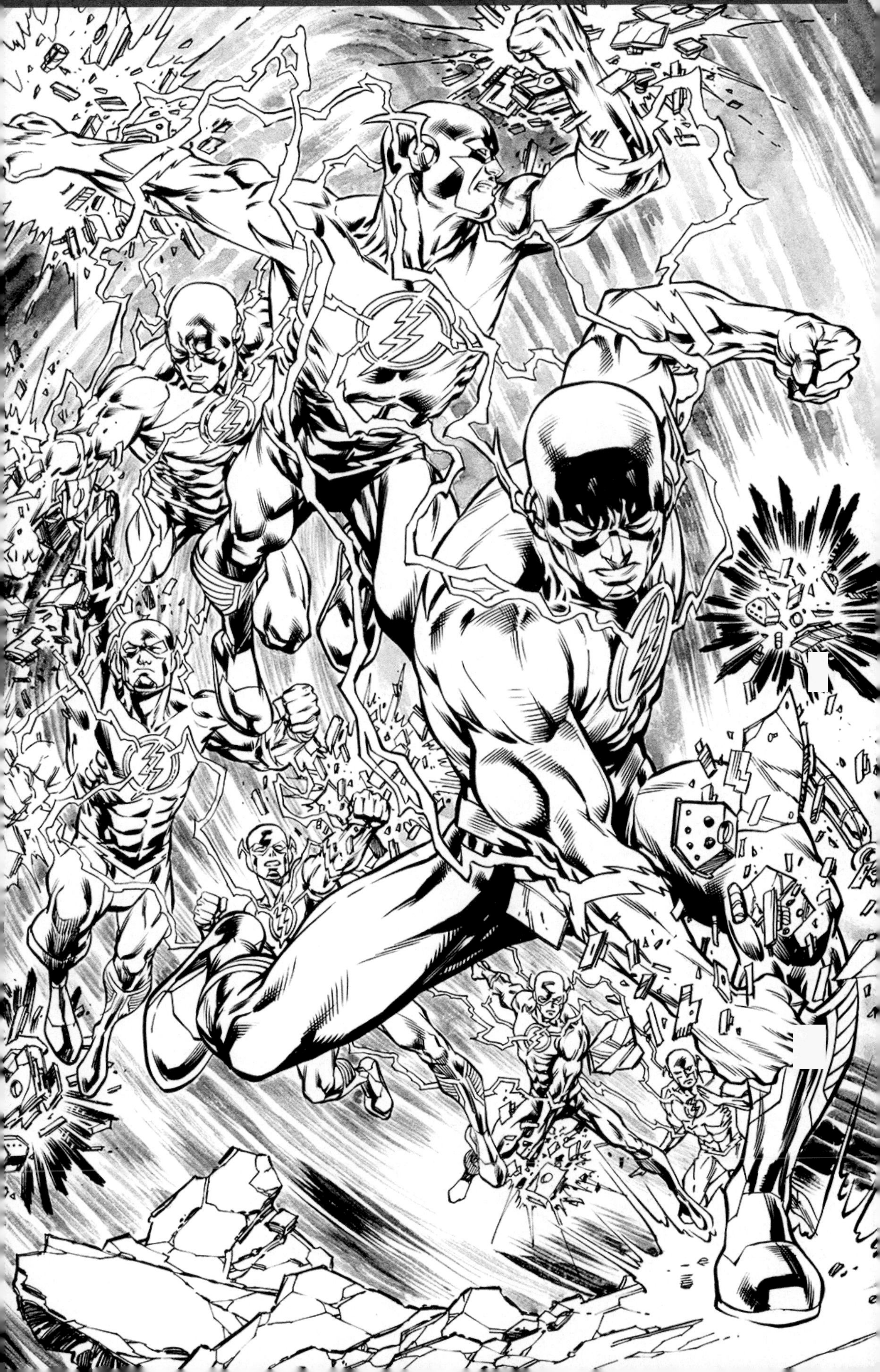

ART BY JESÚS MERINO FOR PAGE 135

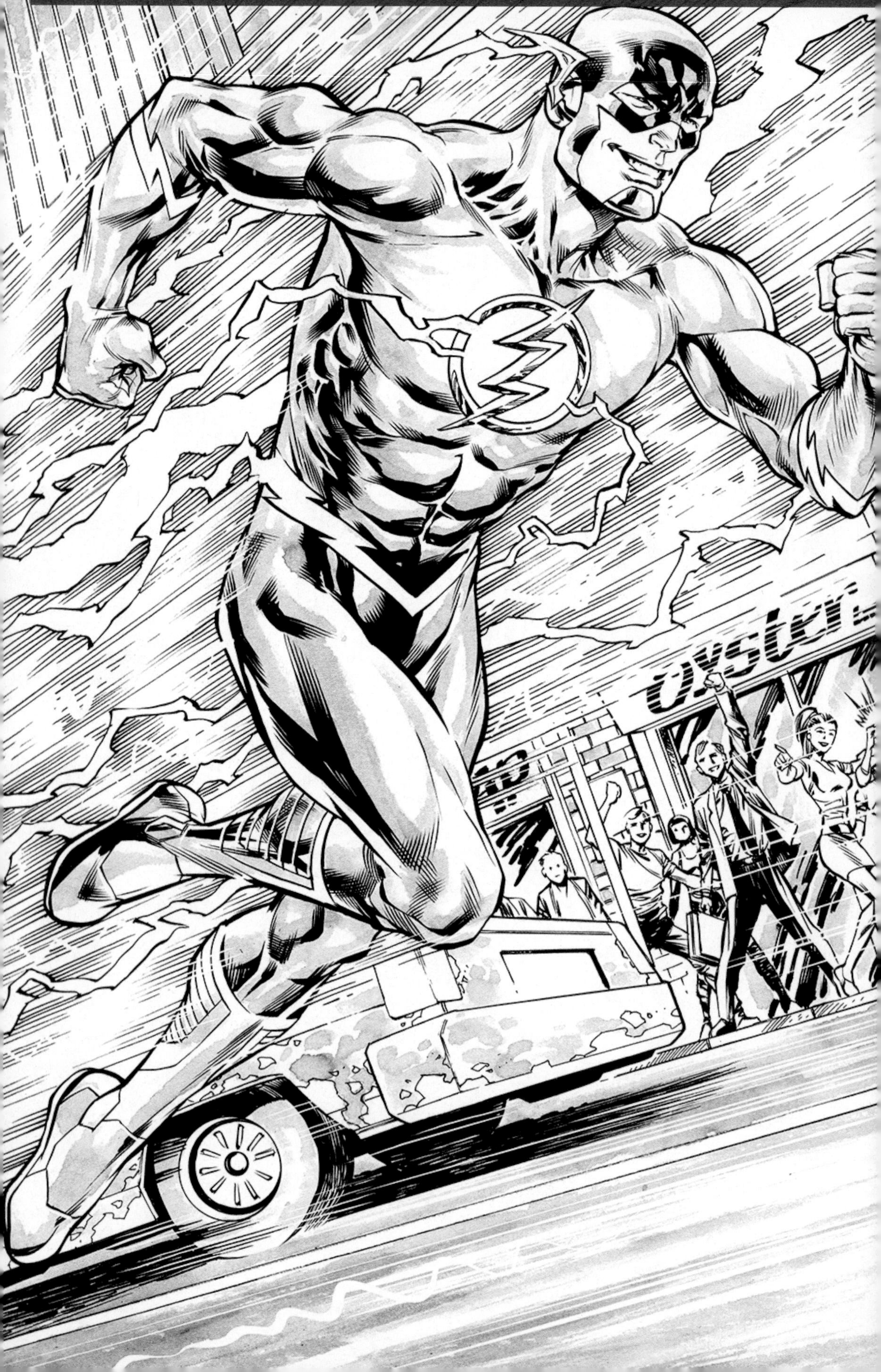
oyster

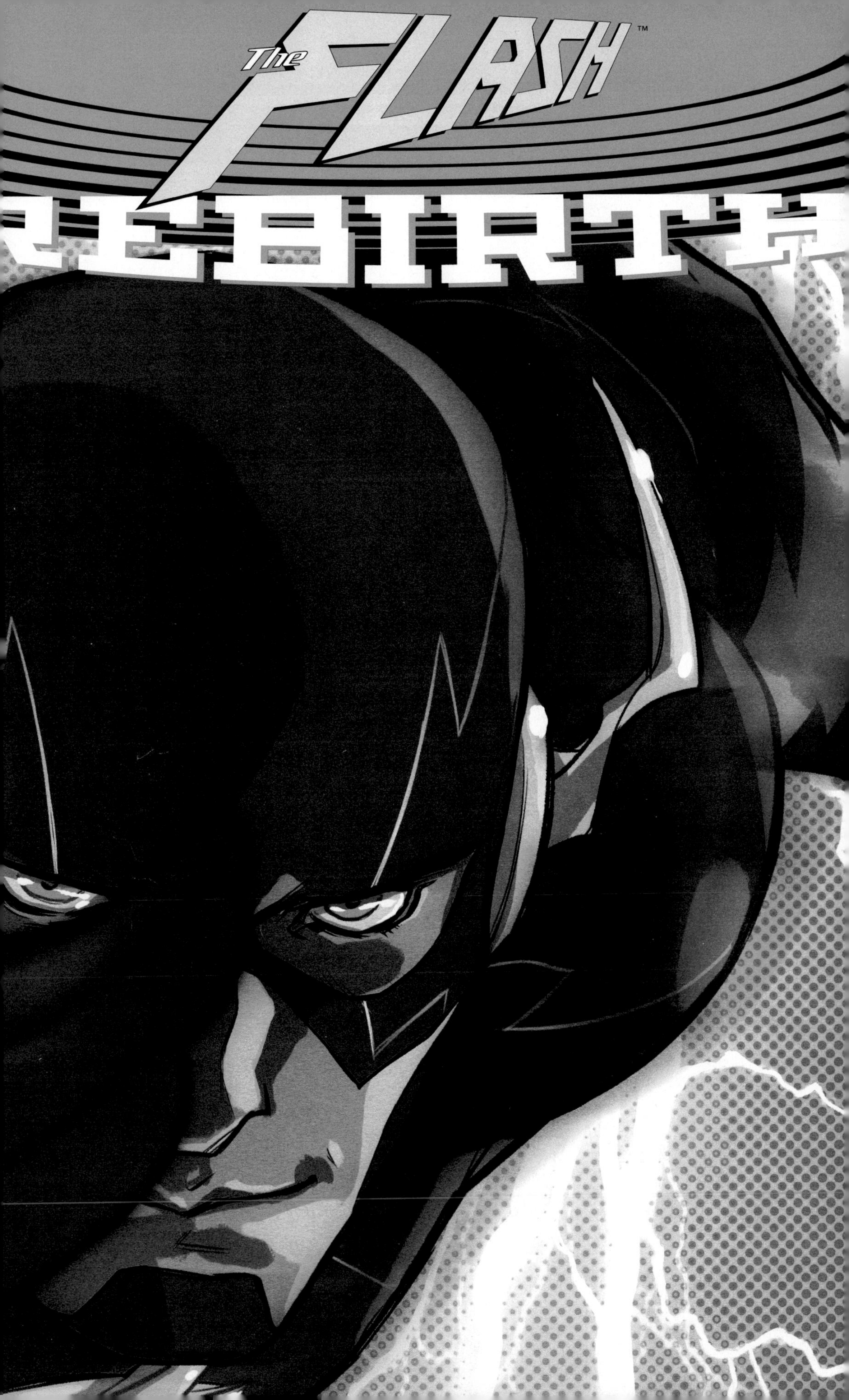
The FLASH™
REBIRTH

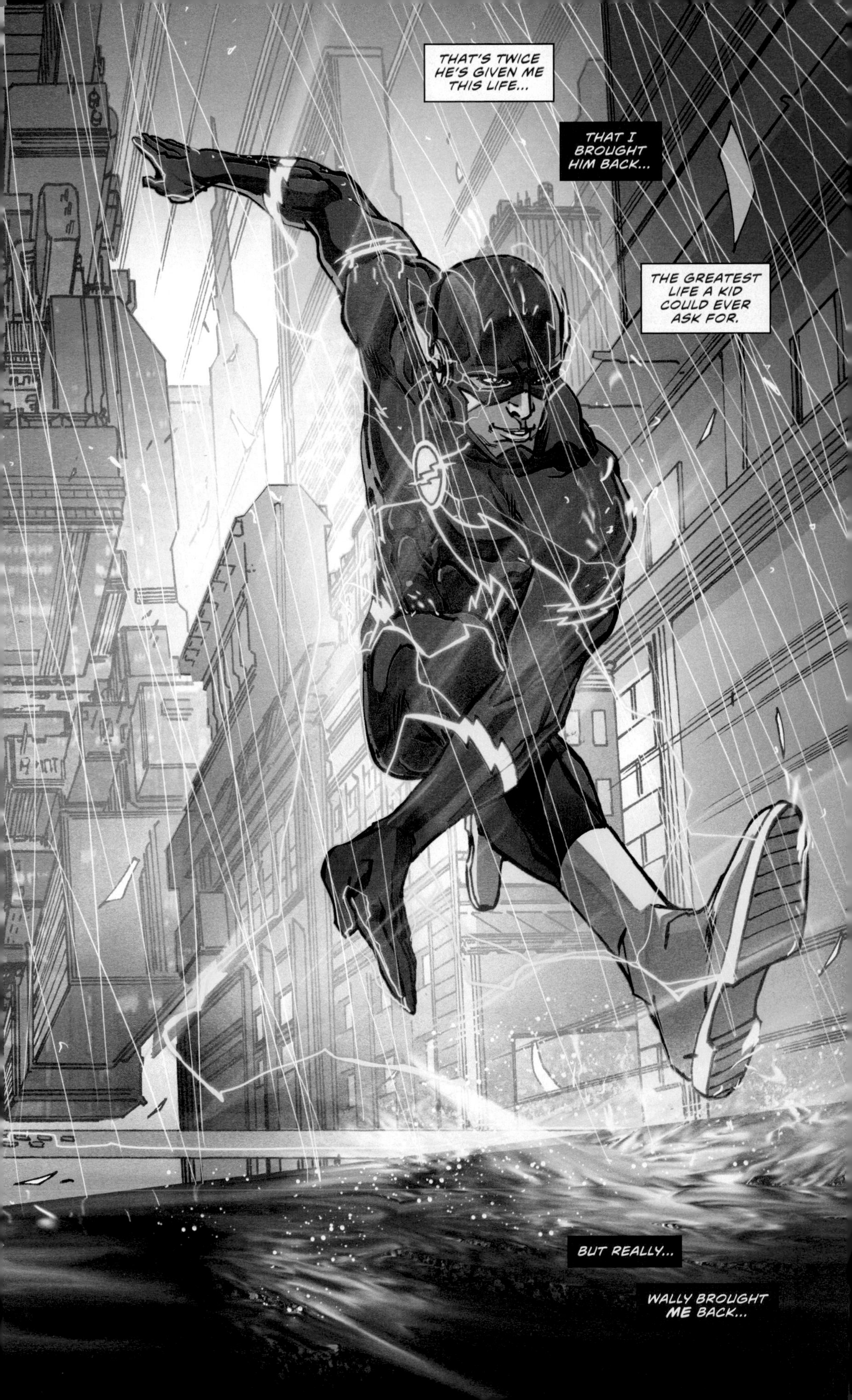
THAT'S TWICE HE'S GIVEN ME THIS LIFE...
THAT I BROUGHT HIM BACK...
THE GREATEST LIFE A KID COULD EVER ASK FOR.
BUT REALLY...
WALLY BROUGHT ME BACK...

I WAS RIGHT. BATMAN IS ALREADY WORKING AN ANGLE.

EVERYONE THINKS OF BRUCE AS A DETECTIVE...

...BUT TO ME... HE'LL ALWAYS BE A SCIENTIST.

HE USES FORENSIC EVIDENCE TO SOLVE CASES, SO I'VE ALWAYS FELT WE WERE KINDRED SPIRITS.

BRUCE TELLS ME THAT A "MAN MADE C LIGHTNING" APPEARE BEFORE HIM EARLIE TONIGHT. IT SOUNDS L WALLY, BUT BRUCE DID RECOGNIZE HIM.

AS THE MAN VANISHED, HIS LIGHTNING EMBEDDED A SMILEY FACE BUTTON WITHIN THE WALL OF THE BATCAVE.

BEFORE RUNNING ANY TESTS, BRUCE FIRST THOUGHT THE JOKER LEFT IT AS A CLUE TO ANOTHER TWISTED GAME. IT WOULDN'T BE THE FIRST TIME.

WE MATCH SAMPL FROM THE LETTE I GAVE HIM AFTE THE FLASHPOINT WITH THE BUTTON AND TRY TO CONNECT THE DOTS...AND SHAR OUR THEORIES.

ONCE I FILL IN BRUCE ON WALLY AND WHAT HE SAID ABOUT THE MISSING YEARS AND HOW WE'RE BEING WATCHED... IT'S CLEAR WE'RE ON THE SAME CASE.

WE TALK FOR A LONG TIME..

FROM THE WRITER OF *JUSTICE LEAGUE*
AND *GREEN LANTERN*

GEOFF JOHNS
with ETHAN VAN SCIVER

THE FLASH:
THE DASTARDLY
DEATH
OF THE ROGUES!

with FRANCIS MANAPUL

THE FLASH: THE ROAD
TO FLASHPOINT

with FRANCIS MANAPUL
and SCOTT KOLINS

FLASHPOINT

with ANDY KUBERT